DIGITAL PRODUCT MANAGEMENT

This book is designed to equip readers with essential knowledge and skills in digital product management. It covers strategic planning and market opportunity, offering a clear and accessible guide to navigating the complex world of digital product management in today's fast-changing environment.

Chapters explore key topics, including understanding digital transformation, identifying market dynamics, and developing a comprehensive product strategy. Readers will learn how to conduct market research, build strong business cases, and define product positioning. The book also covers practical methods for selecting pricing and packaging strategies, as well as crafting a go-to-market plan. Real-world examples, such as the growth of Grab in Southeast Asia, the rise of Zoom during the global pandemic, and Shopify's role in empowering small businesses globally, provide insight into how companies leverage strategic planning and market insights to thrive. The content reflects both current and future trends, making it relevant for global markets and today's digitally driven economy.

This book is especially useful for product managers, entrepreneurs, and business leaders who are keen to refine their strategic planning skills. It offers actionable advice and frameworks that can be applied across various industries, empowering readers to successfully manage digital products and drive business growth.

Boon Kee Lee is a senior lecturer in the Department of Information Systems and Analytics, School of Computing at the National University of Singapore. Boon Kee has 30 years of consulting experience in product management and software development. His research interest is digital product management.

DIGITAL PRODUCT MANAGEMENT

Strategic Planning and Market Opportunity

Boon Kee Lee

CRC Press
Taylor & Francis Group
Boca Raton London New York

CRC Press is an imprint of the
Taylor & Francis Group, an **informa** business

Designed cover image: T&F

MATLAB® and Simulink® are trademarks of The MathWorks, Inc. and are used with permission. The MathWorks does not warrant the accuracy of the text or exercises in this book. This book's use or discussion of MATLAB® or Simulink® software or related products does not constitute endorsement or sponsorship by The MathWorks of a particular pedagogical approach or particular use of the MATLAB® and Simulink® software.

First edition published 2025
by CRC Press
2385 NW Executive Center Drive, Suite 320, Boca Raton FL 33431

and by CRC Press
4 Park Square, Milton Park, Abingdon, Oxon, OX14 4RN

CRC Press is an imprint of Taylor & Francis Group, LLC

© 2025 Boon Kee Lee

Library of Congress Cataloging-in-Publication Data
Names: Kee, Lee Boon, author.
Title: Digital product management : strategic planning and market opportunity / Lee Boon Kee.
Description: First edition. | Boca Raton, FL : CRC Press, 2025. | Includes bibliographical references and index. |
Identifiers: LCCN 2024049989 (print) | LCCN 2024049990 (ebook) | ISBN 9781032776712 (hbk) | ISBN 9781032776705 (pbk) | ISBN 9781003484295 (ebk)
Subjects: LCSH: Product management. | Computer software--Marketing. | Computer software--Development--Management.
Classification: LCC HF5415.15 K44 2025 (print) | LCC HF5415.15 (ebook) | DDC 005.3068/4--dc23/eng/20241226
LC record available at https://lccn.loc.gov/2024049989
LC ebook record available at https://lccn.loc.gov/2024049990

ISBN: 9781032776712 (hbk)
ISBN: 9781032776705 (pbk)
ISBN: 9781003484295 (ebk)

DOI: 10.1201/9781003484295

Typeset in Sabon LT Pro
by KnowledgeWorks Global Ltd.

CONTENTS

1

DIGITAL PRODUCT MANAGEMENT OVERVIEW

1.1 Introduction

In the rapidly evolving landscape of technology and business, digital product management stands at the forefront of innovation and operational strategy. This chapter introduces the concept of digital product management, an area that extends traditional product management into the digital realm, harnessing new technologies to create and enhance products that meet modern consumer demands. As organizations face the imperative to digitalize, the role of the digital product manager becomes increasingly critical, blending technical acumen with strategic foresight. Here, we explore the transformation from conventional product management methodologies to digital-centric practices, setting the stage for a deeper understanding of how digital tools and platforms are revolutionizing product development, customer engagement, and market delivery.

1.2 The Evolution of Product Management into the Digital Realm

The journey of product management from its traditional roots to becoming a pivotal force in digital transformation is both a reflection of and a response to the digital revolution that has reshaped the global business ecosystem. This evolution marks a significant shift from managing the lifecycle of physical goods to orchestrating the development and growth of digital products and services. It underscores the transition towards a world where digital literacy, agility, and customer engagement are not just valued but essential for success.

DOI: 10.1201/9781003484295-1

The demand for skilled product managers has surged as businesses recognize the critical role these professionals play in navigating the complexities of digital product development. They are the architects of change, leveraging digital technologies to unlock new opportunities, redefine customer experiences, and drive strategic innovation. As companies across industries strive to adapt to digital realities, product managers have emerged as indispensable leaders, equipped with the vision and expertise to steer digital initiatives in alignment with overarching business goals.

This transformation has fundamentally altered the product management discipline, expanding its scope and elevating its importance in the digital age. Product managers today are expected to possess a deep understanding of digital markets, user needs, and technological advancements. They are strategists, innovators, and communicators, capable of bridging the gap between technical teams and business stakeholders, ensuring that digital products not only meet but exceed market and customer expectations.

The impact of digital product management extends far beyond the confines of individual organizations, influencing market dynamics, competitive strategies, and the very fabric of the business ecosystem. It has catalysed a shift towards more dynamic, user-centric, and data-driven approaches to product development and management. As the digital landscape continues to evolve, the role of the product manager will only grow in complexity and significance, positioning these professionals as key drivers of business innovation and growth.

Through this exploration of the evolution of product management into the digital realm, we begin our journey into understanding the critical role of digital product management in today's business landscape. This narrative sets the stage for a deeper dive into the methodologies, challenges, and opportunities that define the field, preparing readers to navigate the exciting and complex world of digital product management.

1.3 Understanding Digital Products, Services, and Digitalization

In the realm of digital product management, it is crucial to grasp the fundamental concepts of digital products, services, and the processes driving digital transformation. This section provides a comprehensive overview of these concepts, laying the groundwork for understanding the nuances of managing digital products effectively.

1.3.1 Definitions of Digital Products and Services

Digital products and services are at the core of modern businesses, reshaping industries and revolutionizing the way we interact with technology.

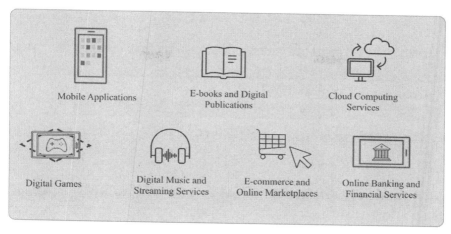

FIGURE 1.1   Digital products and services

Figure 1.1 shows some examples of digital products and services that we are so familiar with.

Here are concise definitions to clarify these essential terms:

1 **Digital Products:** These are intangible goods or services that exist in digital form, typically accessed or consumed through digital devices or platforms. Digital products can range from software applications and multimedia content to online subscriptions and virtual experiences.

Examples of Digital Products:

- Mobile Applications (Apps): Apps for smartphones and tablets, such as social media apps (**Facebook, Instagram**), productivity apps (**Microsoft Office, Evernote**), gaming apps (**Angry Birds, Fortnite**), and entertainment apps (**Netflix, Spotify**).
- E-books and Digital Publications: Electronic versions of books, magazines, newspapers, and academic journals available for download or online reading, such as **Kindle** e-books, digital editions of **The New York Times**, and scholarly articles on platforms like JSTOR.
- Digital Music and Streaming Services: Platforms for streaming and downloading music, including **Spotify, Apple Music, Amazon Music,** and **YouTube Music,** offering access to vast libraries of songs and personalized playlists.
- Digital Games and Virtual Reality (**VR**) Experiences: Video games playable on various devices (PCs, consoles, mobile devices) and immersive **VR** experiences, like virtual reality games (**Beat Saber, Half-Life: Alyx**) and **VR** simulations for training and education.

2 **Digital Services:** Unlike traditional products, digital services primarily involve delivering value through ongoing interactions or engagements facilitated by digital platforms or networks. These can include streaming services, cloud computing solutions, online banking, and digital marketing services.

Examples of Digital Services:

- Cloud Computing Services: Infrastructure as a Service (**IaaS**), Platform as a Service (**PaaS**), and Software as a Service (**SaaS**) offerings provided by cloud service providers like **Amazon Web Services** (**AWS**), **Microsoft Azure**, and **Google Cloud Platform**.
- Streaming Video on Demand (**SVOD**) Platforms: Subscription-based services for streaming movies and TV shows, such as **Netflix**, **Disney+**, **Hulu**, and **Amazon Prime Video**, accessible via internet-connected devices.
- Online Banking and Financial Services: Digital banking platforms and fintech apps for managing accounts, transferring funds, paying bills, and investing, like **Chase Mobile**, **PayPal**, **Venmo**, and **Robinhood**.
- E-commerce and Online Marketplaces: Websites and apps facilitating online shopping and transactions, including **Amazon**, **eBay**, **Alibaba**, **Etsy**, and platforms for food delivery (**Uber Eats**, **DoorDash**) and ride-hailing (**Uber**, **Lyft**).

1.3.2   Understanding Digitalization: Gartner's Perspective

Digitalization, as defined by **Gartner**, refers to the use of digital technologies to transform business processes, operations, and models to improve efficiency, deliver value, and stay competitive in the digital age. It encompasses a broader strategic approach beyond simply adopting digital tools or automating existing processes. Gartner emphasizes the holistic nature of digitalization, which involves reimagining business strategies and customer experiences through digital innovation.

Examples of Digitalization and Digitization:

Digitalization Example: A traditional brick-and-mortar retailer adopts an omnichannel approach, integrating online and offline channels to provide seamless shopping experiences for customers. Through digitalization, the retailer leverages data analytics to personalize recommendations, optimize inventory management, and enhance customer engagement across various touchpoints.

Digitization Example: A library digitizes its collection of books and documents, converting physical texts into electronic formats accessible through digital platforms or e-readers. While this digitization effort improves accessibility and preservation, it represents a foundational step towards broader digitalization initiatives aimed at transforming library services, such as implementing online catalogues, virtual reference services, and digital lending programs.

By understanding the distinctions between digital products, services, and the processes of digitalization and digitization, product managers can better navigate the complexities of managing digital initiatives and driving innovation in today's dynamic marketplace.

1.4   The Role of Product Management in Digital Transformation

In today's rapidly evolving marketplace, the imperative for businesses to adapt and innovate is not just a matter of staying competitive but often of survival. As companies grapple with the digital revolution, product management emerges as a central strategy in navigating the complex process of digital transformation. This transformative journey is not solely about adopting new technologies but fundamentally reshaping how businesses operate, engage with customers, and deliver value in a digital-first world.

Traditional businesses, from bricks-and-mortar retailers to service providers with physical offices, are increasingly shifting towards digital models to align with changing consumer expectations and behaviours. This move to click-and-order business models, leveraging digital channels and delivery methods, is a clear response to the digital threat looming over businesses that fail to adapt. The stark reality is that many companies unable to transition into the digital economy are finding it increasingly difficult to survive, let alone thrive.

The essence of tackling digital transformation lies in adopting a holistic approach that examines every customer interaction with the company, brand, and its offerings. This approach necessitates embracing a product-mindset, focusing on identifying, understanding, and prioritizing customer problems. Successful digital transformation goes beyond the mere adoption of new technologies; it uses technology as a tool to fundamentally transform and enhance customer experiences.

Product management stands at the helm of this transformation, guiding businesses in offering their products and services through innovative digital channels built around user engagement. These channels, seamlessly integrated into consumers' lifestyles, aim to meet needs and deliver exceptional user experiences by addressing six primary customer needs supported by digital technologies: making, finding, exchanging, playing, sensing, and responding. From social media platforms enabling users to create content and form connections to online marketplaces facilitating easy find and exchange of goods, digital technologies are redefining how consumers interact with businesses.

Moreover, the digital threat posed by modern consumers' evolving expectations, competitive startups, and cross-industry entries drives companies to expedite their digital transformation efforts. This shift is not just about digitization but about harnessing digital technologies to better understand and meet customers' growing needs. Here, product managers play a critical role with their deep understanding of digital products and customer insights, enabling traditional businesses to navigate their transformation journeys successfully.

Using strategic product management, companies can ensure market success by developing digital products that resonate with target audiences, engaging customers effectively, and advocating for their needs. In doing so, product managers not only drive the digital transformation of products and services but also empower businesses to navigate the challenges and opportunities presented by the digital age, ensuring long-term success and relevance in an ever-changing digital landscape.

1.5 Digital Technologies and Customer Needs: Catering to the Modern Consumer

In navigating the landscape of digital transformation, understanding how digital technologies cater to customer needs is paramount. Central to this understanding are the six primary ways through which digital innovations support and enhance the customer experience, shaping the core of product management strategies in the digital era.

1 **Making:** Platforms like **Facebook**, **Instagram**, and **TikTok** revolutionize how we communicate, enabling users to create, share, and engage with content. This democratization of content creation and the ability to forge connections across global networks underscore the transformative power of digital technologies in meeting the human need for creation, expression, and interaction.
2 **Finding:** The digital age has transformed how consumers discover products, services, and information. Search engines and review platforms like **Google Reviews** offer a plethora of options, making the process of finding what one needs more accessible and efficient than ever before.
3 **Exchanging:** The ease of completing transactions online marks a significant shift in consumer behaviour. Platforms such as **Amazon** streamline the exchange process, allowing for the seamless purchase and delivery of goods and services with just a few clicks, embodying the convenience and efficiency that digital technologies bring to commerce.

4 **Playing:** Digital products provide value through entertainment and learning, from online games to educational platforms like **Duolingo**. They cater to the human desire for play and personal growth, offering engaging and interactive experiences that enrich users' lives.

5 **Sensing:** Digital products leveraging the use of Internet of Things (**IoT**) sensors to collect data about user interactions or the environment is common in devices like smartphones, smart thermostats, and fitness trackers. These devices can monitor everything from room temperature to heart rates, helping to optimize comfort or health recommendations based on real-time data.

6 **Responding:** The Internet of Things (**IoT**) and artificial intelligence (**AI**) technologies enable a new level of interaction between digital products and the physical world. By sensing and responding to environmental inputs, these technologies create smarter, more intuitive experiences, from facial recognition for security to smart home devices that adjust to user preferences.

Table 1.1 provides a snapshot of the diverse and powerful ways in which digital technologies can meet and support the complex needs and preferences of users. Each example highlights the practical application of digital tools in enhancing various aspects of the user experience, from creation and discovery to interaction and response.

Addressing these needs – making, finding, exchanging, playing, sensing, and responding – digital technologies offer comprehensive support for a wide range of customer desires and activities. This foundation informs product managers as they strategize on using technology not just for innovation's sake but as a means to genuinely enhance and transform the customer experience. By aligning digital product development with these fundamental customer needs, businesses can create meaningful, engaging, and valuable offerings that resonate deeply with their target audiences, driving success in the digital economy.

However, as the digital landscape evolves, additional dimensions of user support and engagement emerge. Here are some additional ways digital technologies can support user needs:

1 **Educating:** Beyond traditional learning platforms, digital technologies can offer just-in-time learning and microlearning opportunities. These allow users to acquire new skills and knowledge precisely when they need them, directly in the flow of work or daily life.

2 **Personalizing:** Advanced data analytics and machine learning enable digital products to offer highly personalized experiences, recommendations, and content. This customization enhances user satisfaction by tailoring services and products to individual preferences, histories, and predicted needs.

TABLE 1.1 Six ways to support and enhance customer experience

Support Way	Examples
Making	Social media platforms like Facebook and Instagram for content creation and sharing.
	Blogging platforms like WordPress and Medium.
	Video sharing sites like YouTube and TikTok.
	Podcast hosting services like Anchor and SoundCloud.
	Digital art tools like Adobe Photoshop and Procreate.
Finding	Search engines like Google and Bing.
	Review platforms like Yelp and TripAdvisor.
	Product comparison websites like Wirecutter and Consumer Reports.
	Location-based services like Google Maps and Apple Maps.
	Hashtag and keyword search functionalities on social media platforms.
Exchanging	E-commerce platforms like Amazon and eBay.
	Digital payment systems like PayPal, Venmo, and Apple Pay.
	Online booking systems for hotels, flights, and restaurants, such as Booking.com and Airbnb.
	Subscription services like Netflix and Spotify.
	Marketplace apps like Etsy and Depop.
Playing	Online gaming platforms like Steam and PlayStation Network.
	Mobile games like Pokémon Go and Candy Crush.
	Educational games and apps like Duolingo and Khan Academy.
	Virtual reality (VR) experiences through platforms like Oculus.
	Streaming services with interactive content, such as Twitch and YouTube Live.
Sensing	Smart home devices like Nest thermostats and Ring doorbells.
	Wearable technology like Fitbit and Apple Watch that monitor health metrics.
	Automotive sensors for self-driving features or parking assistance.
	Environmental monitoring devices that track air quality, noise levels, or weather conditions.
	Augmented reality apps that overlay digital information on the physical world, like IKEA Place.
Responding	Chatbots and virtual assistants like Siri, Alexa, and Google Assistant that provide real-time responses.
	Automated customer service tools that offer instant troubleshooting and support.
	Personalization algorithms that adjust content, recommendations, or settings based on user behaviour and inputs.
	Feedback systems in apps and software that adapt to user preferences and criticisms.
	Predictive text and auto-correct features in messaging apps and word processors.

3 **Facilitating Collaboration:** Digital tools increasingly support real-time collaboration across distances, enabling individuals and teams to work together more effectively. This includes everything from cloud-based workspaces and project management tools to digital whiteboards and real-time editing platforms.

4 **Enhancing Accessibility:** Digital products can significantly improve accessibility for people with disabilities. Technologies such as voice recognition, text-to-speech, and accessible user interfaces make digital content more accessible to people who have visual, auditory, motor, or cognitive impairments.

5 **Providing Security and Privacy:** As users become more concerned about their digital footprints, technologies that enhance security and privacy become crucial. This includes secure communication apps, privacy-enhancing technologies, and features that give users more control over their personal data.

6 **Empowering Creativity:** Digital tools that support creativity, such as graphic design software, music production platforms, and digital art tools, empower users to create in ways that were previously inaccessible to non-professionals. These tools democratize the creative process, allowing anyone with a device to express themselves artistically.

7 **Supporting Health and Wellness:** Digital health technologies, including fitness trackers, telehealth services, and mental health apps, support users' health and wellness goals. These technologies provide tools for monitoring health, accessing healthcare services, and maintaining mental and physical wellbeing.

8 **Enabling Commerce and Entrepreneurship:** E-commerce platforms, digital marketplaces, and fintech solutions empower users to start businesses, sell products, and manage finances more efficiently than ever before.

Each of these additional dimensions not only enhances user experience but also broadens the scope of opportunities for digital product managers to create meaningful and impactful products. As digital technologies evolve, so too will the ways in which they can support and fulfil user needs, continuously offering new avenues for innovation and improvement. Table 1.2 lists eight ways to cater to evolving customer needs.

Table 1.2 extends the scope of digital support beyond the basic functionalities to more sophisticated and specialized needs, reflecting the diverse ways in which digital technologies are integrated into everyday personal and professional activities. Each example demonstrates how these technologies enable users to achieve specific goals, from enhancing personal health and creativity to empowering educational pursuits and entrepreneurship.

TABLE 1.2 Eight ways to cater to evolving customer needs

Support Way	Examples
Educating	Online learning platforms like Coursera and Udemy offering courses from universities and experts.
	Microlearning apps like Blinkist that provide summaries of key concepts from books and articles.
	Virtual reality educational experiences that simulate historical events or scientific experiments.
	Interactive webinars and workshops that allow real-time participation and feedback.
Personalizing	Recommendation engines in streaming services like Netflix and Spotify that suggest content based on past interactions.
	E-commerce websites like Amazon offering personalized shopping experiences based on user behaviour.
	Fitness apps that tailor workout plans to an individual's fitness level and goals.
	News apps that curate articles based on the user's interests and reading history.
Facilitating Collaboration	Project management tools like Asana and Trello that enable team collaboration on tasks and projects.
	Real-time document editing tools like Google Docs that allow multiple users to work simultaneously.
	Virtual meeting platforms like Zoom and Microsoft Teams that facilitate remote team interactions.
	Cloud-based design tools like Figma that support collaborative design processes across locations.
Enhancing Accessibility	Screen readers and accessibility features on websites that help visually impaired users navigate content.
	Speech-to-text applications that assist users with hearing impairments in communication.
	Adaptive controllers for gaming consoles designed for users with limited mobility.
	Websites and applications with high contrast modes, text resizing, and voice navigation options.
Providing Security and Privacy	Encrypted messaging apps like Signal that offer secure communication options.
	VPN services that provide privacy and security for online browsing.
	Anti-malware and antivirus software that protect devices and data.
	Privacy tools that allow users to control their data sharing preferences and manage consent.

(Continued)

TABLE 1.2 (Continued)

Support Way	Examples
Empowering Creativity	Digital painting and illustration apps like Adobe Illustrator and Procreate. Music production software like Ableton Live and GarageBand. Video editing tools like Adobe Premiere Pro and Final Cut Pro. Platforms for publishing and sharing creative work, such as Behance and Dribbble.
Supporting Health and Wellness	Wearable health devices like Garmin and Apple Watch that track physical activities and health metrics. Mental health apps like Headspace and Calm that provide guided meditations and sleep stories. Telehealth services that offer virtual consultations with healthcare providers. Diet and nutrition tracking apps that help users manage their dietary intake and health goals.
Enabling Commerce and Entrepreneurship	E-commerce platforms like Shopify that enable users to create online stores easily. Fintech applications like Square and Stripe that facilitate small business transactions and payments. Crowdfunding websites like Kickstarter and Indiegogo that support entrepreneurial projects. Digital marketing tools that help businesses target and reach potential customers effectively.

1.6 The Digital Product Manager: A New Breed of Leaders

The digital era has ushered in a new breed of leaders in the form of digital product managers. These professionals are pivotal in steering companies through the complexities of digital transformation, bridging the gap between cutting-edge technology and business strategies. Their role is multidimensional, encompassing a blend of technical proficiency, strategic foresight, and customer-centric focus. Figure 1.2 shows key roles of a digital product manager.

Here are the key roles:

1 **Strategic Vision and Execution**: Digital product managers are at the helm of product strategy, aligning product goals with the broader business objectives. They are tasked with envisioning the future of a product, defining its roadmap, and ensuring that every phase of the product lifecycle – from ideation to launch and beyond – is strategically planned and executed. Their ability to foresee market trends and adapt strategies accordingly is

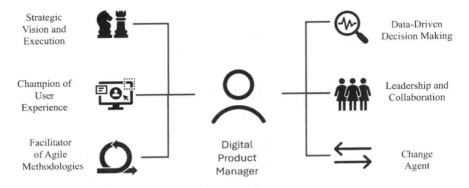

Strategic Vision and Execution

Champion of User Experience

Facilitator of Agile Methodologies

Digital Product Manager

Data-Driven Decision Making

Leadership and Collaboration

Change Agent

FIGURE 1.2   Key roles of a digital product manager

crucial in maintaining competitive advantage in rapidly evolving digital markets.

2 **Champion of User Experience**: At the core of their responsibilities lies a deep commitment to enhancing user experience. Digital product managers advocate for designs and features that meet the actual needs of users, often leveraging user data to make informed decisions. They work closely with design and development teams to ensure that the product not only attracts but also retains users by delivering seamless and engaging experiences. This user-first approach is vital in a digital landscape where user preferences and behaviours change swiftly.

3 **Facilitator of Agile Methodologies**: In an environment where speed and adaptability are paramount, digital product managers promote agile methodologies within their teams. This approach supports rapid iteration based on user feedback and market changes, allowing teams to quickly refine and improve products. By fostering an agile culture, digital product managers ensure that their organizations can pivot and innovate at a pace that matches the demands of the digital age.

4 **Data-Driven Decision Making**: Leveraging data is a fundamental aspect of the digital product manager's role. They utilize analytics to track user engagement, product performance, and market trends, transforming vast amounts of data into actionable insights. This data-driven approach informs every aspect of product development and marketing strategies, ensuring that decisions are grounded in real-world usage and feedback.

5 **Leadership and Collaboration**: As leaders, digital product managers cultivate cross-functional collaboration among teams, including marketing, sales, development, and customer support. Their leadership is characterized by the ability to communicate effectively, influence decision-making, and inspire teams towards a common vision. They play a crucial role in

breaking down silos within the organization, facilitating a more integrated and cohesive approach to product development.

6 **Change Agent**: Beyond their direct responsibilities, digital product managers act as catalysts for change within the organization. They champion digital initiatives and advocate for the adoption of new technologies and practices that can drive the business forward. Their ability to manage change and guide their teams through the uncertainties of digital transformation makes them indispensable in today's business landscape.

Digital product managers embody the leadership qualities necessary to navigate the complexities of modern markets. Their strategic acumen, user-focused approach, and proficiency in agile practices are essential for businesses looking to thrive in the digital economy. This section highlights the transformative role digital product managers play as leaders who not only manage but also inspire innovation and growth.

1.7   Navigating Challenges and Opportunities in the Digital Age

The digital age, while ripe with opportunities, also presents a myriad of challenges that digital product managers must navigate. This section explores both the hurdles and the prospects that arise from operating in such a dynamic environment, highlighting how adept management can transform potential difficulties into strategic advantages.

Here are the challenges and opportunities:

1 **Adapting to Rapid Technological Changes**: One of the most significant challenges in digital product management is the pace at which technology evolves. New tools, platforms, and technologies can quickly render existing products obsolete. Digital product managers must stay abreast of these changes, continually educating themselves and their teams on emerging technologies and industry trends. This constant learning enables them to anticipate shifts and adapt their products accordingly, ensuring relevance and competitiveness in the market.

   • **Example**: A digital product manager at a streaming service, such as **Netflix** or **Spotify**, continuously evaluates emerging technologies to enhance user experiences. This might include integrating new AI algorithms to improve content recommendation systems or exploring the potential of **Augmented Reality (AR)** features to allow users to interact with content in innovative ways. The challenge is to integrate these technologies quickly and seamlessly into existing platforms without disrupting user experiences.

2 **Managing User Expectations**: Today's consumers are more informed and demanding than ever. They expect personalized, seamless, and responsive experiences across all digital platforms. Meeting these expectations requires digital product managers to implement sophisticated user experience and customer service strategies. It's crucial for them to integrate feedback loops into the product development process, allowing for continual adaptation based on user insights. This not only helps in refining the product but also in building strong customer relationships.

  - **Example**: A product manager at an e-commerce company like **Amazon** faces the challenge of managing user expectations around delivery times. During the COVID-19 pandemic, as demand surged and supply chains were disrupted, maintaining customer satisfaction became challenging. To address this, the product manager focused on enhancing the communication features on the platform, providing real-time updates about shipping delays and expected delivery times to manage expectations realistically.

3 **Data Security and Privacy**: As digital products become increasingly integrated with daily activities, concerns about data security and privacy escalate. Digital product managers are tasked with ensuring their products comply with international data protection regulations, such as **GDPR** and **CCPA**, which can be complex and vary by region. By prioritizing security and privacy in the product design, not only do they safeguard user data, but they also enhance trust and credibility among their user base.

  - **Example**: A product manager at a fintech company such as **PayPal** must prioritize data security and privacy due to the sensitive nature of financial data. They face challenges in adhering to global data protection regulations while maintaining a seamless user experience. This often involves deploying advanced encryption methods and multi-factor authentication processes that secure transactions without adding unnecessary friction for the user.

4 **Cross-Functional Coordination**: The interdisciplinary nature of digital products necessitates effective collaboration across various departments – engineering, marketing, sales, and customer support, among others. Digital product managers must excel in cross-functional leadership, facilitating communication and alignment among diverse teams. This coordination ensures that all aspects of the product – from technical development to market launch – are well-integrated and that departmental silos do not hinder progress.

  - **Example**: At a company like **Apple**, a digital product manager working on the latest iPhone must coordinate with hardware engineers, software teams, marketing personnel, and customer service departments to ensure a cohesive product launch. The challenge lies in aligning all these different functions with the product's timeline and quality standards, requiring strong leadership and communication skills.

5 **Scaling Challenges**: As digital products grow, scaling becomes a critical issue. Digital product managers must develop strategies to scale their products effectively, addressing challenges related to infrastructure, operations, and support systems. This includes making decisions about cloud services, data architecture, and customer support tools that will allow the product to grow without compromising performance or user satisfaction.

- **Example**: A digital product manager at a fast-growing cloud storage provider, like **Dropbox**, faces scaling challenges as the user base expands globally. This includes ensuring that the infrastructure can handle increased loads, implementing efficient data management practices, and scaling customer service operations to maintain high service levels. Strategic planning and foresight are critical to manage growth without service disruptions.

6 **Innovation and Disruption**: In an environment where startups can disrupt entire industries overnight, maintaining a competitive edge is crucial. Digital product managers need to foster a culture of innovation within their teams, encouraging the exploration of new ideas and approaches. By continually innovating and potentially disrupting their own products, they can stay ahead of competitors and lead the market.

- **Example**: A product manager at **Tesla** in the autopilot division continuously innovates to maintain its market leader status against fast-catching competitors like **Waymo**. This involves not only enhancing existing autonomous driving features but also foreseeing and developing new ones that meet future safety and regulatory standards, maintaining an edge in a highly competitive market.

7 **Globalization**: Digital products often have a global reach, introducing complexities such as cultural differences, localization needs, and varied regulatory environments. Digital product managers must navigate these international waters deftly, customizing products to meet the diverse needs of global users while complying with local laws and norms.

- **Example**: A product manager at **LinkedIn**, which operates in multiple countries, faces the challenge of localizing content and features to match the cultural and professional norms of each region. This includes translating the interface and localizing the job market data to enhance relevance and usability for global users, requiring a deep understanding of diverse markets.

By effectively managing these challenges and leveraging the inherent opportunities, digital product managers can drive significant value for their organizations. This section not only highlights the hurdles that come with the digital age but also showcases how overcoming these challenges can lead to substantial business growth and innovation. Through strategic thinking, agile adaptation, and proactive leadership, digital product managers play a crucial role in shaping the digital landscape of their companies.

1.8 Conclusion

Digital product management is an essential discipline that adapts traditional product strategies to the demands of the digital age, ensuring that products not only satisfy customer needs but also drive business growth. This chapter has outlined the foundations of digital product management, from the evolution of the field to the roles and challenges faced by digital product managers today. As we have seen, successful digital product management requires a robust understanding of digitalization, a strong grasp of technological trends, and an agile approach to managing both products and people. As the digital landscape continues to expand and diversify, the insights provided here will equip current and aspiring digital product managers with the knowledge and skills needed to lead their organizations towards innovation and success in an increasingly digital world.

2

DIGITAL TRANSFORMATION AND MARKET DYNAMICS

2.1 Introduction

In the rapidly evolving landscape of global business, digital transformation represents both a formidable challenge and a remarkable opportunity. This chapter delves into how companies are not just responding to digital threats but are also harnessing these challenges as catalysts for innovation. By redefining their value propositions and exploring new market spaces, businesses are fundamentally reimagining the future of commerce, entertainment, and personal convenience. Through the lens of transformative examples, we will explore how traditional businesses transition to '**click-and-order**' models, adopting online platforms not merely as an auxiliary channel but as their primary mode of operation. This strategic shift is not only a defensive reaction to digital pressures but also a proactive manoeuvre to capitalize on the expansive opportunities presented by digital engagement and e-commerce.

2.2 The Digital Threat and Business Transformation

In today's rapidly evolving digital landscape, businesses face a significant digital threat – the risk of becoming obsolete if they fail to adapt to new technological advancements and changing consumer behaviours. Digital transformation is no longer optional but a necessity for survival and competitive advantage. This section explores the different types of digital business transformations that companies are adopting to mitigate this threat and capitalize on new opportunities. Figure 2.1 shows some of the key digital business transformations undertaken by many businesses that we will explore in detail in the following sections.

DOI: 10.1201/9781003484295-2

Transformation
from brick and
mortar to digital

Subscription-
based business
model

Digital technologies
in products to
enhance experience

Digital technologies
in engagement
channels

Seamless shopping
experience with
virtual stores

Leveraging
location-based
technologies

Retail reinvention
through mobile
apps

FIGURE 2.1 Digital business transformations

2.2.1 Complete Transformation from Brick-and-Mortar to Almost Entirely Digital

Driven partly by the digital threat, increased competition, and the opportunities that digital technologies provide, traditional brick-and-mortar companies are adopting innovative online business models, such as **click-to-order** or **click-to-pay**, to enhance customer engagement and drive business growth. This trend is exemplified by companies like **Domino's Pizza** and **DBS Bank**, which have embraced digital transformation to not only meet evolving consumer needs but also to improve their operational efficiency and profitability.

Domino's Pizza introduced a platform called 'Domino's Anywhere', which revolutionizes how customers interact with the brand. Through its mobile app, customers can order pizzas to be delivered to non-traditional locations like parks or beaches without needing a specific street address. This service extension caters to the modern consumer's demand for convenience and flexibility, allowing **Domino's** to expand its delivery boundaries and enhance customer satisfaction.

Similarly, **DBS Bank** has undergone a profound transformation with its launch of **'digibank'**, moving from a traditional banking framework to a mobile-first approach. **DBS Digital Bank** exemplifies a seismic shift in the banking industry, transitioning from physical branches to an award-winning digital platform that harnesses mobile technology to provide secure, convenient, and personalized financial services. This digital strategy not only eliminates the need for physical bank visits but also significantly increases the financial throughput of customers engaged with digital banking, compared to those relying on traditional methods.

Both **Domino's** and **DBS Bank** demonstrate how effective digital transformation, guided by strategic product management, can redefine traditional business operations. By adopting digital technologies, these companies have successfully transformed their service delivery models to better align with contemporary market demands and consumer expectations, setting a benchmark for innovation and customer-centricity in the digital era.

2.2.2 *Investing in Digital Technologies in Engagement Channels and Branding*

Disney's Magic Bands are a prime example of how integrating digital technologies into customer service channels can transform the consumer experience. These wearable devices act as an all-in-one digital tool, allowing guests at **Disney** theme parks to access their hotel rooms, enter parks, check in at **FastPass+** entrances, link **Disney PhotoPass** images to their account, and make purchases – all with a simple tap of the band. The bands use **RFID** technology and connect to the **My Disney Experience** app, where guests can plan their visits, select **FastPass+** choices, and utilize other features that enhance their visit.

The **Magic Bands** system collects data on visitor preferences and behaviours, which **Disney** uses to optimize and personalize guest experiences. This data-driven approach not only improves service delivery but also enhances operational efficiency, guest satisfaction, and ultimately, brand loyalty.

The integration of **Augmented Reality (AR)** and **Virtual Reality (VR)** into consumer engagement strategies is gaining momentum across various industries. For example, **IKEA** uses **AR** technology through its **IKEA Place** app, allowing customers to visualize furniture in their own space before making a purchase. This use of **AR** not only simplifies the buying process but also significantly enhances customer satisfaction by reducing the uncertainty associated with online shopping.

Similarly, in the automotive sector, companies like **Audi** have adopted **VR** to enhance the customer experience. **Audi's VR** experience allows customers to configure their new car in a virtual environment, where they can explore different customizations, colours, and features in a way that was never possible before.

Looking ahead, the deployment of **Large Language Models (LLMs)** and **Generative AI** presents new frontiers for digital engagement. These technologies can drive more interactive and personalized customer service channels. For instance, **LLMs** can be utilized to create advanced chatbots and virtual assistants that provide real-time, context-aware customer support and personalized shopping advice, mimicking human-like interactions.

Generative AI can also play a crucial role in content creation, generating personalized marketing materials, product recommendations, and even virtual experiences that are uniquely tailored to each user's preferences and past behaviours. This level of personalization is expected to revolutionize customer engagement by providing experiences that are not only immersive but also deeply integrated with each customer's unique digital footprint.

2.2.3 Integrating Digital Technologies into Products and Services to Enhance Experience

The integration of digital technologies into everyday products and services is revolutionizing how we interact with our environment, bringing convenience and enhanced functionality into our homes, vehicles, and healthcare systems. This trend is particularly evident in Singapore, where the fusion of **AI** with sustainability initiatives and government support is driving the transformation towards smart living and healthcare solutions.

In Singapore, AI-driven smart homes are becoming increasingly common, driven by both consumer demand for smarter living solutions and robust government initiatives such as the **HDB** (Housing & Development Board) **Smart Enabled Home** Initiative. This initiative facilitates the installation of smart devices in public housing to enhance living conditions, improve energy efficiency, and provide residents with a more sustainable lifestyle. These smart homes utilize advanced technologies like **AI** to learn residents' habits and preferences to optimize energy usage and automate systems such as lighting, climate control, and security.

For example, intelligent robotic vacuum cleaners in these smart homes have revolutionized cleaning by autonomously navigating spaces, learning the layout of the home, and being manageable remotely via smartphones. Similarly, smart refrigerators have become interactive hubs within the kitchen, equipped with the capability to track groceries, recommend recipes based on available ingredients, and even facilitate direct grocery orders from the touchscreen, streamlining meal preparation and household management.

The healthcare industry in Singapore is also experiencing significant transformations due to the integration of technology. Digital health tools and platforms are increasingly embedded into healthcare services to improve patient care and operational efficiency. Telemedicine platforms, for instance, allow patients to consult with doctors remotely, leveraging **AI** to help in diagnosing and managing conditions based on digital records and patient data. This technology not only enhances the accessibility of healthcare services but also reduces the burden on physical facilities, aligning with Singapore's sustainability goals.

Moreover, wearable health-monitoring devices are becoming part of routine medical care, enabling continuous monitoring of patients' health metrics such as heart rate, blood pressure, and glucose levels in real-time.

These devices provide critical data that can be analysed to predict potential health issues before they become severe, ensuring timely medical intervention.

The automotive industry is not left behind in this technological integration. Connected vehicles have become a norm, equipped with systems that provide real-time diagnostics, navigation, and personalized in-car entertainment. These vehicles are linked to the user's digital life, allowing for a seamless transition between personal devices and car interfaces, thereby enhancing the driving experience with features such as predictive traffic conditions, route optimization, and voice-controlled media.

The comprehensive integration of digital technologies into homes, healthcare, and automotive sectors in Singapore exemplifies the potential of smart technologies to transform everyday experiences. The government's proactive approach, through initiatives like the Smart Nation project, ensures that these technological advancements contribute to a sustainable, efficient, and highly functional living environment. As these technologies continue to evolve, they promise to redefine our interactions with the world around us, making our lives more connected, convenient, and efficient.

2.2.4 Subscription-Based Business Model

The subscription-based business model has become increasingly popular across various industries, reshaping the way companies deliver products and services to their customers. This model offers consumers a convenient, predictable, and often personalized experience, while providing businesses with a steady revenue stream and enhanced customer engagement. From gourmet coffee to meal kits and streaming services, businesses worldwide are leveraging subscriptions to meet the growing demand for convenience and customization.

Coffee enthusiasts can now enjoy their daily brew with greater convenience and variety through subscriptions from companies like **Blue Bottle Coffee** and **Nespresso**. **Blue Bottle Coffee** offers a subscription service where customers receive freshly roasted coffee beans delivered to their doorstep on a customizable schedule. This service caters to different taste preferences and usage patterns, ensuring that customers never run out of their favourite coffee.

Nespresso, on the other hand, capitalizes on the popularity of its coffee machines and pods by offering a subscription plan that includes a coffee machine for a nominal initial fee. Subscribers commit to a monthly spending amount, which they can use to order coffee pods. This model not only drives the sales of coffee pods but also enhances customer loyalty by simplifying the replenishment process and ensuring Nespresso pods are conveniently delivered to them.

Streaming services are perhaps the most prominent examples of the subscription model's success. Companies like **Netflix, Spotify,** and **Disney+** offer monthly subscriptions that provide unlimited access to vast libraries of movies, TV shows, music, and exclusive content. These services have changed how content is consumed, moving away from physical or digital purchases and rentals to a model where users pay for access rather than ownership. This shift has not only revolutionized the entertainment industry but also set a standard for digital content consumption globally.

Subscription boxes are another area where the model has seen significant success, particularly with meal kits like **Blue Apron**. **Blue Apron** delivers weekly boxes containing ingredients and recipes to its subscribers, making it easy for them to cook healthy and delicious meals at home. This service appeals particularly to busy consumers who want to cook but lack the time to plan meals and shop for ingredients.

In Singapore, the subscription model has been warmly embraced across different sectors. **Circles.Life,** a digital telco, revolutionized the mobile telecommunications landscape with its flexible, no-contract subscription plans that allow customers to tailor their mobile services according to their needs. This customer-centric approach has not only garnered a strong following but also prompted traditional telcos to rethink their service models.

Subscription-based business models offer distinct advantages by fostering customer retention and facilitating predictable financial planning. Whether it's enjoying freshly brewed coffee, streaming favourite shows, preparing home-cooked meals, or customizing mobile services, consumers appreciate the convenience and personalized experience these subscriptions provide. As more businesses across diverse industries adopt this model, the landscape of consumer services continues to evolve, increasingly tailored to the preferences and lifestyles of today's consumers.

2.2.5   Seamless Shopping Experience with Virtual Stores

The concept of virtual stores has been rapidly evolving, blending digital and physical retail spaces to meet the changing needs of consumers. This innovative approach is exemplified not only by large-scale initiatives like **Tesco's** virtual store in Seoul and **Amazon's** 'Just Walk Out' technology but also by industry-specific applications in furniture and athletic apparel, where companies like **Urban Barn** and **Nike** are setting new standards in retail.

Urban Barn has introduced a Virtual Design Studio, enabling customers to visualize how furniture fits within their actual living spaces using 3D modelling. This immersive experience helps reduce uncertainty in online furniture shopping, increasing consumer confidence and satisfaction by allowing customers to see realistic renditions of their furnished rooms before making a purchase.

Similarly, **Nike** has transformed the athletic apparel shopping experience by integrating digital technologies directly into their physical stores. Customers can test products under simulated conditions, receive feedback through digital sensors, and interact with the **Nike** app to scan products for more information, reserve items, and even check out without waiting in line. This seamless integration of digital and physical elements enhances the shopping experience, making it more dynamic and user-friendly.

Building on the foundation laid by earlier initiatives, **Tesco's** virtual store in Seoul allowed commuters to shop using digital screens in subway stations, selecting groceries that would be delivered directly to their homes. This concept paved the way for further innovations like **Amazon Go**, which utilizes a sophisticated system of sensors and **AI** to allow customers to shop without the traditional checkout process, and **Alibaba's Hema** supermarkets in China, which combine the functionalities of both fulfilment centres and physical stores. In **Hema** supermarkets, customers can shop in-person or use the **Hema** app to scan and purchase items for delivery, making the retail experience incredibly flexible and integrated with online shopping capabilities.

These examples collectively highlight how virtual stores are leveraging advanced technologies to redefine the retail experience, making shopping more convenient and adapted to modern lifestyles. By blending online and offline elements, retailers are able to offer unprecedented levels of convenience and efficiency, encouraging a more seamless interaction between consumers and products. As technology continues to advance, the potential for virtual and augmented reality, along with **AI** and mobile applications, to further enhance the shopping experience is immense. Retailers who successfully integrate these technologies can expect to lead the market in innovation, customer satisfaction, and sales performance.

The seamless shopping experience provided by virtual stores represents a significant evolution in retail, driven by the integration of digital innovations. Retailers like **Urban Barn, Nike, Tesco, Amazon**, and **Alibaba** are at the forefront of this transformation, demonstrating the powerful impact of combining digital and physical retail strategies to meet the diverse needs of today's consumers.

2.2.6 *Leveraging Location-Based Technologies*

Location-based technologies, enhanced by artificial intelligence, are revolutionizing the way businesses interact with their environment and customers. By gathering and analysing vast amounts of real-time data, such as user movements, traffic flow, and consumer behaviour, these technologies enable businesses to optimize operations, enhance customer experiences, and drive strategic decisions.

The integration of **AI** algorithms with location-based technologies allows for the real-time processing and analysis of complex data. This capability is crucial for identifying trends and making data-driven decisions that can significantly improve operational efficiency, reduce costs, and boost revenue. For example, retailers can analyse foot traffic patterns to optimize store layouts, product placements, and staff allocation, ensuring that resources are used efficiently to enhance the shopping experience and increase sales.

Location-based technology excels in personalizing user interactions. By understanding the location and behaviour of users, businesses can deliver targeted notifications, personalized recommendations, and efficient routing suggestions that improve the overall customer experience. For instance, a shopping app can notify a user about a sale on a favourite product when they enter a specific part of a store, or a navigation app can suggest the quickest route home based on real-time traffic data.

In the transport hub industry, facility managers utilize location-based technologies to monitor and optimize traffic flow within spaces like airports and train stations. **AI** tools analyse data on traffic patterns and weather conditions to make real-time adjustments that enhance flow efficiency and reduce wait times. AI-powered chatbots also play a crucial role by providing passengers with real-time updates on their flights or train statuses, thereby improving communication and passenger satisfaction.

Businesses are increasingly adopting location-based marketing strategies to provide customers with highly relevant and timely promotions. Major retailers such as **Walmart** and **Target** deploy beacons and geo-fencing technologies to send personalized offers directly to customers' smartphones when they are nearby or even within the store. This method not only enhances the customer experience by making it more relevant and convenient but also significantly increases the likelihood of conversions.

For example, **Starbucks** uses geo-fencing technology around its outlets to trigger reminders for mobile orders as customers approach, making the purchase process as seamless as possible. This approach not only streamlines operations but also boosts customer loyalty by reducing wait times and enhancing the overall service experience.

The strategic use of location-based technologies combined with **AI** is transforming industries by enabling more connected, responsive, and efficient business practices. Whether it's optimizing the layout of a retail store, enhancing navigational efficiencies in transport hubs, or personalizing marketing efforts, these technologies are proving invaluable in adapting to the dynamic needs of customers and the operational demands of modern business environments. As these technologies continue to evolve, they will offer even greater opportunities to innovate and compete in a digitally connected world.

2.2.7   *Retail Reinvention Through Mobile Apps*

Mobile applications have rapidly ascended to become central elements in the strategic transformation of the retail sector. They not only facilitate the traditional purchasing process but also enhance the entire customer journey, providing a platform where interactive technology meets consumer convenience. From fashion to sports equipment to beauty products, mobile apps are reshaping how retailers connect with their customers and revolutionizing the in-store experience.

Uniqlo and **Decathlon** are prime examples of how mobile applications are being used to streamline operations and enrich the customer experience. **Uniqlo's** mobile app includes a barcode scanning feature that allows customers to quickly check out products, verify prices, view available sizes, or locate alternative colours without needing to interact directly with staff. This feature significantly speeds up the shopping process, reduces waiting times, and improves overall customer satisfaction.

Decathlon's app serves as a comprehensive digital tool, providing users with detailed product information, user reviews, and availability status both online and in-store. It enhances the shopping experience by ensuring that customers are well-informed, enabling them to make purchasing decisions confidently. The app also supports **Decathlon's** inventory management by showing real-time stock levels, thus helping to manage customer expectations and reduce potential frustrations over out-of-stock items.

Sephora's app represents a leap forward in integrating technology with customer service by incorporating **Augmented Reality (AR)**. This feature allows customers to try on makeup virtually using their mobile device's camera, effectively merging the online shopping experience with the tactile in-store environment. By enabling customers to see how products look on them before making a purchase, **Sephora's** app reduces the uncertainty often associated with buying cosmetics online. Additionally, it offers personalized product recommendations based on the user's interactions, further tailoring the shopping experience to individual preferences.

Beyond enhancing individual shopping experiences, mobile applications are becoming a holistic service platform. They facilitate a deeper engagement by incorporating loyalty programs, personalized notifications, and exclusive offers that incentivize repeat visits and foster a strong brand connection. For instance, apps often allow users to accumulate points that can be redeemed for discounts on future purchases or gain early access to sales and special events, enhancing customer loyalty and retention.

Looking ahead, the potential for mobile apps in retail continues to expand as technology advances. Features like AI-driven chatbots for personalized shopping assistance, machine learning algorithms for predictive shopping behaviours, and integration with other smart technologies like **IoT** for a seamless shopping experience are on the horizon. These innovations will continue to build on the strong foundation laid by current applications, driving further transformations in the retail landscape.

Mobile applications have evolved from simple transactional tools to complex platforms that enrich the retail experience. By leveraging these digital tools, retailers like **Uniqlo, Decathlon,** and **Sephora** are not only enhancing operational efficiencies and customer satisfaction but also setting new standards in how technology can be used to revolutionize the retail industry.

2.3 Navigating the Digital Threat: The Catalyst for Transformation

In today's business landscape, the digital threat looms large as a powerful catalyst for transformation, pushing companies to adapt or risk obsolescence. This threat, driven by rapid technological advancements and evolving consumer expectations, presents both challenges and opportunities. Industries across the board, from transportation to retail, are experiencing unprecedented disruption as new digital-first entrants redefine the norms and set new standards. This section explores how businesses are navigating the digital threat, highlighting the essential shifts in strategy that are critical for survival and growth in the digital era. Through real-world examples, we will examine how companies are transforming their operations and market approaches to not only withstand but also capitalize on the challenges posed by digital disruption.

2.3.1 Understanding the Digital Threat in Modern Business

A crucial driver of digital transformation across industries is the looming presence of the digital threat. This threat originates from various sources including modern consumers, emerging startups, intense competition, and the rapid evolution of technology itself. This reality is evident in the disruption caused by companies like **Uber** and **Airbnb**, which have leveraged technology to reshape the transportation and hospitality industries, respectively. These companies exploited the digital gap left by traditional firms, offering more efficient, scalable, and user-friendly alternatives that better meet modern consumer expectations.

2.3.2 Changing Consumer Behaviours and Expectations

Over the last decade, consumer behaviour has undergone significant changes, largely influenced by the maturation of digital technologies. As digital devices and platforms become more ingrained in daily life, consumers increasingly expect businesses to offer services that incorporate these technologies.

The demand for convenience, speed, and personalization is higher than ever, pushing companies to innovate continually to meet these evolving needs. For example, **Amazon** has set a high standard with its Prime service, offering same-day or next-day delivery, which has recalibrated consumer expectations for delivery speed across all retail sectors. Consumers now expect fast, seamless, and highly personalized shopping experiences, pressuring traditional retailers to innovate rapidly. Companies like **Nike** have responded by integrating apps like Nike+ to offer personalized training advice, product recommendations, and direct marketing, which enhances customer engagement and loyalty.

2.3.3 Impact of Digitization on Market Dynamics

Digitization – the process of converting information from a physical to a digital format – has notably lowered the barriers to entry in many markets. This shift facilitates cross-border and cross-industry competition, enabling new market entrants and startups to scale rapidly and at a fraction of the traditional cost. The agility and innovation capacity of these newcomers often allow them to outpace established players, especially those reliant on outdated brick-and-mortar models. An illustrative example is the fintech industry, where companies like **Revolut** and **TransferWise** have disrupted traditional banking services by offering quick and cost-effective international money transfer services without the need for physical branches. These fintech startups utilize digital platforms to provide enhanced customer experiences with better rates, faster services, and higher transparency compared to traditional banks.

Similarly, in media and entertainment, streaming services such as **Netflix** and **Spotify** have utilized digitization to change how content is distributed and consumed. These platforms bypass traditional distribution channels like broadcast television and physical stores, offering vast libraries of content directly to consumers on-demand, which traditional cable providers and media outlets struggled to compete with initially.

In the retail sector, the digitization process has allowed companies like **IKEA** to enhance customer experiences by integrating augmented reality into their app. This technology enables customers to visualize furniture in their homes before making a purchase, effectively bringing the showroom into their living rooms.

2.4 Transforming Industry Norms with Innovative Service Models

As digital technologies reshape markets and consumer expectations, businesses are increasingly adopting innovative service models that enhance customer engagement and provide ongoing value. This shift from product-centric to service-centric business models marks a significant transformation in how companies operate and generate revenue. By focusing on services rather than just products, companies are not only responding to changing consumer preferences but are also creating more sustainable and scalable business models. This section explores how various industries are embracing this paradigm shift, highlighting key examples of companies that have successfully transitioned to these new service models, thereby securing competitive advantages and stronger customer relationships in their respective markets.

2.4.1 Rolls Royce's Power-by-the-Hour: Revolutionizing Aerospace Maintenance

Rolls Royce has innovated its business model by shifting from selling aircraft engines to offering a holistic service package. Their '**Power-by-the-Hour**' approach encompasses complete engine lifecycle management, covering everything from routine maintenance to detailed performance assessments. This service-centric model provides a stable financial structure for airlines by smoothing out the traditionally erratic expenses of engine procurement and major repairs. Airlines can then redirect their focus and resources towards primary business functions. For **Rolls Royce**, this strategy results in scale benefits. The company's continuous oversight and maintenance of a vast fleet of engines enable it to accumulate a wealth of data on engine health and efficiency, positioning **Rolls Royce** as a leader not just in engine production but also in comprehensive engine care and operational optimization.

2.4.2 Industries Embracing Subscription and Service-Based Models for Strategic Growth

The service model exemplified by **Rolls Royce** is becoming increasingly prevalent across a range of industries, signalling a shift in how companies approach product delivery and customer engagement. In the software industry, the SaaS (Software as a Service) model is a prime example of this trend. Instead of the traditional model where software is purchased as a static product, companies like **Adobe** and **Microsoft** have redefined their offerings by adopting subscription-based models.

These models offer a continuous service in exchange for regular payments, effectively turning software into an ongoing service. Customers benefit from a dynamic product that evolves through regular updates, enhancements, and new features, all delivered seamlessly through the cloud. This approach not only ensures that users always have access to the latest advancements in software technology but also affords them a degree of flexibility and scalability previously unattainable in the era of one-time purchases.

For the providers like **Adobe** and **Microsoft,** the subscription model represents a transformation in their revenue architecture, introducing predictability and stability into their financial planning. The consistent revenue generated from subscriptions mitigates the unpredictability associated with one-off sales and software piracy. Moreover, it establishes a long-term relationship with customers, who become ongoing recipients of the company's services.

Additionally, this model provides companies with a wealth of data on how their software is used, enabling them to refine their products in alignment with user behaviour and preferences. It's a virtuous cycle where continuous feedback informs product development, leading to higher customer satisfaction and retention rates.

The proliferation of the **SaaS** model is evident in the widespread use of cloud-based platforms for tasks ranging from document creation and collaboration to complex data analysis and machine learning. As more companies transition to this model, it is reshaping entire industries, promoting a culture of innovation, and setting new standards for delivering value to customers.

Table 2.1 lists some key industries with subscription and service-based models.

TABLE 2.1 Industries with subscription and service-based models

Industry	Company	Service Model	Description
Automobile	Tesla	Subscription for Self-Driving	Offers a subscription model for its advanced self-driving feature.
	Volvo	Subscription Service (Volvo Care)	Provides an all-inclusive subscription that covers car, maintenance, insurance, and concierge services.
	BMW	BMW Subscription	Offers flexible vehicle subscriptions, including insurance, maintenance, and roadside assistance.
	Audi	Audi on Demand	Provides premium car rental services with flexible time frames from hours to months.
	GetGo	Car Rental Subscription	Allows users in Singapore to rent cars on a flexible subscription basis, enhancing mobility solutions.

(*Continued*)

TABLE 2.1 (Continued)

Industry	Company	Service Model	Description
	BlueSG	Electric Car Subscription	Offers electric cars for rent on a subscription basis in Singapore, with numerous pick-up points.
	TribeCar	Pay-as-you-go Car Rental	Provides car rental services in Singapore, billed by the hour or day, catering to casual users.
Air Travel	Surf Air	All-you-can-fly Membership	Offers unlimited flights within their network for a monthly fee.
	Delta	Delta Sky Club Membership	Provides access to exclusive airport lounges, enhancing the travel experience with various amenities.
	FlyLine	Airfare Subscription	Provides a club membership that offers access to wholesale prices on flights with a booking guarantee.
	United Airlines	Subscription Services	Offers subscriptions for baggage fees, United Club access, and preferred seating.
	JetBlue	Mosaic Membership	Offers accelerated earning potential, bonus rewards, and additional flight benefits to subscribers.
Retail	Amazon Prime	Membership Subscription	Combines free shipping, streaming video, music services, and more, enhancing customer loyalty.
	Style Theory	Fashion Subscription Service	Provides a monthly subscription service for renting designer apparel and accessories.
	Sephora	Beauty Subscription Box	Offers a monthly subscription box of sample beauty products tailored to user preferences.
	Stitch Fix	Personalized Shopping Subscription	Delivers personally tailored clothing items based on user style preferences and feedback.
Technology	Adobe	Software as a Service (SaaS)	Transitioned to a subscription-based model offering access to its suite of creative software.
	Microsoft	Office 365	Provides its office suite on a subscription basis, offering regular updates and cloud storage.

(*Continued*)

TABLE 2.1 (Continued)

Industry	Company	Service Model	Description
	Salesforce	CRM as a Service	Delivers a customer relationship management system on a subscription basis, enhancing business operations.
	Slack	Collaboration Tools Subscription	Offers business communication tools on a subscription basis, facilitating workplace collaboration.
	Xbox Game Pass	Gaming Subscription	Provides access to a library of games for Xbox and PC, including new releases and discounts.
Gaming	GameSpot	Gaming News and Discounts Subscription	Offers premium content, early access to new releases, and exclusive discounts to subscribers.
	PlayStation Now	Game Streaming Subscription	Offers on-demand game streaming services for PlayStation games on console and PC.
	EA Access	Game Subscription	Provides access to a selection of EA's best games, discounts, and exclusive trials of new releases.
	Google Play Pass	App and Game Subscription	Offers access to hundreds of apps and games without ads or in-app purchases, enhancing mobile gaming.
Fitness	Peloton	Interactive Fitness Subscription	Offers live and on-demand fitness classes that are integrated with their equipment.
	Mirror	Fitness Content Subscription	Offers interactive workout classes through a reflective display that acts as a personal trainer.
	Tonal	Smart Home Gym Subscription	Combines equipment purchase with a subscription for personalized strength training programs.
	Fitbit Premium	Health and Fitness Guidance Subscription	Provides personalized workout plans, detailed health insights, and guided programs based on user data.
Healthcare	CureVac	Subscription for Vaccine Supply	Offers countries subscriptions for priority access to vaccines produced, ensuring supply ahead of demand.

(*Continued*)

TABLE 2.1 (Continued)

Industry	Company	Service Model	Description
	One Medical	Membership-based Medical Care	Provides membership-based healthcare services, offering enhanced doctor access and health management.
	Healthway Medical	Membership-based Healthcare Services	Offers comprehensive healthcare packages in Singapore, providing priority services and health screening.
	Ping An Good Doctor	Digital Health Subscription	Provides online health consultation and management services in China, leveraging a massive digital platform.
Home Appliances	Miele	Subscription for Appliances	Provides high-end appliances for a monthly fee, including maintenance and upgrades as part of the subscription.
	Bosch	Subscription for Home Appliances	Offers a range of home appliances for rent, including options to swap, upgrade, or purchase outright at the end of the subscription period.
	Dyson	Dyson Cordless Vacuum Subscription	Provides cordless vacuums on a subscription basis, with regular maintenance and the option to upgrade to the latest model.
	Whirlpool	Appliance as a Service	Offers washing machines and dryers on a pay-per-use basis, integrating smart technology to track usage and optimize operations.
	LG	Smart Appliance Subscription	Provides smart home appliances with a subscription that includes regular updates, remote diagnostics, and premium customer support.
	Levande	Home Appliance Subscription	Offers a variety of home appliances on a subscription model, enabling consumers to access modern equipment without hefty upfront costs.

Table 2.1 shows a detailed and comprehensive list of examples across various industries where companies are utilizing innovative subscription-based and service-oriented business models to meet modern consumer demands and market trends.

2.5 Conclusion

This chapter provides a comprehensive exploration of the evolving roles and challenges faced by digital product managers in the midst of rapid technological change and market evolution. This chapter has dissected how businesses transform from traditional to digital entities, navigating the myriad threats and seizing opportunities that arise during this transformative process. It has illustrated that success in digital markets isn't merely about adopting new technologies but also about fundamentally understanding and integrating these technologies in ways that align with consumer expectations and market needs.

The discussion on the digital threat and the adaptation strategies employed by companies highlights the critical nature of agility and foresight in business planning. Similarly, the concept of creative destruction has been presented as a catalyst for innovation, pushing companies to continually evolve or risk obsolescence. Through examples of digital natives and immigrants, the chapter underscores the varied approaches businesses might take depending on their legacy, culture, and market positioning.

Moreover, the juxtaposition of product success stories and failures provides valuable lessons on the importance of customer-centricity, clear vision, and persistent innovation. It becomes clear that understanding the reasons behind product failures is as crucial as celebrating successes, as both provide crucial learning points for future endeavours.

As the digital landscape continues to expand and integrate into every facet of business, product managers and their teams are urged to harness the insights provided in this chapter to build resilient strategies that not only respond to immediate challenges but also anticipate future trends. Embracing the dynamics of digital transformation is not just about survival, but about thriving in an era of digital economies where change is the only constant.

3
MANAGING EXPECTATIONS
AND STAKEHOLDER DYNAMICS

3.1 Introduction

In the rapidly shifting landscape of digital business, managing expectations and navigating stakeholder dynamics become pivotal to sustaining growth and fostering innovation. This chapter delves into the critical strategies and practices necessary for effectively managing market and user expectations in a digital reality. It also explores how businesses can navigate the complex dynamics of stakeholders amidst the ongoing phenomenon of creative destruction, a process where innovation disrupts existing market norms.

3.2 Managing Market and User Expectations in a Digital Reality

In the rapidly evolving digital landscape, managing market and user expectations has become increasingly complex but essential for maintaining competitiveness and ensuring customer satisfaction. This section explores the challenges digital product managers face in aligning product offerings with the dynamic expectations of modern consumers and markets, and how they can effectively navigate these challenges.

1 **Understanding Market Dynamics**
   Digital markets are characterized by rapid changes in technology, consumer behaviour, and competitive strategies. For product managers, staying ahead requires a deep understanding of market trends and the agility to adapt quickly. This includes recognizing shifts in consumer preferences, such as the increasing demand for personalized experiences and instant

DOI: 10.1201/9781003484295-3

gratification, and anticipating technological advancements that could disrupt or enhance product offerings.

2 **Aligning Product Development with User Expectations**
The digital consumer expects products that are not only functionally rich but also highly user-friendly, personalized, and accessible across multiple devices and platforms. Digital product managers must ensure that their product development strategies are user-centred, incorporating user feedback continuously through data analytics, user testing, and direct interactions. This iterative approach helps refine product features and functionalities to better meet user needs.

For example, streaming services like **Netflix** and **Spotify** have excelled in this area by using algorithms to personalize content recommendations based on individual user behaviours. This not only enhances user satisfaction but also increases engagement and retention.

3 **Communicating Effectively with Users**
Effective communication with users is critical, especially when rolling out new features or making changes to existing ones. Digital product managers must develop clear communication strategies that inform users about updates, address concerns, and manage expectations. This can be achieved through various channels such as email updates, in-app notifications, and active engagement on social media platforms.

4 **Leveraging Customer Data for Improved Service Delivery**
With access to extensive customer data, digital product managers have a unique opportunity to understand and predict user behaviour. By leveraging analytics tools, they can identify patterns and preferences, which can inform product enhancements and marketing strategies. However, with great data comes great responsibility, and it is crucial to handle user data ethically and in compliance with data protection regulations.

5 **Adapting to Global Market Variations**
Digital products often have a global reach, which means product managers must consider diverse user expectations and regulatory environments across different regions. Localization of products – including language, content, and functionality – must be managed carefully to cater to local tastes while maintaining a consistent brand experience globally.

6 **Dealing with Change and Uncertainty**
In a digital reality where market conditions and technologies evolve rapidly, product managers must cultivate a culture of flexibility and resilience within their teams. This involves being prepared to pivot strategies in response to new market information or feedback, and fostering an organizational mindset that embraces change rather than resists it.

3.3 Navigating Stakeholder Dynamics Amidst Creative Destruction

In today's rapidly evolving business landscape, the concept of creative destruction, introduced by Austrian economist Joseph Schumpeter, vividly captures the essence of innovation's disruptive power. As digital technologies continue to reshape industries, they introduce new challenges and opportunities for businesses of all types. This dynamic often creates a stark divide between **'digital natives'**, who are inherently equipped to thrive in a digital environment, and **'digital immigrants'**, established entities now scrambling to adapt to new technological realities.

This section explores how businesses can effectively manage the complex stakeholder dynamics that arise in the face of such transformative changes. We will delve into the unique challenges and strategies of both digital natives and immigrants, examining how these groups navigate the disruptive waters of technological innovation. Through real-world examples, we will contrast how emerging startups and multinational corporations adjust their strategies to not only survive but excel amidst the ongoing digital revolution. By understanding and addressing the concerns of diverse stakeholders – ranging from employees and customers to investors and partners – companies can forge a path to sustained success and growth in an era defined by continuous change.

3.3.1 Understanding Creative Destruction

The concept of 'creative destruction', coined by Austrian economist Joseph Schumpeter in the 1940s, captures the essence of how technological advancements can simultaneously drive economic progress and disrupt existing systems. This dynamic not only impacts industries but also differentiates between individuals and companies categorized as digital natives and digital immigrants.

3.3.2 Contemporary Examples of Creative Destruction

In recent years, the travel, hospitality, retail, and media industries have experienced profound transformations due to digital technologies, as shown in Figure 3.1.

1 **Travel Agencies:** Online platforms like **Expedia, Kayak,** and **Travelocity** have largely supplanted traditional human travel agents by offering convenient, one-stop solutions for comparing and booking travel.
2 **Hospitality: Airbnb** and **HomeAway** have disrupted the traditional hotel and motel industry by enabling homeowners to rent out private accommodations, often providing more personalized and cost-effective alternatives.

FIGURE 3.1   Contemporary examples of creative destruction

3 **Media and Publishing:** The rise of digital media has severely impacted traditional newspapers, with many seeing a steep decline in circulation and revenue. Increasingly, news content is being produced by algorithms, particularly for routine reporting on local events and sports.

4 **Retail Bookstores: Amazon** and other online bookstores have led to the closure of many brick-and-mortar booksellers. The rise of e-books and the ease of self-publishing have also diminished the roles of traditional publishers and printers.

5 **Recruitment and Classifieds:** Digital platforms like **LinkedIn, Indeed.com,** and **Monster** have transformed job recruitment, reducing the reliance on human recruiters and print classified ads. Similarly, **Craigslist** has replaced many traditional forms of classified advertising.

6 **Educational Platforms:** Educational sites like **Khan Academy, Udemy,** and university-provided **Massive Open Online Courses** (**MOOCs**) are transforming traditional education. These resources enable students to access quality education online at minimal costs, potentially diminishing the need for traditional teaching roles. As this trend continues, it is plausible that future students will complete their undergraduate studies largely online, significantly reducing educational expenses and democratizing access to learning.

3.3.3   Digital Natives vs. Digital Immigrants

At the individual level, digital natives are those who have grown up with digital technology, thus, they are inherently comfortable with navigating and embracing new tech innovations. Digital immigrants, on the other hand, are those who have had to adapt to these technologies later in life, often facing steeper learning curves. This distinction is also apparent at the company level, where many multinational corporations (**MNCs**) are digital immigrants, having to retrofit digital solutions into their established ways of doing business, while many startups are digital natives, built with digital technologies and business models from their inception.

3.3.4 Examples and Strategic Differences

1 **Digital Native Companies**: Startups like **Snapchat** and **Revolut** exemplify digital natives. **Snapchat**, for instance, has continually innovated with augmented reality and interactive content to engage its largely Gen Z audience, who are digital natives themselves. **Revolut**, started in 2015, disrupts traditional banking by offering a completely app-based banking experience, resonating with customers accustomed to managing their lives via smartphones.
2 **Digital Immigrant Companies**: Traditional **MNCs** like **General Electric** (**GE**) and **Ford** serve as examples of digital immigrants. **GE** has been transitioning towards becoming a '**digital industrial**' company, investing heavily in **GE Digital** and integrating IoT capabilities into its industrial products. **Ford** has embraced digital transformation by investing in autonomous vehicles and mobility solutions, attempting to keep pace with newer, more agile competitors like **Tesla**.

3.3.5 Strategies Employed by Digital Natives and Immigrants

1 **Innovation Speed and Adoption**: Digital native companies often have the advantage of speed and flexibility. They can innovate rapidly and are not hindered by legacy systems or traditional business models. In contrast, digital immigrants must often undergo significant transformations, which can be costly and time-consuming, to integrate new digital technologies.
2 **Customer Engagement and Experience**: Digital natives typically focus intensely on user experience and customer engagement, leveraging data analytics and user feedback to continuously refine their offerings. Digital immigrants, meanwhile, may struggle with transforming their customer engagement models to meet the expectations of a digital-first audience.
3 **Organizational Culture and Agility**: Startups usually boast a culture of agility and innovation, readily experimenting and adapting to market changes. In contrast, **MNCs** might battle entrenched cultures and bureaucracies that resist change, necessitating more deliberate strategies for fostering a digital-first mindset.

4 **Technology Integration**: Digital natives build their operations around modern technologies and thus can seamlessly integrate the latest advancements into their products and services. Digital immigrants have to retrofit new technologies into existing infrastructures, which can lead to compatibility issues and disruptions.

3.3.6 Strategies for Managing Stakeholder Dynamics

In the rapidly changing landscape of digital transformation, effectively managing stakeholder dynamics is crucial for sustaining business growth and innovation. This sub-section explores various strategies that organizations can employ to engage and align stakeholders with their digital transformation initiatives, providing real-world examples to illustrate these approaches in action.

1 **Communication and Transparency**

Keeping stakeholders informed about changes, the reasons behind them, and expected outcomes is essential. Clear and continuous communication can mitigate resistance and build trust, ensuring that stakeholders feel involved and valued.

Example: Microsoft's Shift to Cloud Computing

When **Microsoft** transitioned from traditional software products to cloud services, it adopted a product-led approach, centralizing its offerings around Azure and Office 365 to better meet customer needs. This shift required **Microsoft** to reimagine its operations and product development to ensure seamless integration and delivery of its cloud services. The company placed significant emphasis on transparent communication to mitigate scepticism among stakeholders. Regular updates and clear explanations of the long-term benefits of cloud computing were essential in aligning employees, customers, and investors with the new strategic direction.

This open line of communication helped transform potential resistance into widespread support, easing the transition into cloud services. **Microsoft's** approach not only facilitated smoother adoption but also bolstered stakeholder trust and commitment to the company's vision, demonstrating effective management during a major digital transformation. By focusing on a product-led strategy, **Microsoft** ensured that its cloud solutions were not only technologically advanced but also directly aligned with the evolving needs of the market, enhancing customer satisfaction and driving business growth.

2 **Stakeholder Involvement**

Involving stakeholders in the planning and implementation phases of digital projects can foster a sense of ownership and buy-in. Engaging them early and often ensures that their insights and concerns are addressed, which can enhance the outcomes of transformation efforts.

Example: Adobe's Subscription Model Transition

Adobe's transition to a subscription-based model with its Creative Cloud was a significant shift that required meticulous planning and robust stakeholder engagement. The company initially maintained its traditional software sales alongside the new subscription service, ensuring a smooth transition by not alienating existing customers who were accustomed to the perpetual license model. This dual-offering phase was crucial in providing stakeholders time to see the benefits of the new model, such as more frequent updates and better security.

Stakeholder engagement was vital, not just in alleviating concerns but also in gathering feedback that helped **Adobe** refine its offerings to better meet user expectations. The approach helped transform potential customer scepticism into acceptance and approval, illustrating how critical stakeholders are to the success of major strategic shifts.

By successfully engaging stakeholders and managing the transition carefully, **Adobe** set itself up for increased subscription growth and recurring revenue, demonstrating the effectiveness of strategic stakeholder management in corporate transformations.

3 **Training and Support**
Providing stakeholders with the necessary training and support to adapt to new technologies and processes is critical. This strategy helps mitigate fears about obsolescence and builds competency and confidence among employees and customers.

Example: AT&T's Future Ready Workforce Initiative

AT&T's Future Ready Workforce Initiative is a strategic response to the rapid advancements in digital technology and the evolving demands of the telecom industry. With a significant investment of $1 billion, **AT&T** embarked on retraining nearly half of its workforce, which consists of about 250,000 employees, to equip them with necessary skills for future digital and data-driven roles. This extensive program leverages online courses from platforms like **Coursera** and **Udacity**, and also includes partnerships with universities to provide tailored educational programs.

The initiative goes beyond just providing training; it introduces a holistic approach to career development. This includes a career centre that helps employees identify future job roles within **AT&T** and understand the skills required for these positions. **AT&T's** commitment extends to fostering a culture of continuous learning and adaptability, encouraging employees to proactively manage their professional growth. Employees are supported in assessing their current skills, understanding future needs, and accessing the tools needed to achieve their career goals.

This proactive approach not only helps **AT&T** manage its workforce's transition but also ensures the company retains valuable talent while aligning employee growth with its broader strategic objectives, exemplifying a forward-thinking method to handle technological transformation in the corporate world.

4 **Personalization of Experience**

Tailoring the digital experience to meet the specific needs and preferences of different stakeholder groups can significantly enhance engagement. Personalization ensures that each stakeholder group receives relevant content and interactions, making the digital transformation more relevant and valuable to them.

Example: Sephora's Personalized Shopping Experience

Sephora's approach to personalizing the shopping experience utilizes advanced data analytics and AI, successfully merging online and in-store interactions. Through its comprehensive mobile app, customers can check product availability, book in-store services, and access a wealth of personalized features. The app enhances the in-store experience by allowing customers to virtually try on products, receive tailored recommendations, and even log the products used during in-store makeovers directly into their profiles. This integration ensures that every aspect of the customer's journey is remembered and accessible for future interactions.

Additionally, **Sephora's** commitment to a seamless customer experience extends to its loyalty program, **Beauty Insider**, which enriches customer engagement by offering tiered rewards. These include early access to new products, exclusive event invitations, and free beauty services for top-tier members. The loyalty program effectively uses customer data to deliver customized communications and offers, ensuring that promotions and recommendations are highly relevant and personalized.

Sephora's strategy has proven highly effective, with its loyalty program boasting about 25 million members, who contribute to 80% of the company's total transactions. This success is underscored by **Sephora** consistently ranking high in retail personalization indexes, demonstrating the effectiveness of its customer-centric approach. This method not only fosters customer loyalty but also sets a high standard for retail personalization, significantly enhancing the overall consumer experience.

5 **Monitoring and Feedback Mechanisms**

Establishing mechanisms to continuously monitor the impact of digital initiatives and gather feedback is essential. This ongoing evaluation allows businesses to make iterative improvements, addressing any issues promptly and adapting strategies as needed.

Example: Zara's Real-Time Retail Strategy

Zara's real-time retail strategy employs advanced data analytics to effectively monitor sales trends and customer feedback, ensuring swift responses that align product offerings and store layouts with current fashion trends and customer preferences. By utilizing technologies such as **RFID** tags for inventory management and sensors to track foot traffic and popular areas within stores, **Zara** not only optimizes inventory levels but also enhances the overall store experience. This strategic use of data allows **Zara** to anticipate customer needs dynamically, offering a personalized shopping experience and maintaining a competitive edge in the fast-paced fashion industry.

The company's ability to rapidly adjust its collections to the latest consumer demands significantly reduces lead times and keeps it ahead of industry trends. This agility is supported by a comprehensive data system that collects insights on everything from sales figures to customer preferences and even the local demographics' average body measurements to ensure the right stock of sizes. **Zara's** commitment to data-driven decision-making extends beyond simple sales tracking; it involves analysing returns, customer feedback, and online discussions to refine every aspect of its business operations, from physical storefronts to online platforms.

Zara's approach not only exemplifies how real-time data can be leveraged to streamline operations but also illustrates the potential of a well-integrated data analytics system to transform the core of retail business strategies. This methodology has proven crucial in enabling **Zara** to maintain its status as a leader in the global fashion retail market, continuously evolving to meet the dynamic demands of its diverse customer base.

3.4 Conclusion

This chapter has thoroughly explored the multifaceted challenges and strategies involved in managing expectations and stakeholder dynamics in digital product management. By understanding the nuanced requirements of different stakeholders and aligning these with the product vision, digital product managers can foster an environment conducive to successful product development.

We have seen how effective communication plays a pivotal role in harmonizing stakeholder interests with project goals. Strategies such as regular updates, transparent feedback mechanisms, and inclusive decision-making processes are vital for maintaining alignment and building trust among all parties involved. The chapter highlighted the importance of empathy and understanding in managing diverse expectations, ensuring that all voices are heard and considered in the product development process.

Moreover, conflict resolution has been identified as a critical skill for product managers. The ability to navigate disagreements and find solutions that align with the product's best interests can determine the success of a project. This involves a deep understanding of each stakeholder's perspective and finding common ground that supports the project's objectives.

In conclusion, managing expectations and stakeholder dynamics is not just about balancing demands but about creating a collaborative environment where innovation can thrive. Digital product managers who master these skills are better equipped to lead projects that not only meet but exceed the expectations of their users and stakeholders, driving the product to greater success in the competitive digital marketplace.

4

LESSONS FROM MARKET SUCCESSES AND CHALLENGES

4.1 Introduction

This chapter delves into how companies like **Apple, Tesla, Nespresso, Netflix**, and **Amazon** have mastered the art of combining visionary leadership with strategic operations and technological innovation to excel in the digital economy. Through case studies, we explore their methods for overcoming industry challenges and delivering exceptional value, highlighting the importance of strategic resource management and market differentiation. By examining their approaches to customer focus and innovative problem-solving, this chapter offers valuable insights on how businesses can thrive by effectively navigating the complexities of the digital marketplace, setting new standards, and ensuring long-term growth in competitive environments.

4.2 Analysing Product Failures: Lessons from the Marketplace

In the dynamic world of product development, not every launch can translate into a market success. Understanding why some products fail while others flourish is crucial for businesses aiming to innovate effectively and sustainably. This section explores various cases of product failures across different industries, analysing key factors that contributed to their lack of success. From the infamous case of **Google Glass**, which stumbled due to privacy concerns and social acceptability, to the ambitious yet financially unsustainable business model of **MoviePass**, each example provides invaluable lessons on the complexities of meeting market demands. Additionally, the story of **Keurig Kold** illustrates how even well-established companies can misjudge consumer readiness and market conditions, leading to significant financial

DOI: 10.1201/9781003484295-4

FIGURE 4.1   Failure examples of products launched

and reputational setbacks. By examining these examples, we aim to uncover common pitfalls and strategic missteps that can derail even the most promising products. This analysis not only highlights the importance of aligning product offerings with consumer expectations and existing market trends but also emphasizes the need for continuous adaptation and responsive business strategies in today's ever-evolving marketplace.

Figure 4.1 shows some of the product failures that will be explored in details in the following section.

4.2.1   Google Glass – A Case of Poor User Experience

4.2.1.1   Background

Google Glass was introduced as an innovative wearable technology with the potential to revolutionize how people interact with the digital world. Featuring a head-mounted display, the device was designed to deliver augmented reality experiences, provide hands-free computing, and integrate various **Google** services like maps and search.

4.2.1.2   The Ambitious Vision

Google's vision for **Glass** was to create a seamless integration of technology into daily life. The device was capable of taking pictures, recording videos, accessing email, and retrieving information via voice commands. It aimed to provide users with real-time information overlays in their visual field, enhancing interaction with their environment without the distraction of a handheld device.

4.2.1.3 Design and User Experience Challenges

Despite its groundbreaking technology, **Google Glass** faced significant user experience challenges that ultimately led to its downfall as a consumer product:

- **Social Acceptance and Privacy Concerns:** The most critical issue was privacy. The ability to record pictures and videos discreetly led to public and media backlash, resulting in bans in various establishments and creating a stigma around its wearers.
- **User Interface and Aesthetics:** The design of **Google Glass**, while technologically advanced, was perceived as intrusive and socially awkward. The device's appearance made users stand out uncomfortably, deterring everyday use.
- **Limited Battery Life and Functionality:** The practicality of **Google Glass** was hampered by its short battery life, which could not support prolonged use. Additionally, the limited number of apps and the device's functionality did not meet the high expectations set by smartphones, reducing its perceived value.

4.2.1.4 Market Response and Commercial Reception

Google Glass initially generated significant interest and anticipation within the tech community. However, as the practical and social implications became apparent, the excitement waned. The high price point of $1,500 also made it inaccessible to a broad audience, limiting its adoption to tech enthusiasts and early adopters.

4.2.1.5 Lessons Learned and Subsequent Developments

The experience of **Google Glass** taught several valuable lessons in product development:

- **Importance of User-Centric Design:** Products must not only advance in terms of technology but also align with user expectations and social norms.
- **Gradual Introduction and Community Feedback:** Had **Google** opted for a more phased approach and sought broader public input during development, many of the privacy and design issues could have been mitigated.
- **Iterative Design Based on User Feedback:** Learning from the initial feedback, **Google** did not abandon the project but instead shifted its focus towards specialized applications, such as helping workers in various industries like manufacturing and logistics, where hands-free data access improves productivity and safety.

4.2.1.6   Outcome and Lessons Learned

Google Glass' journey from a consumer product to a niche industrial tool underscores the complexities of introducing new technologies into the consumer market. It highlights the need for balancing innovation with user-centric design and societal norms. The pivot towards industrial applications demonstrates adaptability and responsiveness to market feedback, positioning **Google Glass** as a useful tool in specific contexts rather than a widespread consumer gadget.

4.2.2   Segway – A Case of Market Misalignment

4.2.2.1   Background

Introduced in the early 2000s, the **Segway Personal Transporter** was hailed as a revolutionary step in personal mobility. The two-wheeled, self-balancing electric vehicle was expected to transform urban transport by providing an efficient, eco-friendly alternative to traditional vehicles.

4.2.2.2   Vision and Innovation

The **Segway** was the brainchild of inventor Dean Kamen, who envisioned a world where cities would be built around personal transporters, reducing congestion and pollution. Its innovative technology allowed for intuitive movement controls, where the rider could steer by leaning in the desired direction.

4.2.2.3   Challenges and Market Reception

Despite its innovative appeal, the **Segway** faced several hurdles:

- **Regulatory and Safety Issues**: The **Segway's** use was restricted in many cities due to safety concerns and regulatory limitations. Its classification as neither a vehicle nor a pedestrian mode of transport created significant legal challenges.
- **High Costs and Practicality Issues:** With a price tag often exceeding $5,000, the **Segway** was too expensive for the average consumer. Additionally, the practicality of using **Segways** in crowded urban environments, where infrastructure was not adapted for such vehicles, was questionable.
- **Public Perception and Adoption:** The **Segway** did not live up to the mass-market hype. It found niche markets in tours, law enforcement, and mobility assistance for warehouses and large facilities, but it failed to become the urban mobility revolution it aimed to be.

4.2.2.4 Analysis of Failure and Strategic Shifts

- **Understanding Consumer Needs:** The **Segway's** failure highlights the importance of aligning product capabilities with actual consumer needs and existing infrastructure.
- **Adaptation to Market Feedback:** In response to limited consumer uptake, **Segway** Inc. shifted its focus towards markets that found real value in the product, such as commercial applications where mobility and efficiency are critical.

4.2.2.5 Outcome and Lessons Learned

The **Segway's** case provides critical insights into the challenges of introducing radical innovations to the market. It emphasizes the need for thorough market research to ensure product features meet real-world needs and an understanding of the consumer landscape to ensure new innovations find a viable market. **Segway's** pivot to commercial and specialized markets demonstrates a strategic adaptation that many companies might learn from when faced with similar challenges.

4.2.3 MoviePass – A Case of an Unsustainable Business Model

4.2.3.1 Background

Launched in 2011, **MoviePass** aimed to revolutionize the cinema-going experience by offering an unlimited movie ticket subscription. The service allowed subscribers to watch one movie per day for a monthly fee, initially set at different rates based on geographical location and usage but famously dropped to $10 per month in 2017.

4.2.3.2 The Vision and the Hype

MoviePass's vision was to generate revenue by driving more people to theatres, where they would presumably spend on concessions, from which **MoviePass** would take a cut, and by selling user data for marketing purposes. The idea was that once a massive subscriber base was built, leverage with theatres and distributors would follow.

4.2.3.3 Flawed Execution and Financial Downfall

The drop to a $10 monthly fee saw subscriptions skyrocket from about 20,000 to more than three million. However, this growth was a double-edged sword:

- **Unsustainable Cost Structure: MoviePass** paid full price for each ticket to theatres, which often cost more than the monthly subscription fee itself.

This meant that every additional movie watched by a subscriber led to increasing losses.

- **Cash Burn:** The company's cash reserves dwindled as expenses massively outstripped income. Attempts to modify the terms of service to stem losses, such as preventing repeat viewings of the same movie or introducing additional fees, led to customer dissatisfaction and churn.
- **Lack of Viable Revenue Streams:** The anticipated revenue from partnerships and data sales never materialized to a sufficient extent. The business model relied heavily on an uncertain future leverage that failed to develop.

4.2.3.4 Analysis of Strategic Missteps

MoviePass's strategy underscores several critical business lessons:

- **Testing and Iteration:** The importance of testing pricing models before wide-scale implementation could not be overstressed. **MoviePass's** initial pricing experimentation lacked comprehensive strategic planning.
- **Financial Sustainability:** Startups, especially in the tech and service sectors, must ensure their business model can sustain initial growth phases without compromising long-term viability.
- **Customer Relationship Management:** Changes to service terms must be managed sensitively to maintain trust and satisfaction, particularly when the business model is radically altered post-subscription.

4.2.3.5 Outcome and Lessons Learned

MoviePass serves as a cautionary tale about the dangers of a growth-at-all-costs strategy without a sustainable business model or clear, viable revenue paths. The failure of **MoviePass** highlights the critical need for startups to have robust financial models and a deep understanding of their cost structures and market dynamics before scaling.

Each of these expanded analyses illustrates the multifaceted reasons products fail and provides a nuanced look into strategic adjustments that can inform future business and product decisions. By understanding these failures, companies can better navigate the complexities of product development and market integration, ensuring more sustainable success.

4.2.4 Keurig Kold – A Case of Product-Market Fit Misstep

4.2.4.1 Background

Keurig Kold was an ambitious venture by **Keurig Green Mountain**, aimed at tapping into the cold beverage market by allowing consumers to make sodas, iced teas, and other cold drinks at home with the convenience and technology similar to what the original **Keurig** machines did for hot drinks. Introduced in 2015, the product sought to capitalize on the brand's success in the single-serve coffee market.

4.2.4.2 The Vision and Market Entry

Keurig Kold represented a significant investment in technology and marketing to expand the brand's footprint into the cold beverage space, traditionally dominated by soda giants like **Coca-Cola** and **Pepsi**. **Keurig** partnered with **Coca-Cola** and **Dr Pepper** to offer recognizable brands in its flavour pods, aiming to replicate the model that had made its hot beverage machines a household name.

4.2.4.3 Challenges and Market Reception

Despite the initial excitement, **Keurig Kold** faced several challenges that contributed to its downfall:

- **High Costs:** The **Keurig Kold** machine was priced at around $370, significantly higher than other beverage making machines. The pods themselves were also costly compared to traditional soda options, making it an expensive proposition for the average consumer.
- **Bulky Design:** The machine took up considerable counter space, which was a significant deterrent for customers with smaller kitchens or those who prioritized minimalistic kitchen designs.
- **Convenience vs. Necessity:** While the original **Keurig** machines offered a clear advantage over traditional coffee brewing methods in terms of convenience, the value proposition was less clear for cold beverages, which do not require the same preparation time or effort as coffee.
- **Environmental Concerns:** Similar to its coffee machines, the disposable nature of the pods raised environmental concerns among eco-conscious consumers, which affected the brand's image.

4.2.4.4 Market Withdrawal and Strategic Learnings

Keurig discontinued **Keurig Kold** in 2016, less than a year after its launch, due to poor sales and lacklustre market response. This decision led to a significant financial loss and layoffs, signalling a misjudgement in consumer demand and market readiness.

4.2.4.5 Analysis of Strategic Missteps

- **Assessing Consumer Demand:** **Keurig** failed to accurately gauge consumer interest and willingness to invest in a high-cost, niche product, especially when cheaper and more convenient alternatives were available.

- **Pricing Strategy:** The pricing of both the machine and the pods was out of step with market expectations, particularly given the non-essential nature of the product.
- **Product Design and Usability:** The large size and design of the machine did not appeal to the broader market, which had come to expect more compact and sleek appliances.

4.2.4.6   Outcome and Lessons Learned

The failure of **Keurig Kold** serves as a cautionary tale about the importance of understanding consumer behaviour, needs, and the competitive landscape before launching a new product. It highlights the need for rigorous market research, realistic pricing strategies, and environmental considerations in product development. **Keurig's** experience underscores that even established brands must carefully evaluate new markets and consumer trends to avoid costly missteps.

This analysis shows how crucial it is for businesses to align product features with consumer expectations and market conditions. **Keurig Kold's** case illustrates that without a clear advantage or necessity, high-tech and innovative products may still fail if they do not meet practical consumer needs or fit into existing lifestyle patterns.

4.2.5   Concorde Jet – A Case of Pricing Issues

4.2.5.1   Background

The **Concorde** was an iconic supersonic passenger airliner developed jointly by aircraft manufacturers in Great Britain and France. With capabilities of flying at speeds over twice the speed of sound, **Concorde** epitomized luxury air travel and was a symbol of technological prowess.

4.2.5.2   Vision and Market Entry

The vision behind **Concorde** was to drastically reduce flight times across the Atlantic, transforming international travel by making it possible to travel from New York to London in just under three and a half hours. Introduced in 1976, **Concorde** targeted wealthy business travellers and celebrities who valued time savings over cost.

4.2.5.3 Challenges and Market Perception

Despite its technological innovations, **Concorde** faced significant challenges related to its economic viability:

- **High Operational Costs:** Concorde's fuel consumption and maintenance were substantially higher than conventional jets, leading to high operational costs.
- **Ticket Pricing:** To cover these costs, ticket prices were exorbitantly high, limiting the potential customer base to the very affluent. A round-trip ticket could cost upwards of $12,000, which was far beyond what average consumers could afford.
- **Environmental and Regulatory Issues:** The aircraft also faced environmental concerns due to its loud sonic boom, leading to restrictions on its flight routes that limited its commercial use.

4.2.5.4 Outcome and Lessons Learned

Concorde was ultimately retired in 2003 due to a combination of factors including diminished demand following the 9/11 attacks, ongoing high operating costs, and the lack of broader market appeal due to its prohibitive pricing. The **Concorde's** case illustrates the critical importance of aligning pricing strategies with broader market capabilities and demands, as well as the need for sustainable operational economics in luxury markets.

4.2.6 Blockbuster – A Case of Poor Adaptation and Evolution

4.2.6.1 Background

Blockbuster was once a dominant force in the video rental industry, with thousands of stores worldwide offering film and video game rentals.

4.2.6.2 Vision and Market Entry

Blockbuster's initial success was built on a widespread network of retail outlets that offered convenient access to a wide range of video titles. The company capitalized on the growing popularity of home movie watching in the 1980s and 1990s, becoming synonymous with movie rentals.

4.2.6.3 Challenges and Market Perception

As the digital age dawned, **Blockbuster** faced critical challenges that it failed to effectively navigate:

- **Technological Shifts:** The rise of digital streaming technologies fundamentally changed how people consumed media. Companies like **Netflix** introduced streaming services that provided instant access to a broad array of content without the need to visit a physical store.

- **Failure to Adapt: Blockbuster** was slow to recognize and respond to these technological shifts. While it eventually launched an online rental service, the effort was half-hearted and failed to compete effectively with more agile and technologically adept competitors.
- **Customer Convenience: Blockbuster** continued to rely on its physical store model long after consumers began showing a clear preference for the convenience of online access.

4.2.6.4 Outcome and Lessons Learned

Blockbuster declared bankruptcy in 2010, overtaken by competitors that had embraced digital models and adapted more effectively to changing consumer preferences. The company's decline is a stark reminder of the importance of staying attuned to technological advancements and evolving market trends. It underscores the necessity for continuous innovation and adaptability in business strategy to remain competitive in rapidly changing industries.

4.3 Success Stories: Strategies That Shaped the Market

This section shifts focus to the triumphant stories of companies like **Nespresso, Netflix, Amazon, Apple,** and **Tesla.** This section explores how visionary leadership, innovative business strategies, and a strong emphasis on customer experience and technology integration have propelled these companies to the forefront of their industries. Each case study provides a blueprint for success, highlighting the importance of adapting to market changes and continually engaging with technological advancements to maintain competitive advantage.

Figure 4.2 shows some of the successful companies that will be explored in details in the following section.

4.3.1 Nespresso: Elevating Coffee to a Luxury Experience

4.3.1.1 Background

Launched as part of the **Nestlé Group, Nespresso** began as a daring project to market coffee as a premium product, distinguishing itself through quality and innovation.

4.3.1.2 Vision and Market Entry

Nespresso aimed to transform coffee drinking into a sophisticated, enjoyable experience. Its strategy focused on high-quality coffee capsules and stylish, easy-to-use machines, initially targeting affluent consumers and boutique hotels.

FIGURE 4.2   Success stories of visionary companies

4.3.1.3   Challenges and Market Perception

Initially, consumers were hesitant about the concept of machine-specific capsules and the higher cost compared to traditional coffee. The market was sceptical of the need for another home appliance and the long-term cost associated with capsule purchases.

4.3.1.4   Customer Experience

Nespresso addressed these concerns by offering an exceptional customer experience, including personalized services, easy online ordering, and exclusive member benefits. Its boutique stores provided hands-on experiences and expert staff to educate consumers about coffee varieties.

4.3.1.5   Business Strategy

The company's strategy involved creating an aspirational brand image through sleek design and celebrity endorsements. It built a direct-to-consumer sales model that maintained high-quality control and customer intimacy.

4.3.1.6   Technology Lever

Nespresso's success was partly due to its continuous innovation in machine technology and capsule design, ensuring convenience and consistency in coffee preparation.

4.3.1.7 Outcome and Lessons Learned

Nespresso transformed into a global leader in coffee, learning the importance of brand positioning and the value of a premium customer experience in differentiating a product in a crowded market.

4.3.2 Netflix: Streaming Success Through Innovation

4.3.2.1 Background

Netflix revolutionized the entertainment industry with its streaming service, which began as a DVD rental business.

4.3.2.2 Vision and Market Entry

The vision was to provide a convenient and continuous viewing experience without the limitations of physical rentals. **Netflix** introduced streaming technology, which allowed users to watch a vast array of content anytime.

4.3.2.3 Challenges and Market Perception

The major challenge was the initial resistance from traditional media companies and slow broadband speeds that affected streaming quality. Consumers were also slow to change their habits from scheduled programming to on-demand viewing.

4.3.2.4 Customer Experience

Netflix focused on user-friendly interfaces and algorithms that personalized recommendations based on viewing habits, significantly enhancing user satisfaction and engagement.

4.3.2.5 Business Strategy

Its strategy included significant investments in original content to differentiate from competitors and control its programming. **Netflix** also adopted a global expansion strategy early on, adapting its content and marketing to diverse cultural tastes.

4.3.2.6 Technology Lever

Advancements in cloud computing and data analytics enabled **Netflix** to stream high-quality video efficiently across devices and to optimize its content library based on rich user data.

4.3.2.7 Outcome and Lessons Learned

Netflix became a dominant player in the global entertainment market, learning that adaptive technology and content customization are key to staying relevant and leading in a rapidly evolving industry.

4.3.3 Amazon: Defining Modern E-commerce

4.3.3.1 Background

Started as an online bookstore, **Amazon** quickly expanded to become the 'everything store', offering a wide range of products across the globe.

4.3.3.2 Vision and Market Entry

Jeff Bezos envisioned a shopping platform that could offer unprecedented convenience, variety, and customer service. **Amazon** aimed to leverage internet technology to make buying easier and more consumer-oriented.

4.3.3.3 Challenges and Market Perception

Early challenges included consumer scepticism about online shopping security, the feasibility of large-scale e-commerce logistics, and the initial financial viability of the low-margin, high-volume business.

4.3.3.4 Customer Experience

Amazon invested in customer experience by streamlining the purchasing process, providing comprehensive product information, user reviews, and personalization features like tailored recommendations.

4.3.3.5 Business Strategy

Its strategy focused on aggressive pricing, vast selection, and a strong focus on customer service. **Amazon** also diversified into cloud computing with **Amazon Web Services** (**AWS**), which supported its e-commerce infrastructure and became a profitable business unit.

4.3.3.6 Technology Lever

Innovations such as **Amazon Prime**, one-click shopping, and predictive analytics tools to manage inventory and personalize shopping experiences have kept **Amazon** at the forefront of e-commerce technology.

4.3.3.7 Outcome and Lessons Learned

Amazon's approach solidified its leadership in e-commerce, demonstrating the importance of customer-centricity, scalability in business operations, and foresight in technological investment.

4.3.4 Apple: Pioneering Innovation in Technology

4.3.4.1 Background

Apple Inc., established in 1976, has become a symbol of innovation and high-quality product design in the technology industry, known for its comprehensive ecosystem of devices and services.

4.3.4.2 Vision and Market Entry

Apple's vision was to develop easy-to-use, aesthetically pleasing products that enhance everyday life. The introduction of the **Apple I** computer set the stage for the future of personal computing with a focus on user interface and experience.

4.3.4.3 Challenges and Market Perception

Apple faced significant challenges, including competitive pressure from Microsoft in the PC market and internal struggles that led to the departure of Steve Jobs in 1985. Initially, **Apple** was perceived as a premium brand with limited market share due to its higher price points and closed ecosystem.

4.3.4.4 Customer Experience

Apple excels in creating an intuitive user experience across its product lines, emphasizing design and functionality. Its seamless ecosystem allows products to work together flawlessly, enhancing user convenience and brand loyalty.

4.3.4.5 Business Strategy

The company's approach includes controlling the hardware and software to ensure optimal performance and user experience. **Apple's** retail stores provide direct customer engagement and support, further solidifying its brand presence.

4.3.4.6 Technology Lever

Apple consistently pushes technological boundaries, from pioneering the first graphical user interface in **Macintosh** to removing the headphone jack and introducing facial recognition in **iPhones**. These innovations often set new industry standards.

4.3.4.7 Outcome and Lessons Learned

Apple's resurgence under Steve Jobs' leadership with products like the **iPod**, **iPhone**, and **iPad** revolutionized multiple industries, including music, phones, and personal computing. The key lesson from **Apple's** success is that innovation, coupled with great design and a focus on user experience, can lead to market domination.

4.3.5 Tesla: Accelerating the World Towards Sustainable Energy

4.3.5.1 Background

Founded in 2003, **Tesla, Inc**. has redefined the automotive industry by proving that electric vehicles (**EVs**) can be desirable and profitable.

4.3.5.2 Vision and Market Entry

Tesla's mission was to accelerate the world's transition to sustainable energy. This began with high-performance sports cars and expanded to more affordable consumer models, demonstrating the viability of **EVs**.

4.3.5.3 Challenges and Market Perception

Tesla faced scepticism about the market readiness for **EVs**, concerns over battery life, vehicle range, and the initial high cost of production. Early on, the market perceived Tesla as a niche luxury brand that might not achieve mass-market success.

4.3.5.4 Customer Experience

Tesla focuses on the customer driving experience, offering cutting-edge technology like autopilot and over-the-air software updates that improve vehicle functionality over time. The direct sales model eliminates traditional dealerships, enhancing the overall buying experience.

4.3.5.5 Business Strategy

Tesla's strategy includes building its own extensive network of **Superchargers**, vertical integration of battery production, and expanding into renewable energy solutions like solar panels and home batteries.

4.3.5.6 Technology Lever

Leveraging technology has been crucial for **Tesla**, not just in terms of vehicle design but also in manufacturing processes and energy management solutions. Its commitment to software and hardware development leads to continuous improvements in performance and efficiency.

4.3.5.7 Outcome and Lessons Learned

Tesla has not only become the most valuable carmaker but also changed public perception and industry standards regarding electric vehicles. **Tesla's** success illustrates the importance of visionary leadership and relentless innovation in driving technological adoption and environmental change.

4.4 Overcoming Resource Constraints in High-Pressure Digital Markets

In the fast-paced and competitive digital marketplace, startups and established companies alike often face significant resource constraints. These can range from limited financial resources and manpower to technological limitations. Successfully navigating these challenges is crucial for sustaining growth and fostering innovation. This section delves into effective strategies and real-world examples of businesses that have adeptly managed resource constraints to maintain competitive advantage and drive success.

4.4.1 Strategic Prioritization and Lean Operations

Lean principles are fundamental for companies aiming to maximize efficiency. By focusing on eliminating waste – whether in terms of time, capital, or materials – businesses can streamline operations and focus resources on areas that generate the most value.

1 **Lean Principles and Practices: Spotify**
   Spotify utilizes lean methodologies in its software development process, enabling quick deployment of new features and ensuring efficient use of resources. By continuously testing and refining its product, **Spotify** maintains technological relevance and user engagement without overextension.
2 **Cloud Computing: Dropbox**
   Dropbox leveraged cloud services like **Amazon Web Services** (**AWS**) to handle its data storage needs. This strategic decision allowed **Dropbox** to scale its services efficiently without the upfront cost of building and maintaining extensive physical infrastructure.

3 **Agile Project Management: Airbnb and Uber**
   Airbnb employs agile practices to incrementally and quickly adapt its offerings based on user feedback and changing market conditions, helping the company innovate while managing resource allocation. **Uber** uses agile methodologies to enhance its app and service features, ensuring rapid implementation and adaptation to user needs and market dynamics.

4.4.2 Partnerships and Collaborations

In the realm of product management, partnerships and collaborations offer substantial benefits that can dramatically enhance a product's market reach and functional capabilities. By strategically aligning with other businesses, companies can leverage complementary strengths, which can lead to the co-creation of products that are more innovative and appealing to a broader customer base. For instance, through partnerships, a product management team can access new technologies and platforms that might otherwise be out of reach, enabling them to integrate advanced features without the associated R&D costs and time delays. This collaborative approach not only speeds up the product development cycle but also distributes the financial risk involved in new product innovations. Moreover, partnerships can expand a product's ecosystem, enhancing its value proposition through seamless integrations that improve user experience and satisfaction. In essence, by fostering the right collaborations, product managers can tap into new expertise, technologies, and markets, making their products more competitive and adaptable to changing market demands.

1 **Google and Android Development: Fostering an Open Ecosystem**
   Overview: Google's strategic unveiling of the Android operating system in 2007 marked a pivotal move to challenge the dominance of **Apple's** iOS. Android was introduced as an open and customizable platform, significantly contrasting **Apple's** more restrictive ecosystem. This approach empowered **Google** to cultivate broad-based collaborations with a variety of hardware manufacturers.
   Strategic Impact: Android's open-source model facilitated rapid adoption across the mobile manufacturing industry. Major players like **Samsung, HTC,** and **Sony** embraced Android, allowing them to offer a competitive alternative to **Apple's** iPhones without the need to develop their own operating systems. This widespread adoption quickly established Android as the global leader in mobile operating systems.
   Benefits: The open-source nature of Android significantly lowers costs and entry barriers for hardware manufacturers. It enables them to innovate on their device offerings by customizing the OS to fit different market segments – from budget smartphones to premium devices. For **Google,**

widespread Android adoption expanded the reach of its services, such as **Google Play** and **Google Maps,** enhancing revenue streams from app sales, advertising, and data analytics. The platform's openness also fosters a dynamic developer community that continuously enriches Android's capabilities and applications, driving further innovation and user engagement.

2 **IBM and Red Hat Collaboration**

Overview: In 2018, **IBM** announced its acquisition of **Red Hat** for $34 billion, one of the largest technology deals. More than just an acquisition, this move represented a strategic collaboration to enhance **IBM's** cloud offerings with **Red Hat's** open-source software capabilities.

Strategic Impact: This collaboration allows **IBM** to leverage **Red Hat's** open-source innovations, particularly in the **Linux** and **Kubernetes** environments that are pivotal in enterprise cloud solutions. This partnership strengthens **IBM's** position in the hybrid cloud market, offering more flexibility and broader options to customers transitioning to cloud environments.

Benefits: For **Red Hat,** the deal provides vast scalability under **IBM's** umbrella, allowing them to reach a wider audience while maintaining their core principles of open-source development. For **IBM,** this move accelerates its hybrid cloud growth strategy and reinforces its commitment to open-source technology and development, which are crucial for future innovations in cloud computing.

3 **Starbucks and Microsoft: Reinventing Customer Experience**

Overview: Starbucks and **Microsoft** partnered to create a series of innovative technological solutions to streamline operations and enhance the customer experience. This includes integrating blockchain **technology** for coffee traceability, deploying predictive analytics for inventory management, and utilizing **Microsoft's Azure and AI** capabilities to personalize customer interactions.

Strategic Impact: The collaboration aims to transform the coffee giant into a more efficient digital enterprise. By using **Microsoft's AI** technology, Starbucks personalizes the marketing efforts directed towards customers, enhances mobile app functionalities, and improves sales forecasting and supply chain operations.

Benefits: For **Starbucks,** this technology integration helps maintain its competitive edge by enhancing customer loyalty and operational efficiency. For **Microsoft,** this partnership serves as a powerful case study of how its **Azure** and **AI** technologies can be employed in the retail industry to drive digital transformation.

4.4.3 Outsourcing and Offshoring

Outsourcing and offshoring are critical strategies within product management that enable businesses to streamline operations, reduce costs, and focus on core competencies. By delegating non-core activities such as **IT, HR,** and **customer service** to **external providers**, companies can leverage specialized expertise, scale quickly, and improve service quality without significant capital investment. Offshoring allows businesses to tap into global talent pools at a lower cost, optimizing budget allocations and enhancing competitive advantage through cost efficiency.

Here are the key benefits:

1 **Cost Efficiency:** Outsourcing and offshoring can significantly reduce operational costs. Lower labour costs in offshoring countries and the ability to pay only for services needed in outsourcing agreements contribute directly to the bottom line. Companies like **Apple** outsource their manufacturing to countries like China to capitalize on lower labour costs, which contributes directly to their high profit margins.

2 **Access to Expertise:** Companies benefit from specialized skills and technologies without the need for in-house development. This is particularly valuable in areas like software development, customer support, and data analysis, where expertise is crucial but difficult to build internally. For instance, **IBM** and **Microsoft** outsource software development to India, benefiting from the region's vast pool of IT talent.

3 **Focus on Core Business:** By offloading routine or non-core tasks, product teams can focus on strategic activities that drive innovation and product development, such as market research, product design, and customer experience improvement. **Google**, for example, outsources less critical components of its operations, allowing it to focus on core product development and market expansion strategies.

4 **Scalability and Flexibility:** Outsourcing and offshoring provide the flexibility to scale operations up or down based on market demands without the constraints of local labour markets or capital investments. **Amazon** uses this strategy to handle customer service peaks during holidays by outsourcing to call centres across different regions.

5 **Speed to Market:** With round-the-clock operations possible through global outsourcing, companies can accelerate product development cycles, allowing faster response to market changes and quicker product launches. **HP**, for instance, outsources parts of its **R&D** to accelerate innovation and maintain competitive advantage.

Here are two strategies of outsourcing:

1 **Software Development Outsourcing:** Many tech companies, particularly startups, outsource software development to regions with a strong tech talent pool but lower wage rates, such as Eastern Europe or Southeast Asia. This approach not only cuts costs but also taps into a broader range

of technological expertise, accelerating product innovation. Strategic impact includes the ability to rapidly develop and deploy features that meet evolving customer needs, maintaining a competitive edge in fast-paced markets. For example, **GitHub** outsources certain development projects to Eastern European companies to tap into advanced coding skills at lower rates than in the US, enhancing their platform's capabilities without escalating costs.

2 **Customer Support Offshoring:** Large corporations often offshore their customer support operations to countries like India or the Philippines, where English-speaking skills are high and labour costs are low. This strategy allows them to offer 24/7 support services without a significant increase in cost. The strategic benefit lies in enhanced customer satisfaction through timely support and the capacity to handle high volumes of customer interactions without compromising quality. For example, **American Express** has offshored parts of its customer service operations to the Philippines, allowing for cost-effective 24/7 service to customers globally. This strategic move improves customer satisfaction and service efficiency.

Each of these strategies enables businesses to optimize their operations and focus on high-value tasks in product management, ultimately contributing to better product offerings and increased market competitiveness.

4.4.4 *Innovative Funding Models*

Innovative funding models provide essential financial support for businesses to develop, launch, and scale products without relying solely on traditional funding sources such as bank loans or venture capital. These models allow businesses to tap into diverse funding streams, engage with their customer bases directly, and validate product ideas early in the development cycle. They can catalyse rapid growth and innovation by providing the capital needed to respond quickly to market demands and changes, enhancing the agility of product management teams.

Here are some examples of **Innovative Funding Models**:

1 **Crowdfunding**
   Overview: Crowdfunding platforms like **Kickstarter** and **Indiegogo** enable businesses to raise funds directly from customers by pre-selling products or offering unique perks.
   Strategic Impact: Crowdfunding not only raises capital but also serves as a powerful marketing tool and a platform for market validation. It allows product managers to gauge consumer interest and gather feedback before full-scale production.

Benefits: For example, the **Pebble Smartwatch** used **Kickstarter** to fund its initial production, raising over $10 million from 68,929 backers. This not only provided the necessary capital to start production but also demonstrated significant market demand, guiding product development with direct customer input.

2 **Bootstrapping**

Overview: Bootstrapping involves funding the business through internal cash flow and is less reliant on external investors. This method allows companies to grow at their own pace and maintain greater control over their operations. Also sometimes known as self-funding, bootstrapping is funding your business with your own money, income from your company's sales and, occasionally, money from friends and family. You can also think of it as funding your startup without taking venture capital investment.

Strategic Impact: By minimizing external interference, bootstrapping allows product managers to focus deeply on customer and product alignment without the pressure of investor expectations.

Benefits: GoPro is a prime example of a successfully bootstrapped company. The company's product idea originated from founder Nick Woodman's need to capture high-quality action photos during sports activities. Starting with a wrist strap for cameras in 2002, he bootstrapped **GoPro** by selling belts from his van and living with his parents. The company launched its first 35mm analogue camera in 2004, evolving quickly to digital models. **GoPro** cameras, known for their durability and high-definition capabilities, expanded from surfing to various action sports, revolutionizing personal video production in extreme environments. Woodman's relentless innovation and niche market focus catapulted **GoPro** into a leading position in the action camera industry.

3 **Revenue-Based Financing**

Overview: This funding model allows businesses to receive upfront capital from investors in exchange for a percentage of ongoing gross revenues up to a predetermined amount.

Strategic Impact: It aligns the interests of investors and business owners because investors only succeed when the business's revenue grows, encouraging support in areas like marketing and customer acquisition.

Benefits: Clearbanc (now **Clearco**) offers revenue-based financing primarily to e-commerce companies. It provides funds for ad spend and inventory without diluting the business owners' equity, facilitating growth while allowing product managers to retain control over the product vision and execution. Examples of startups in Singapore and the Southeast Asia region include **Jenfi, Choco Up,** and **Aspire. Jenfi,** based in Singapore, provides revenue-based financing to high-growth digital-native businesses across Southeast Asia. They offer non-dilutive capital to companies like SaaS providers and e-commerce sellers, helping them scale efficiently. **Choco Up**, another Singaporean platform, offers revenue-based financing to small businesses that are often overlooked by traditional venture capitalists. **Choco Up** provides flexible repayment terms, allowing businesses to pause repayments when they are not earning. Although primarily known for its financial services, **Aspire** has also utilized revenue-based financing to support its growth. The company focuses on providing financial solutions to small and medium-sized enterprises (**SMEs**) in Southeast Asia.

The above innovative funding models offer flexibility and strategic benefits that traditional funding methods often lack, enabling product management teams to operate with more autonomy and a sharper focus on creating products that truly resonate with their target markets.

4.4.5 Adapting with Minimum Viable Products (MVPs)

In the fast-paced digital marketplace, the concept of the **Minimum Viable Product** (**MVP**) is crucial for companies aiming to innovate quickly and efficiently. An **MVP** is the most pared-down version of a product that can still be released to market. It includes only the essential features that allow the product to be deployed and no more. This approach helps businesses test their product hypotheses with minimal resources, gather user feedback early in the development process, and iterate based on that feedback.

Here are the key benefits of using **MVPs**:

1 **Speed to Market:** MVPs allow companies to launch their products quickly, enabling them to capture market share and learn from customer interactions without fully developing the product.
2 **Reduced Costs:** By developing only the necessary features, companies can minimize initial development costs, focusing their expenditures on aspects of the product that are critical to user acceptance and satisfaction.
3 **Enhanced Flexibility:** With an **MVP**, companies can adapt their product development in response to user feedback and changing market conditions, making it easier to pivot or adjust features based on actual customer needs and desires.

Here are some examples where **MVPs** have been used to validate the product idea and have driven the startups to success:

1 **Dropbox:** Initially, **Dropbox** launched a simple video explaining its file-syncing concept, gauging interest by the number of sign-ups

received. This early prototype wasn't a fully functional product but was enough to validate user interest and secure funding for further development.

2 **Zappos:** The founder of **Zappos**, Nick Swinmurn, tested his hypothesis about whether customers would buy shoes online by setting up a simple website with pictures of shoes from local stores without any inventory. Once an order was placed, he would buy the shoes from the store and ship them, validating the market need.

3 **Buffer: Buffer**, a social media scheduling tool, began as a two-page website. The first page explained the value proposition and pricing, while the second page was a payment page. Initially, there wasn't even a product; the founder wanted to see if people would pay for the service. The interest received from users helped in deciding to build the actual product.

Incorporating **MVP** strategies can significantly impact a company's ability to innovate efficiently, making it an essential component of the modern digital product management toolkit.

4.5 Competitive Strategies and Market Differentiation in Digital Economies

Success in the digital economy hinges not just on entering the market, but on standing out within it. As industries become more saturated and consumer preferences shift rapidly, businesses must devise and implement innovative strategies that highlight their unique value propositions. This section explores how various companies have successfully differentiated themselves by honing in on niche markets, enhancing user experiences, and leveraging sustainability as a competitive advantage.

4.5.1 Leveraging Niche Markets

Square revolutionized payment processing for small businesses and independent vendors by providing an easy-to-use, portable point-of-sale (**POS**) system. Initially focusing on small merchants who found traditional credit systems inaccessible or too costly, **Square** offered a simple plug-in device that turned smartphones into credit card readers. This approach not only opened up a new market but also allowed **Square** to later expand into a comprehensive suite of financial services tailored to small businesses, including business loans and payroll services. By addressing the specific pain points of a niche market, **Square** built a strong foundation that supported expansive growth.

4.5.2 Adapting to Consumer Needs

Zoom's rise to prominence in the video conferencing sector was fuelled by its focus on simplicity and reliability – key consumer demands. During the **COVID-19** pandemic, when reliable video communication became crucial, **Zoom's** platform offered superior performance with minimal setup, distinguishing it from competitors. Unlike other platforms that required more complex installations and configurations, **Zoom** facilitated instant connectivity, which was essential for schools, businesses, and personal communications during lockdowns. This responsiveness to fundamental consumer needs for simplicity and reliability drove its rapid adoption and brand loyalty.

4.5.3 Sustainability as a Competitive Advantage

Beyond Meat has effectively differentiated itself in the highly competitive food industry by offering plant-based meat alternatives that appeal to a broad demographic. By focusing on sustainability and health, **Beyond Meat** targets not only vegetarians and vegans but also meat-eaters looking to reduce their environmental impact and improve their diet. The company's use of proteins derived from peas and other plants to mimic the taste and texture of meat addresses environmental concerns and taps into the growing trend of sustainable eating. This clear focus on sustainability has not only carved out a niche for **Beyond Meat** but has also positioned it as a leader in a new, rapidly growing industry segment.

4.5.4 Customer Experience and Engagement

Warby Parker disrupted the traditional eyewear industry by focusing heavily on customer experience. By offering home try-on kits, a user-friendly website, and interactive retail spaces, **Warby Parker** made shopping for eyewear as hassle-free and enjoyable as possible. Additionally, for every pair sold, the company donates a pair to someone in need, which resonates with socially conscious consumers. This commitment to customer service and social responsibility has engendered strong customer loyalty and set **Warby Parker** apart from its competitors.

4.5.5 Building Brand Ecosystems and Community Engagement

Peloton has transformed at-home fitness by not just selling exercise equipment but by creating an integrated digital community. **Peloton** users gain access to live and on-demand fitness classes, competitive leaderboards, and a community of users with whom they can connect and compete. This strategy of creating a comprehensive fitness ecosystem has turned **Peloton** into a lifestyle brand, fostering a loyal community of users who are invested in the brand not just for its products but for the entire experience it provides.

4.6 Conclusion

This chapter has provided a comprehensive analysis of the critical factors that contribute to both the successes and failures in the digital market landscape. By examining a range of case studies, this chapter has offered valuable insights into the strategic decisions and management practices that can lead to a product's triumph or downfall in competitive digital environments.

The successes discussed illuminate the importance of innovation, customer engagement, and adaptive business models. These success stories demonstrate that understanding market needs, coupled with agile responses to technological advancements and consumer trends, is foundational to achieving and sustaining market leadership. Meanwhile, the examination of failures highlights the significance of risk assessment, the need for market validation before full-scale product launches, and the critical role of continuous learning and improvement.

For product managers and digital strategists, this chapter serves as a crucial resource, providing lessons that are essential for navigating the complexities of the digital marketplace. It emphasizes that while the paths to success can be diverse, the ability to learn from both past successes and mistakes is what truly empowers companies to innovate and evolve effectively.

By integrating these lessons into their strategic frameworks, businesses can better position themselves to capitalize on opportunities and mitigate risks, ensuring not only survival but also prosperity in the ever-changing digital economy. This chapter encourages a proactive approach to product management, where continuous adaptation and learning are seen as key drivers of long-term success.

5

PRODUCT TEAM MODEL

5.1 Introduction

Traditionally, product development teams were often siloed, with each function operating independently. This approach is becoming increasingly inadequate as it fails to address the interconnected nature of modern digital products. The evolving digital landscape demands that companies move away from isolated, vertical silos of function, which have proven to be less effective in today's dynamic market environment.

Today, effective product management requires a holistic view of the product lifecycle, emphasizing that products are not merely collections of features but complete experiences shared among the product team, customers, and the company. In today's dynamic business environment, the composition and operation of product teams are crucial for driving product innovation and market success.

This chapter delves into the **Product Team Model**, emphasizing the importance of cross-functional and self-organizing teams with broader organizational function integration that are essential for managing the complexities of product lifecycles in a cohesive and agile manner.

5.2 Cross-Functional Team Dynamics

In a digital economy, cross-functional teams comprise diverse roles including user experience designers, product developers, engineers, marketers, and more. These teams are characterized by their ability to work beyond traditional boundaries, sharing skills, knowledge, and resources across the board. This fluid exchange enhances coordination and fosters a unified approach to achieving the shared goal of delivering exceptional products and

DOI: 10.1201/9781003484295-5

services. This cross-functional nature ensures that different perspectives are considered during product development, enhancing creativity and problem-solving. Team members from different disciplines work together from the initial stages of product conception through to launch, which improves communication and reduces the time needed for decision-making and revisions.

5.3 Agile Self-Organizing Teams

Self-organizing teams operate on principles of autonomy and empowerment, with minimal top-down control. They organize their own workflow and make decisions collaboratively, which boosts innovation and accelerates product development. Such teams rely on the diverse expertise of their members to meet complex challenges, often adapting more quickly to market changes than centrally managed teams. This aspect of the model is rooted in **Agile** methodologies, where teams are encouraged to adapt quickly to changing conditions without constant oversight from management. Self-organizing teams are empowered to experiment, take initiative, and learn from their failures, which accelerates the development process and leads to innovative solutions.

5.4 Broader Organizational Function Integration

While the core product team focuses on direct product outcomes, integral functions such as sales, legal, and finance also play critical roles. Although these units do not directly engage in product development, their input and collaboration are essential for comprehensive product strategies. For example, legal and finance teams ensure compliance and viability, while sales teams provide market feedback crucial for iterative development. This ensures that product strategies are aligned with business objectives and that all necessary resources are available to support the product lifecycle. Integrating these broader functions helps in scaling the product effectively, managing budgets, and ensuring compliance with industry standards and regulations.

5.5 Product Team Model Components

Figure 5.1 shows the components in a **Product Team Model**.

1 Core Team Roles

- **Product Manager (PM):** The PM is responsible for defining the product vision, strategy, and roadmap. They collaborate with stakeholders, prioritize features, and ensure the product aligns with business goals.
- **UX Designer:** The UX designer focuses on user experience, creating wireframes, prototypes, and ensuring the product is intuitive and user-friendly.

FIGURE 5.1 Product Team Model components

- **Software Engineers:** Engineers write code, develop features, and maintain the product. They work closely with other team members to implement functionality.
- **Scrum Master/Agile Coach:** In an **Agile** environment, the Scrum Master facilitates the team's processes, removes obstacles, and ensures efficient development.
- **Product Security Champion:** Responsibilities include advocating for security best practices, conducting security reviews, and ensuring that security considerations are integrated into the product development lifecycle.
- **Quality Assurance (QA) Tester:** QA testers verify that the product works as expected, finding and reporting bugs. They ensure high-quality releases.
- **Data Analyst:** Data analysts analyse data collected from product usage to inform improvements and understand user behaviour.

2 **Extended Team Roles**

- **Marketing Specialist:** Marketing specialists promote the product, create campaigns, and analyse market trends.
- **Sales Representative:** Sales representatives sell the product, engage with customers, and gather feedback.
- **Customer Support Agent:** Customer support agents assist users, handle inquiries, resolve technical issues, and ensure customer satisfaction.
- **Compliance Specialist:** Compliance specialists ensure that the product complies with relevant regulations (e.g., GDPR, HIPAA). Collaborates with legal and privacy experts.

- **Finance Analyst:** Finance analysts manage budgets, pricing strategies, and forecast financial impacts related to the product.
- **Legal Advisors:** Legal advisors ensure that the product complies with relevant laws, regulations, and standards.

5.6 Building Effective Product Teams

Successful product teams are not just about grouping people together; they require careful selection and management to ensure they are effective. The following lists some strategies for success:

- **Clear Roles and Responsibilities:** Each team member needs a clear understanding of their roles and what is expected of them.
- **Empowerment and Autonomy:** Teams that are empowered to make decisions tend to move faster and innovate more. This includes autonomy in problem-solving and prioritizing tasks.
- **Regular Communication:** Regular updates and communication are vital to keep everyone aligned and moving in the same direction.
- **Cross-Functional Collaboration:** Encouraging collaboration across different functions can lead to innovative solutions and a more cohesive product strategy.

5.7 Agile Methodology in Product Teams

Many modern product teams employ **Agile** methodologies to enhance flexibility and responsiveness. **Agile** promotes an iterative development process, regular feedback, and adaptability to change. The following are the benefits of **Agile** practices:

- **Increased Flexibility:** Allows teams to adapt to changes in market conditions or customer preferences quickly.
- **Enhanced Customer Focus:** Frequent iterations and continuous feedback loops keep the product aligned with customer needs.
- **Improved Team Productivity:** Short sprints and clear milestones keep the team focused and productive.

5.8 Case Study: Spotify and Amazon

5.8.1 Spotify's Approach to Product Innovation

5.8.1.1 Background

Spotify, the global music streaming service, has become synonymous with **Agile** practices in a corporate environment. Its innovative approach to product development and team management through **Agile** methodologies has been widely discussed and serves as a model for many organizations aiming for agility and effectiveness.

5.8.1.2 Squad Model

Spotify's organizational structure is famous for its unique take on **Agile** practices, known as the '**Spotify Model**' or '**Squad Model**'. This model divides the workforce into small, autonomous '**squads**' that are cross-functional and aligned with a specific feature or product area. Each squad operates like a mini-startup within the company, complete with its own autonomy and tools to design, develop, test, and release features.

5.8.1.3 Roles and Responsibilities

In **Spotify's** model, squads are composed of various roles including developers, product managers, data analysts, and designers. The company emphasizes leadership through influence rather than hierarchy, with **Agile** Coaches supporting squads in process and continuous improvement rather than traditional managers directing tasks.

5.8.1.4 Tribes, Chapters, and Guilds

To maintain alignment and quality while promoting exchange across squads, **Spotify** organizes **squads** into larger groups called '**tribes**', which are focused on larger product areas. Within **tribes**, '**chapters**' and '**guilds**' provide platforms for individuals sharing similar skills or facing similar challenges to collaborate and share knowledge across squad borders. This structure helps in scaling Agile practices while maintaining a shared knowledge base and culture. Figure 5.2 depicts the **Spotify's Squad Model**.

1 **Squads: The Foundation of Spotify's Innovation**
   At the heart of the **Spotify Model** are **squads**, which are small, cross-functional teams of 6 to 12 people. **Squads** operate much like mini-startups within **Spotify**, with end-to-end responsibility for a specific feature, component, or user experience. Each **squad** is autonomous and fully empowered to make decisions on what to build, how to build it, and how to deliver it.

   • **Autonomy and Ownership:** Squads have a high degree of autonomy. Each **squad** owns a specific aspect of **Spotify's** product and is responsible for designing, developing, testing, and deploying it. This ownership empowers squads to experiment and make decisions quickly, without needing approval from higher management.

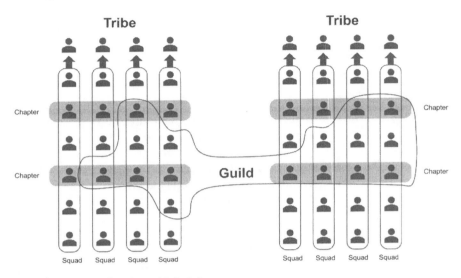

FIGURE 5.2 Spotify's Squad Model

- **Cross-Functional Teams:** A **squad** typically includes all the roles necessary to deliver a feature, such as developers, designers, product owners, and testers. This cross-functional composition enables squads to work independently and avoid dependencies on other teams, which can slow down progress.
- **Agile at Scale:** Squads use **Agile** methodologies like **Scrum** or **Kanban** to deliver continuous improvements. The team works in sprints, delivers product increments regularly, and adapts based on user feedback and data.

Some of **Spotify's** most popular features have emerged from this dynamic structure:

- **Discover Weekly:** This personalized playlist, which generates a unique list of songs for each user every week, was born out of the innovative environment created by **Spotify's Squad Model**. The autonomy granted to **squads** allowed for rapid prototyping and testing, leading to the fine-tuning of the algorithm that drives this highly successful feature. The **squads** were able to experiment with different models of user engagement and personalization, ultimately delivering a product that has become a staple for millions of **Spotify** users.
- **Spotify Wrapped:** The popular **Spotify Wrapped**, an annual recap of each user's listening habits, is another example of how the **Squad Model** drives creative and engaging user experiences. The cross-functional **squads** working on this feature were able to tap into the user

data that **Spotify** collects throughout the year, combining design, engineering, and marketing expertise to create a viral, personalized experience that has become a cultural phenomenon each year.

2 **Tribes: Grouping Squads with a Shared Mission**
While **squads** operate independently, they don't work in isolation. **Squads** that work in related areas or on similar products are grouped into **tribes**. A **tribe** is a collection of **squads** that share a common mission, such as working on **Spotify's** recommendation engine or its user interface.

- **Size and Collaboration**: A **tribe** can consist of up to 150 people (a number inspired by **Dunbar's Number**, which suggests that people can maintain stable social relationships with about 150 individuals). **Tribes** facilitate coordination and collaboration between **squads** working towards the same overarching goal.
- **Tribe Leaders**: Each **tribe** has a **tribe leader** whose role is to support the **squads**, remove roadblocks, and ensure alignment with the broader product strategy. The **tribe** leader doesn't dictate what **squads** do but instead ensures that they have the resources and support they need to succeed.
- **Tribe Meetings**: **Tribes** hold regular meetings or **tribe councils** where **squads** showcase their progress, share learnings, and discuss challenges. This ensures alignment between **squads** and fosters a collaborative environment where teams can share ideas and best practices.

Example: A **tribe** focused on **Spotify's** user interface (UI) might include multiple **squads**, each working on different aspects of the UI, such as the desktop app, mobile app, and web player. The tribe structure allows these **squads** to coordinate their efforts and maintain a cohesive user experience across platforms.

3 **Chapters: Fostering Alignment Across Squads**
While **squads** are autonomous, there still needs to be alignment and consistency in how certain roles operate across the organization. This is where **chapters** come into play. **Chapters** are groups of people with similar skills and roles, such as frontend developers, UX designers, or data analysts, who are spread across different **squads** within a **tribe**.

- **Role-Based Alignment**: Each **chapter** brings together individuals with the same skillset to share knowledge, set standards, and ensure consistency in their work. For instance, all frontend developers across various **squads** might belong to the same **chapter**. They meet regularly to discuss technical challenges, share new techniques, and ensure that the frontend development across squads follows best practices.

- **Chapter Leads:** **Chapters** are led by **chapter leads** who are also working members of a **squad** but have additional responsibilities for ensuring that members of the **chapter** have the necessary skills and tools. The **chapter lead** is responsible for professional development and mentoring within the chapter, helping to maintain technical excellence across the organization.
- **Consistency and Innovation:** **Chapters** are crucial in maintaining alignment without centralizing decision-making. For example, while each **squad** might implement their solution independently, **chapter** meetings ensure that all developers are aware of the latest advancements, trends, and internal best practices, allowing **squads** to remain consistent in technical implementation while still innovating.

Example: If multiple **squads** are working on different parts of Spotify's recommendation engine, the **data science chapter** might ensure that all data scientists across these squads use the same algorithms or methodologies, ensuring consistency while allowing for flexibility in implementation.

4 **Guilds: Sharing Knowledge Across the Organization**
   Lastly, **Spotify** has **guilds**, which are informal communities of interest that cross both **squads** and **tribes**. **Guilds** are not tied to a specific function or team but instead focus on shared interests or areas of expertise, such as machine learning, security, or **Agile** methodologies.

- **Knowledge Sharing:** Guilds are a way to connect employees who are passionate about a specific topic, even if they belong to different **squads** or **tribes**. For example, a **DevOps guild** might include engineers, product owners, and testers from various parts of the organization who come together to discuss best practices, share tools, and provide advice on improving **DevOps** processes.
- **Voluntary Participation:** Participation in **guilds** is voluntary, and they often serve as a forum for innovation, experimentation, and continuous learning. **Guilds** encourage cross-functional collaboration, breaking down silos across the company.
- **Cross-Company Impact:** **Guilds** often work on initiatives that span the entire organization. For instance, a **security** guild might work to improve security standards and protocols across all products, ensuring that **squads** across different tribes are aligned on security best practices.

Example: Spotify's **Agile Guild** is composed of members who are passionate about continuously improving **Agile** processes. This **guild** allows teams across the company to share experiences and learn how to better implement **Agile** practices in different contexts.

5.8.1.5 Innovation and Adaptation

Spotify's Agile environment encourages rapid experimentation, prototyping, and a fail-fast mentality. **Squads** frequently deploy **A/B** tests and use data-driven decision-making to innovate and iterate on product features swiftly. This methodology allows **Spotify** to adapt quickly to changing consumer preferences and technological advancements.

5.8.1.6 Outcome and Impact

By adopting this model, **Spotify** has achieved remarkable flexibility and responsiveness, enabling it to stay competitive in the fast-paced music streaming industry. The model fosters a strong sense of ownership and motivation among employees, as they feel directly connected to the product's success and are empowered to influence outcomes.

Through this model, **Spotify** exemplifies how empowering teams to work independently with minimal bureaucratic overhead enables faster innovation and keeps the company at the forefront of the music streaming industry. By allowing squads to rapidly test and implement new ideas, **Spotify** has been able to adapt to the evolving needs of its users, all while maintaining its position as a leader in digital music.

5.8.2 Amazon's Approach to Product Innovation

5.8.2.1 Background

Amazon's agility and innovative capacity across its business segments are anchored in a unique corporate structure and a strong emphasis on **Agile** methodologies. This foundation facilitates the rapid development and launch of products that consistently push industry boundaries.

5.8.2.2 Decentralized Decision-Making

Amazon's 'two-pizza teams' are small, autonomous groups responsible for specific features or services. This structure promotes quick decision-making and high levels of innovation, as teams are empowered to operate independently, reducing the bottlenecks typically associated with larger organizational hierarchies.

5.8.2.3 Roles and Responsibilities

Teams at **Amazon** are cross-functional, equipped with all the necessary roles to take a product from concept to market. This includes developers, product managers, marketers, and customer support, allowing for seamless product development and launch processes.

5.8.2.4   Leadership Principles and Cultural Emphasis on Innovation

Amazon's leadership principles like customer obsession and ownership are deeply ingrained in team operations, ensuring decisions align with broader business goals. The culture of experimentation is crucial, with teams encouraged to take calculated risks to innovate and learn from outcomes, fostering an environment where failure is seen as a step towards innovation.

5.8.2.5   The Working Backwards Method

Central to **Amazon's** product development strategy is the 'Working Backwards' method, which begins with drafting an internal press release for a new product idea. This hypothetical press release is written as if the product has already launched, detailing the benefits and customer impacts rather than technical features. This approach ensures the product development focuses on customer needs and the ultimate user experience from the outset. The press release is a tool to envision the final product's impact and to articulate its value proposition clearly before any development begins. It acts as a litmus test to validate the idea's potential to meet customer expectations and solve real problems.

5.8.2.6   Operational Scalability and Efficiency

The ability to deploy rapidly and reliably is enhanced by **Amazon's** technological infrastructure, particularly **AWS**, which supports these **Agile** teams with the necessary tools to scale operations efficiently. The integration of automated systems and robust cloud solutions ensures that even small teams can manage large-scale services effectively.

5.8.2.7   Outcome and Impact

This strategic approach has enabled **Amazon** to launch products that have significantly altered consumer behaviours and expectations across various industries, from cloud computing with **AWS** to smart home devices like **Amazon Echo**.

5.9   Conclusion

The **Product Team Model** is essential for navigating the complexities of product development in a competitive landscape. By examining the roles within cross-functional and self-organizing teams, and how they collaborate across various stages of a product's lifecycle, we gain a comprehensive understanding of the dynamics that drive innovation and efficiency.

The case studies of industry leaders like **Spotify, Amazon,** and others illustrate practical applications of these theories in real-world settings. These examples highlight the importance of Agile methodologies, the empowerment of teams, and the strategic use of technology to enhance collaboration and adaptability. Companies like **Amazon** with its '**Working Backwards**' approach, or **Spotify** with its autonomous '**squads**', exemplify how aligning team structures and processes with overarching business goals can dramatically improve product outcomes and customer satisfaction.

Moreover, this chapter emphasizes that the effectiveness of product teams is not solely determined by the skills and knowledge of individual team members, but also by how well these members can integrate their efforts towards a unified goal. The integration of customer feedback loops, iterative development processes, and continuous learning and adaptation is crucial for maintaining relevance and competitiveness in the market.

As businesses continue to navigate the complexities of digital transformation, the insights provided in this chapter offer valuable guidelines for structuring product teams that are not only efficient but also resilient and responsive to market demands. Embracing the principles of the **Product Team Model** can lead to significant improvements in product innovation, faster time-to-market, and enhanced customer engagement, ultimately contributing to sustained business success.

6

THE DIGITAL PRODUCT MANAGER

6.1 Introduction

In the dynamic realm of digital product management, the role of the **digital product manager** is pivotal. This chapter explores the multifaceted responsibilities and skills required for this critical position. From strategic planning to driving product development and managing stakeholder communications, the **digital product manager** is at the heart of transforming ideas into successful digital products. By understanding the breadth and depth of this role, this chapter provides insights into how digital product managers can effectively influence product outcomes and drive business success.

6.2 The Role and Responsibilities of the Digital Product Manager

The **digital product manager's** role is central to coordinating and leading product strategy, planning, development, marketing, and support, as shown in Figure 6.1. This section explores how the product manager orchestrates the various product management process groups and engages with different organizational functions to ensure the product's success.

1 Product Strategy

- **Gain Buy-In for Business Case:** The product manager begins by demonstrating the benefits of the product to secure buy-in from key stakeholders. This involves using reciprocity and showcasing how the product aligns with the organization's broader goals.

DOI: 10.1201/9781003484295-6

FIGURE 6.1 Digital product manager's roles and responsibilities

- **Share Product Vision and Strategy:** It's crucial to communicate the product vision and strategy clearly to both core and extended team members to ensure alignment and commitment throughout the product lifecycle.
- **Establish Brand Identity:** Developing a strong, consistent brand identity that resonates with the target market is a fundamental responsibility. This includes crafting a compelling product positioning statement and a unique selling proposition (**USP**) to differentiate the product in the market.

Example: Apple iPhone

On 9 January 2007, **Apple** unveiled the **iPhone**, dramatically shifting the landscape of mobile technology by integrating three distinct products into one: a mobile phone, a widescreen **iPod** with touch controls, and a ground-breaking internet communications device. This innovative integration allowed for desktop-class email, superior web browsing, and advanced map functionality, all accessible through a multi-touch interface, pioneering a new approach to user interaction that relied solely on the user's fingers.

The **iPhone** not only merged multiple devices into one but also introduced several industry-first features that set new standards for mobile communication. Features like Visual Voicemail transformed how users interact with traditional voicemail by allowing them to select and listen to messages out of sequence – akin to email usability. The integration of a full **QWERTY** soft keyboard and predictive text input streamlined **SMS** and email communication, enhancing usability over the cramped keyboards of typical smartphones of that time.

The strategy behind the **iPhone's** product launch was meticulously planned to ensure it resonated with potential users. By establishing a clear, compelling product vision that was communicated effectively to both internal stakeholders and the global market, **Apple** managed to create substantial buy-in and anticipation. The product's strategic positioning was bolstered by **Apple's** reputation for high-quality, innovative products, ensuring the **iPhone** was seen not just as a new gadget, but as a revolutionary development in mobile technology.

Moreover, **Apple's** choice to tightly integrate hardware with software allowed for seamless functionality that was unmatched at the time, setting a benchmark for what consumers could expect from their mobile devices. This holistic approach to product strategy and planning was pivotal in the **iPhone** becoming a transformative product in the tech industry, leading to widespread adoption and setting the stage for future innovations.

2 Product Planning

- **Stakeholder Involvement:** The product manager must engage with executives, the product team, sales, marketing, and support services. Regular updates keep all parties aligned on the progress and developments of the product.
- **Customer Voice:** Listening to the customer voice through the development of personas and grounding requirements prioritization with customer validation ensures the product meets the market's needs and expectations.

Example: Tesla

Tesla's product planning exemplifies a comprehensive and vertically integrated approach, making them a standout in the automotive industry. They manufacture a significant portion of their vehicle components in-house, including batteries and drivetrain systems, which not only ensures quality control but also reduces dependency on external suppliers. This vertical integration extends to their software updates, which are delivered digitally via the cloud, ensuring that all Tesla vehicles on the road are up-to-date with the latest features and improvements.

One of **Tesla's** most significant investments has been in advanced robotic technology for their production lines. This technology, paired with thousands of human workers, helps **Tesla** maintain high production flexibility and lower costs, making their products, like the **Model 3**, more affordable and competitive. This approach contrasts sharply with traditional automakers who rely on complex networks of suppliers and manufacturers spread across different countries. **Tesla** consolidates much of its manufacturing and supply chain operations within its factories and service centres.

Tesla's Gigafactory, a cornerstone of its strategy to make electric vehicles more accessible and affordable, has dramatically increased its production capabilities since its inception. Initially projected to reduce battery cell costs significantly by more than 30% at the start of its mass market vehicle production, the **Gigafactory** has exceeded expectations. Today, it produces more batteries in terms of kWh than any other plant worldwide. This achievement is critical in supporting **Tesla's** scaling up of electric vehicle production, aiming to meet the growing demand more sustainably.

Additionally, **Tesla's** direct-to-consumer sales strategy eliminates traditional dealerships, allowing for a more direct feedback loop with customers and reducing inventory costs. This model not only streamlines operations but also enhances customer experience by simplifying the car buying process and ensuring **Tesla** maintains direct control over sales and customer interactions.

Overall, **Tesla's** approach to product planning integrates high levels of in-house production with innovative manufacturing techniques and a direct sales model, setting a new standard in the automotive industry for integrating technology and sustainability with business operations.

3 Product Development

- **Agile Collaboration:** Adopting an agile approach, the product manager collaborates closely with business stakeholders and users to ensure that development efforts are closely aligned with user needs and business goals.
- **MVP and Validation:** Utilizing a **Minimum Viable Product** (MVP) approach involves engaging beta users to validate and refine the product based on actual customer feedback. This iterative process helps to keep the product development focused on solving the right problems.

Example: Spotify's Use of Agile Development

The **Spotify** model exemplifies a progressive approach to **Agile** product development, seamlessly integrating UX design, continuous delivery, and a robust product stack to foster an environment conducive to innovation and scalability. Introduced by Henrik Kniberg and Anders Ivarsson in 2012 through the 'Scaling Agile @ Spotify' whitepaper, this model diverges from conventional **Agile** methodologies by prioritizing team autonomy and adaptability over rigid structures.

Central to **Spotify's** strategy are 'squads', autonomous, cross-functional teams akin to mini-startups, each tasked with a specific long-term mission. These **squads** embrace various **Agile** methodologies, such as **Scrum** or **Kanban**, to suit their project needs, which allows for flexibility in tackling diverse product challenges. This autonomy is balanced with a structured approach through 'tribes', groups of **squads** that collaborate on related product areas, ensuring alignment and facilitating cross-pollination of ideas and practices.

UX design is deeply embedded in the product development process at **Spotify**. **Squads** focus on creating intuitive, user-centred designs, iterating based on direct user feedback to refine and enhance the user experience continuously. This focus is supported by **Spotify's** use of continuous delivery practices, enabling squads to rapidly deploy updates and improvements, thereby reducing time-to-market and increasing responsiveness to user needs.

Furthermore, **Spotify's** product stack is designed to support this dynamic environment, with tools and technologies that enable efficient workflow management, robust data analysis, and seamless integration across different platforms. The deployment of a comprehensive tech stack ensures that the technical infrastructure can keep pace with the fast-evolving product requirements.

By integrating UX design deeply into the development process, committing to continuous delivery for quick market response, and utilizing a flexible product stack, **Spotify's** model not only supports its growth ambitions but also sets a benchmark in **Agile** practices, making it a paragon of modern software development.

4 **Product Marketing:**

- **Launch Preparation:** The product manager coordinates with marketing, sales, and support to ensure everyone is prepared for the product launch. This includes finalizing the product release dates, ensuring the product's value and differentiation are clearly communicated, and leveraging third-party sales channels.
- **Launch Support Materials:** Ensuring that all teams are equipped with the necessary training resources, pricing information, packaging, collaterals, and press materials is vital for a successful launch.

Example: Dropbox's Referral Program

Dropbox's referral marketing strategy exemplifies how effectively executed product marketing can lead to exponential growth, especially for **SaaS**

companies operating fully online. By engaging existing users to spread the word through an easy-to-use referral program, **Dropbox** achieved a staggering 3,900% growth in just 15 months. The program was ingeniously simple and highly effective: users were encouraged to refer others via email, social media, or by sharing a direct link, and both the referrer and the new user received additional storage space as a reward. This not only incentivized current users to bring in new ones but also enhanced their engagement and loyalty by improving their service experience with more storage.

The timing of the referral invites was crucial; **Dropbox** sent these invites right after onboarding new users, capitalizing on their peak interest. Additionally, the company made it seamless for users to track the progress of their referrals and reinforced the cycle of positive feedback by promptly notifying them when a referral was successful. This strategic approach not only optimized user engagement but also maintained the program's relevance and attractiveness over the years. As a result, today, a significant 35% of **Dropbox** users are acquired through referrals, which underscores the enduring effectiveness of their referral program in driving user base growth. **Dropbox's** ongoing commitment to refining their product based on user feedback further sustains the program's success, demonstrating the power of integrating product development with dynamic marketing strategies to fuel long-term growth.

5 **Product Support:**

- **Support Team Collaboration:** Building and maintaining strong relationships with the service and support teams is essential. The product manager provides these teams with the necessary training and documentation to help them deliver excellent customer service.
- **Feedback Loop:** Utilizing feedback from the service and support teams allows the product manager to gather insights into customer experiences and areas for product improvement.

Example: Adobe's Customer Support

Adobe's approach to **SaaS** product support exemplifies a holistic and customer-centric strategy, focused not just on resolving issues but on fostering long-lasting relationships with users. At the heart of **Adobe's** support philosophy is the aim to deliver an uninterrupted, gratifying user experience, achieved through a blend of advanced support techniques, clear guidelines, and measurable success metrics. This ensures a responsive, knowledgeable, and dedicated service that consistently aims for customer delight and aligns closely with broader business objectives, enhancing user retention and opening avenues for upselling.

Adobe's infrastructure for customer support is meticulously designed to address user needs proactively. By choosing the right support channels based on customer demographics – such as live chat for tech-savvy users or more traditional channels like email and phone for corporate clients – **Adobe** ensures accessibility and satisfaction across its user base. The inclusion of comprehensive self-service options, like a detailed knowledge base and dynamic FAQs, empowers users to find solutions independently, enhancing the efficiency of the support process.

Moreover, **Adobe's** commitment to a seamless multi-channel support experience guarantees that user interactions are consistent and high-quality, regardless of the communication platform. This approach is complemented by an extensive repository of user guides, manuals, and video tutorials that cover common functionalities and troubleshooting steps, reducing the volume of direct support requests and allowing users to learn at their own pace.

The continuous training and development of **Adobe's** support team are crucial in maintaining an expert-level understanding of the products, ensuring that customer inquiries are handled expertly and efficiently. Regular updates and skill enhancements for the support staff keep them aligned with the latest product developments and customer expectations, further reinforcing **Adobe's** reputation for exceptional customer support.

In essence, **Adobe's** robust support system is a testament to their commitment to not only solving problems but also enhancing the user experience, making it a cornerstone of their long-term relationship with users.

6.3 Strategic Planning and Execution

In the realm of digital product management, strategic planning and execution form the backbone of a product manager's responsibilities. This section delves deeper into how digital product managers use strategic planning to steer products from conceptualization to market success, ensuring alignment with business goals and user expectations.

1 **Market Analysis and Opportunity Identification**
   Strategic planning begins with a thorough market analysis. Digital product managers must identify and interpret market trends, user needs, and potential gaps that the product can fill. This involves collecting and analysing data from market research, user feedback, and competitive analysis. Tools like **SWOT (Strengths, Weaknesses, Opportunities, Threats)** analysis and **Porter's Five Forces** are commonly used to frame these insights and identify strategic opportunities.

2 **Defining the Product Vision**

The product vision articulates the long-term mission of the product and its intended impact on the market. It acts as a guiding star for all product-related decisions. A clear, compelling vision helps unify the team and stakeholders around a common goal. It is the product manager's job to communicate this vision effectively and ensure it resonates with both the team and the target customers.

3 **Roadmapping and Prioritization**

With the vision defined, digital product managers develop a product roadmap that outlines the major milestones and timelines for the product's development cycle. This roadmap must balance market demands, technical feasibility, and business priorities. Prioritization frameworks such as the **MoSCoW** method (**Must have, Should have, Could have, Won't have**) or the **Kano** model help in deciding which features to develop first based on their expected impact and feasibility.

4 **Stakeholder Alignment and Collaboration**

Ensuring stakeholder alignment is crucial for seamless execution. This involves regular updates and strategic meetings with key stakeholders across the organization – such as marketing, sales, engineering, and customer support – to ensure everyone is aligned with the roadmap and the strategic goals. Effective use of communication tools and regular stakeholder engagements help in mitigating risks and preempting resistance by keeping everyone informed and involved.

5 **Continuous Strategy Evaluation**

The digital landscape evolves rapidly, and strategies that are relevant today may become obsolete tomorrow. Thus, continuous evaluation and iteration of the strategy are crucial. This involves setting up feedback loops with users, analysing product performance metrics, and staying updated with technological advancements. **Agile** methodologies often facilitate this dynamic approach, allowing strategies to evolve based on real-time data and user feedback.

6 **Leveraging Technology and Innovation**

In today's competitive environment, leveraging cutting-edge technology and fostering innovation are key components of strategic planning. Digital product managers need to explore and integrate new technologies such as AI, machine learning, and blockchain where appropriate to enhance product features and create a competitive edge.

In conclusion, strategic planning and execution in digital product management demand a meticulous, data-driven approach that aligns closely with both user needs and business objectives. Through careful analysis, clear communication, and agile responsiveness to market changes, digital product managers can drive their products to succeed in the fast-paced digital marketplace.

6.4 Driving Product Development

Effective product development is the cornerstone of a digital product manager's responsibilities. It involves translating strategic plans into actionable steps and overseeing the end-to-end development of the product. This section explores the various facets of driving product development, from team collaboration and **Agile** methodologies to user feedback integration and product iteration.

1 **Agile Methodology and Team Collaboration**

   Digital product managers often adopt **Agile** methodologies to manage product development. **Agile** allows for flexibility and rapid iteration based on user feedback and changing market conditions. Within this framework, product managers work closely with cross-functional teams – comprising developers, designers, and quality assurance specialists – to ensure that each sprint delivers incremental value to the product.

2 **Feature Prioritization and Backlog Management**

   One of the key roles of a digital product manager in the development phase is to prioritize features. This involves deciding which features to build first based on their potential impact on user satisfaction and business objectives. Tools like a prioritized backlog, which lists all the features, bugs, and technical work in priority order, help keep the development team focused and productive.

3 **MVP Development and Market Testing**

   The concept of the **Minimum Viable Product** (**MVP**) is central to Agile development. Digital product managers push for the development of **MVPs** to quickly launch a product with enough features to satisfy early adopters. The feedback received from this initial market testing is crucial for further development and refinement.

4 **Incorporating User Feedback**

   Continuous feedback is vital. Digital product managers establish mechanisms such as beta tests, usability testing sessions, and customer interviews to gather feedback. This feedback is essential for understanding user needs and preferences and is incorporated into the development lifecycle to refine and improve the product.

5 **Iterative Development and Continuous Improvement**

   Product development is an ongoing process that extends beyond the initial launch. Digital product managers lead the charge in ensuring the product evolves by managing iterative cycles that enhance functionality, address user pain points, and introduce innovations. This ongoing process of refinement helps the product stay relevant and competitive in the market.

6 **Technological Integration**

   Staying abreast of new technologies is a critical part of a digital product manager's role in product development. Whether it's integrating AI to personalize user experiences, using big data to drive decisions, or adopting new cloud services for enhanced performance, digital product managers need to leverage technology to enhance product offerings and user satisfaction.

7 **Risk Management**

Identifying potential risks and developing mitigation strategies is another important aspect of driving product development. Digital product managers assess risks related to technology, user adoption, and market dynamics. They work closely with the risk management team to implement strategies that minimize potential impacts on the product's success.

Driving product development requires a blend of technical knowledge, strategic thinking, and leadership. By effectively managing the development process, incorporating Agile methodologies, and integrating user feedback, digital product managers ensure that the product not only meets but exceeds user expectations while contributing to the business's success. This ongoing commitment to innovation and quality drives the product forward in a competitive digital landscape.

6.5 User Experience and Customer-Centric Approach

A digital product manager's role crucially involves ensuring an excellent user experience (**UX**). This section explores how successful digital product managers prioritize customer needs and create products that are not only functional but also enjoyable and easy to use.

1 **Incorporating User-Centric Design**

Digital product managers often work closely with UX/UI designers to incorporate user-centric design principles. This involves understanding the user's journey, identifying pain points, and continuously seeking to improve the design to enhance usability. A prime example is the redesign of **Airbnb's** booking platform. Initially, user feedback indicated confusion and a lack of trust during the booking process. In response, **Airbnb** revamped their platform to simplify the user interface and enhance transparency, which significantly increased bookings and user satisfaction.

2 **Iterative Design and Prototyping**

Iterative design processes allow product managers to test and refine concepts quickly. For instance, **Google** often employs rapid prototyping followed by user testing to refine its products continually. **Google Maps** has evolved significantly over time, adding features like real-time traffic updates and integration with public transit, directly based on user feedback and iterative testing.

3 **Personalization and Customization**
  Digital product managers also focus on personalization to enhance user engagement. **Netflix** provides a strong example of this through its recommendation algorithm, which personalizes content suggestions based on individual viewing habits. This not only improves user satisfaction but also increases the time spent on the platform.

4 **Accessibility and Inclusivity**
  Ensuring that digital products are accessible to all users, including those with disabilities, is another critical aspect overseen by product managers. **Microsoft's** inclusive design initiative is a leading example. They develop products with accessibility features like the Narrator and Magnifier for Windows, which help users with visual impairments navigate and use their software effectively.

5 **Leveraging User Feedback**
  Consistent collection and analysis of user feedback are pivotal. **Slack's** approach to user feedback exemplifies this well. They maintain open channels of communication with their users through various platforms, and continuously iterate their product based on the insights gained. This responsiveness to user needs has been instrumental in their growth and user retention.

Digital product managers play a fundamental role in weaving **UX** into the fabric of product development. By emphasizing a customer-centric approach and utilizing real-world feedback, they ensure the product not only meets functional requirements but also delivers a superior user experience. These efforts lead to higher user engagement, satisfaction, and ultimately, product success.

6.6 Data-Driven Decision Making

In today's digital economy, being data-driven is not just an advantage – it's a necessity for survival and success. Digital product managers play a pivotal role in ensuring that product decisions are grounded in data, enhancing the product's effectiveness and market fit. This section explores how successful product managers use data to inform their strategies, featuring real-world examples from leading tech companies.

1 **Using Analytics to Drive Product Decisions**
  Amazon stands out for its use of big data to drive decision making across its vast ecosystem. By analysing customer purchase data, browsing habits, and search history, **Amazon** optimizes its product offerings and user experience. This extensive data analysis allows for personalized product recommendations, a feature that significantly boosts customer satisfaction and sales.

2 **Experimentation and A/B Testing**

Netflix is renowned for its culture of experimentation. The company conducts hundreds of **A/B** tests annually to determine which features enhance viewer satisfaction and retention. This approach allows **Netflix** to make informed decisions that substantially impact its user interface and content algorithms, ensuring viewers receive a personalized and engaging experience.

3 **Feedback Loops and Continuous Improvement**

Spotify utilizes user data to refine its music recommendation algorithms continuously. By analysing listening habits, playlist data, and user ratings, **Spotify** adjusts its algorithms to deliver more precise and personalized music recommendations. This ongoing refinement process keeps users engaged and helps **Spotify** maintain a competitive edge in the music streaming industry.

4 **Predictive Analytics for Forecasting Demand**

Uber uses predictive analytics to revolutionize transportation logistics. By analysing various data points such as traffic patterns, user demand, and local events, **Uber** forecasts rider demand and directs drivers accordingly. This not only improves user wait times but also maximizes efficiency for drivers, balancing supply and demand effectively.

5 **Enhancing Customer Support with Data**

Salesforce leverages data to enhance its customer support services. By analysing customer interaction data, **Salesforce** identifies common issues and bottlenecks, enabling them to proactively improve their support processes. This data-driven approach helps in crafting more effective customer service strategies, increasing customer satisfaction and loyalty.

Data-driven decision making empowers digital product managers to refine their products continuously, anticipate market trends, and respond effectively to user needs. By leveraging analytics, conducting robust testing, and utilizing feedback loops, product managers can ensure that their decisions lead to tangible improvements and sustained product success. These examples illustrate the transformative power of data in crafting successful digital products that resonate well with users and thrive in competitive markets.

6.7 Stakeholder Management and Communication

Effective stakeholder management and communication are crucial for the success of any digital product. Digital product managers must navigate complex networks of stakeholders, from internal teams to external partners and customers. This section explores strategies for effective stakeholder engagement, illustrated with real-world examples from leading companies.

1 **Understanding Stakeholder Needs**
Digital product managers start by identifying and understanding the diverse needs and influences of their stakeholders. For example, at **Apple**, stakeholder mapping is a critical step when launching a new product like the **iPhone**. The product manager coordinates between design teams, engineering, marketing, and external supply chain partners to align goals and expectations, ensuring that each stakeholder's needs are considered in the product development process.

2 **Regular and Transparent Communication**
Regular updates and transparent communication channels are vital. Google, known for its transparent culture, regularly conducts all-hands meetings where product updates, challenges, and successes are shared. This approach ensures that everyone from engineers to marketers is on the same page, fostering a collaborative environment.

3 **Involving Stakeholders in Decision Making**
Involving stakeholders in decision-making processes can lead to better outcomes. **Microsoft**, for example, uses collaborative tools like **Microsoft Teams** to facilitate real-time feedback and decision-making with stakeholders across different geographic locations. This inclusive approach helps ensure that decisions are well-rounded and supports the broader business objectives.

4 **Managing Expectations**
Setting realistic expectations is key to maintaining stakeholder satisfaction. **Amazon** excels in this area by using detailed product roadmaps and clear communication to set and manage expectations with its stakeholders, particularly when integrating new technologies or launching new services like **Amazon Prime**.

5 **Leveraging Feedback Mechanisms**
Feedback mechanisms are essential for continuous improvement. **Salesforce** uses sophisticated **CRM** tools to gather stakeholder feedback, which is then analysed and used to improve product offerings and customer service strategies. This feedback loop not only enhances product quality but also builds stronger relationships with stakeholders.

6 **Building Advocacy**
Building advocates among stakeholders can drive success and facilitate smoother implementations. **Adobe**, through its **Adobe Insiders** program, cultivates relationships with key influencers in the digital marketing space. These insiders provide valuable insights and advocate for **Adobe's** products within their networks, enhancing product credibility and reach.

Effective stakeholder management and communication require a proactive and strategic approach. By understanding and addressing stakeholder needs, maintaining open lines of communication, involving stakeholders in the decision-making process, and leveraging feedback, digital product managers can build strong relationships that are essential for the success of their products. These examples from leading tech companies demonstrate the benefits of strategic stakeholder engagement in achieving business goals and driving product innovation.

6.8 Adapting to Technological Advances

In the fast-evolving tech landscape, staying abreast of technological advances is crucial for digital product managers. This section examines how top product managers integrate cutting-edge technologies to enhance product capabilities and user experiences.

1 **Incorporating Emerging Technologies**
   Tesla's integration of AI and machine learning in their vehicles exemplifies technological adaptation. By using these technologies, **Tesla** enhances autonomous driving features, improves battery efficiency, and offers predictive maintenance, which significantly elevates the user experience and product performance.
2 **Leveraging Big Data and Analytics**
   Netflix's use of big data and analytics to personalize viewing recommendations illustrates the power of data-driven product enhancements. By analysing vast amounts of user data, **Netflix** can tailor content to individual preferences, thereby increasing user engagement and satisfaction.
3 **Utilizing Cloud Computing**
   Adobe's shift to a cloud-based subscription model with **Adobe Creative Cloud** revolutionized how it delivers software. This move not only improved accessibility and collaboration capabilities for users but also allowed **Adobe** to roll out updates more smoothly and frequently.
4 **Blockchain for Enhanced Security**
   IBM's deployment of blockchain technology in supply chain management solutions showcases how digital product managers can leverage new tech to enhance product integrity and transparency. This technology provides immutable records and enhanced security features, appealing to industries that require robust traceability systems.

Staying ahead in digital product management requires a keen eye on technological trends and an understanding of how to seamlessly integrate these into product offerings. Successful product managers not only follow trends but also anticipate them, positioning their products at the forefront of innovation.

6.9 Regulatory Compliance and Ethical Considerations

As digital products become increasingly complex, ensuring compliance with regulations and ethical standards is more critical than ever. This section highlights how leading companies manage these aspects through proactive strategies.

1 **Data Privacy and Security**
   Google's approach to data privacy and security provides a benchmark in regulatory compliance. With products that handle sensitive user data, **Google** implements rigorous data protection protocols and regularly updates its privacy policies to comply with global standards like **GDPR**.

2 **Ethical AI Usage**
   Microsoft's commitment to ethical **AI** demonstrates how digital product managers can incorporate ethical considerations into product development. **Microsoft** establishes clear guidelines and uses **AI** responsibly to avoid biases and ensure fairness, fostering trust among users.

3 **Accessibility Standards**
   Apple's dedication to making products accessible to people with disabilities illustrates adherence to both ethical standards and regulatory requirements. Features like VoiceOver and closed-captioning not only comply with regulations like the Americans with Disabilities Act but also embody **Apple's** commitment to inclusivity.

Navigating the complex landscape of regulatory compliance and ethical considerations is essential for maintaining user trust and safeguarding the company's reputation. By prioritizing these aspects, digital product managers ensure their products are not only successful but also responsible and inclusive.

6.10 Measuring Success and ROI

Effectively measuring success and return on investment (**ROI**) is vital for justifying product decisions and planning future strategies. This section explores how successful digital product managers use metrics and **KPIs** to track performance and guide product evolution.

1 **Setting Clear Metrics and KPIs**
   Amazon's use of detailed performance metrics to gauge the success of its retail and **AWS** services exemplifies this practice. Metrics like customer satisfaction scores, conversion rates, and average revenue per user provide insights that drive decisions on product enhancements and marketing strategies.

2 ROI Calculation

Salesforce demonstrates the importance of calculating **ROI** by assessing the effectiveness of its cloud-based solutions in helping businesses increase productivity and sales efficiency. This assessment helps justify the investment in Salesforce products and demonstrates clear value to stakeholders.

3 **Continuous Improvement Based on Metrics**

Spotify's iterative approach to product development, guided by user engagement metrics and subscription growth rates, showcases how continuous improvement can be driven by data. This approach ensures that **Spotify** remains responsive to user needs and market dynamics.

By rigorously measuring success and **ROI**, digital product managers can provide concrete evidence of their product's impact, justify investments, and refine their strategies. This data-driven approach is crucial for maintaining competitiveness and achieving long-term success in the digital product landscape.

6.11   Conclusion

In conclusion, the role of a digital product manager is crucial and dynamic, demanding a blend of technical expertise, strategic foresight, and effective communication. As the linchpin of product strategy and execution, digital product managers must adeptly navigate the intersection of user needs, technological opportunities, and business goals. The examples discussed in this chapter demonstrate the significant impact of adept product management on a company's ability to innovate and compete in the digital age. Effective digital product managers not only adapt to changing market dynamics and emerging technologies but also anticipate future trends, thereby positioning their products – and their companies – for success. The insights provided in this chapter serve as a guide for current and aspiring product managers to refine their skills and strategies, fostering products that resonate with users and excel in increasingly competitive markets.

7

DIGITAL PRODUCT MANAGEMENT FRAMEWORK

7.1 Introduction

This chapter delves into the **Digital Product Management Framework**, a structured approach that guides product managers through five core process groups: **Product Opportunity, Product Planning, Product Development, Product Launch, and Product Support**. Each process group consists of key activities designed to ensure that digital products meet market demands, align with business objectives, and achieve sustained success. This framework is instrumental for product managers navigating the complexities of the digital landscape, providing them with a blueprint for systematic product management from conception to market delivery and beyond.

7.2 The Digital Product Management Framework

More and more companies are transforming their organizations to make use of technological innovation and are becoming more product-centric. Companies are shifting from a project- to a product-centric approach. This requires adopting a **Product Operating Model (POM)**. A **POM** is a comprehensive framework designed to manage and deliver products or services effectively and efficiently. Its primary purpose is to align product development efforts with an organization's overarching strategic objectives, ensuring efficient delivery and high-quality outputs that meet customer needs and drive business success.

Think of the **POM** as the backbone that helps your organization manage products or services in an efficient, strategic way. It's not just about having

DOI: 10.1201/9781003484295-7

a plan – it's about making sure every part of the product process, from brainstorming an idea to supporting customers after a product launch, runs smoothly and in sync with the company's broader goals.

At its heart, the **POM** ensures that everyone knows their role, responsibilities, and workflows. It creates clarity, which is essential for efficiency. Without a clear structure, you're left with confusion, inefficiencies, and gaps in the process. The **POM** sets up that structure, offering guidance on everything from product strategy and development to lifecycle management and even the technologies and tools you'll use along the way. It's like having a roadmap to help everyone stay on track.

What makes the **POM** so useful is its focus on **scalability and flexibility**. As companies grow, markets change, and technology evolves, the **POM** helps an organization adapt seamlessly, without causing chaos in day-to-day operations. Whether you're scaling up a product to meet higher demand or adapting to new market realities, the **POM** ensures the product journey is smooth.

Why is this important? Because product failures often stem from poor market research, unclear positioning, or weak planning. By adopting a solid **POM** and leveraging the skills of product managers, organizations can avoid these common pitfalls. It provides the necessary foundation to support both digital transformation and the evolving role of product management in today's business landscape.

In short, a well-structured **POM**, supported by the **Digital Product Management Framework**, helps your business align its product development efforts with its overall objectives, ensuring that every product is designed, launched, and supported in a way that drives success.

The **Digital Product Management Framework** as shown in Figure 7.1 includes five clusters of processes, grouped together into 'process groups'.

1 Firstly, product managers engage in **Product Opportunity**, in which they are responsible for the product strategy, which determines a product's vision to shape the product direction. This process group includes processes and tasks, where product managers and their teams build clear, realistic plans to reach a desired outcome. In their role, product managers begin by establishing a clear direction and overarching goals for their product, ensuring these align with broader business objectives. They then delve into assessing potential opportunities and gaps in the market, gathering insights to inform their strategy. This role involves justifying new initiatives or significant strategic shifts through well-articulated business cases. Product managers craft messaging that positions their product distinctively in the consumer's mind. They also determine pricing structures that optimize financial returns while delivering value to customers. Ultimately, they spearhead the launch

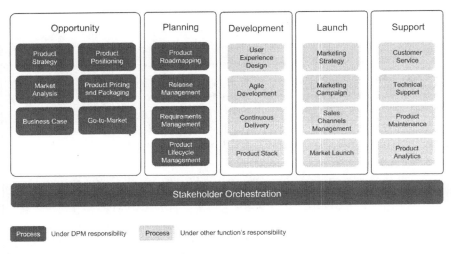

Opportunity		Planning	Development	Launch	Support
Product Strategy	Product Positioning	Product Roadmapping	User Experience Design	Marketing Strategy	Customer Service
Market Analysis	Product Pricing and Packaging	Release Management	Agile Development	Marketing Campaign	Technical Support
Business Case	Go-to-Market	Requirements Management	Continuous Delivery	Sales Channels Management	Product Maintenance
		Product Lifecycle Management	Product Stack	Market Launch	Product Analytics

Stakeholder Orchestration

Process — Under DPM responsibility   Process — Under other function's responsibility

FIGURE 7.1 Digital Product Management Framework

planning, ensuring a coordinated approach to bring the product to market effectively.

There are six key activities in **Product Opportunity**

- *Product Strategy*: Create a product vision to shape your product direction and build a clear, realistic plan of how to reach the desired result.
- *Market Analysis*: Evaluate a market opportunity for a product in a target market based on market trends, target market segments, challenges, frustrations, and unmet needs.
- *Business Case*: Build a business case to justify the proposal for a new product or a business strategy change to an existing product.
- *Product Positioning*: Develop product positioning to guide and communicate how you want your customer to think and feel about your product.
- *Product Pricing* and *Packaging*: Choose a pricing strategy to maximize profits and value for both shareholders and customers.
- *Go-to-Market*: Formulate a go-to-market strategy to successfully launch a product in the market.

2 Secondly, product managers perform processes related to **Product Planning**. Here, they need to shape the direction and path for the product, using a product roadmap. They typically work with various stakeholders and teams to prioritize product requirements, and plan how, and when, a product will be released. These processes are carried out prior to releasing the product to market, although these processes are in fact iterative.

They therefore require product managers to adapt continually and revise their plans during the later stages of the lifecycle.

There are four key activities in **Product Planning**:

- *Product Roadmapping*: Create the Product Roadmap to map out the vision and direction of your product offering over time.
- *Release Management*: Plan and communicate your product releases to the market or customers.
- *Requirements Management*: Managing market requirements in alignment with the product plan and roadmap, including how to identify, analyse, and prioritize requirements.
- *Product Lifecycle Management*: Apply product iterations throughout the product lifecycle in the context of fast-moving digital world today.

3 Thirdly, product managers orchestrate various stakeholders involved in **Product Development** processes. Here, they need to design and develop the product, with a focus on customer experience. They should leverage modern, Agile methods, and adopt a continuous delivery approach to deliver products in short cycles. Product development is performed before the introduction of the product to the market. But, crucially, it's also performed continually throughout the four phases of the product lifecycle (Introduction, Growth, Maturity, Decline).

There are four key activities in **Product Development**:

- *User Experience Design*: Design product or service with a focus on customer experience through the various touchpoints through which customers interact with the product or service.
- *Agile Development*: Leverage modern Agile methods to develop a digital product through multiple iterations in collaboration with each other and with customers.
- *Continuous Delivery*: Adopt a continuous delivery approach to delivering a product digital product in short cycles to achieve greater speed, accuracy, and frequency.
- *Product Stack*: Evaluate your product stack that comprise apps, technologies, and other resources product managers use to bring their products to market.

4 Fourthly, product managers must manage various processes related to **Product Launch**. This entails creating awareness of the product, ensuring that marketing campaigns reach the intended audience, developing a sales channel strategy to maximize customer reach, and crafting a launch plan to introduce the product to the market. These processes are performed during the introduction phase of the product lifecycle, but can also be performed throughout the product lifecycle whenever a new upgrade or extension is made to the product.

There are four key activities in **Product Launch**:

- *Marketing Strategy*: Formulate a marketing strategy to acquire customers for your product using value messaging.
- *Marketing Campaign*: Design a marketing campaign to drive a specific goal through various channels and touchpoints.
- *Sales Channels Management*: Develop a distribution channel strategy through provisioning the right level of support and control.
- *Market Launch*: Craft a product launch plan to introduce your product to the market.

5 Lastly, product managers are responsible for managing various stakeholders involved in providing Product Support. They are also responsible for customer service and technical support, as well as maintaining, tracking, and measuring product performance metrics for continuously improving a product. These processes are performed throughout the four phases of the product lifecycle.

There are four key activities in **Product Support**:

- *Customer Service*: Provide great customer experience through a proactive approach to support customers to get the most out of your product.
- *Technical Support*: Create an effective technical support structure to assist customers with technical issues in your product.
- *Product Maintenance*: Explore how continuous product maintenance helps to keep up with customer needs.
- *Product Analytics*: Examine the use of product analytics to assess adoption and usage of product and the performance of the digital experiences built around it.

The **Digital Product Management (DPM) series** is divided into two volumes to cover the key areas of the **DPM framework**.

Volume 1	Digital Product Management: Strategic Planning and Market Opportunity
Volume 2	Digital Product Management: Managing Product Development, Launch, and Support

Volume 1 focuses on **Product Opportunity** and **Product Planning** – the two core process groups where product managers hold direct responsibility. These areas involve identifying opportunities, defining strategies, and creating product roadmaps. Volume 2 shifts the focus to the operational aspects, covering **Product Development**, **Product Launch**, and **Product Support**. While product managers may not directly control these phases, their role in orchestrating stakeholders and guiding cross-functional teams is critical for successful execution.

7.3 Companies Leveraging Digital Product Management Framework

Table 7.1 demonstrates how companies can effectively apply different aspects of the Digital Product Management Framework to achieve success in the digital marketplace. These strategies not only cater to immediate business needs but also build a foundation for long-term innovation and market leadership.

TABLE 7.1 Companies leveraging digital product management processes for digital marketplace

Process Groups	Company and Key Activities
Product Opportunity	Apple's introduction of the iPhone in 2007 showcases an exemplary product strategy that revolutionized the mobile phone industry. The strategy was built on a clear vision to integrate three devices into one – a phone, an iPod, and an internet communicator. Apple conducted extensive market research to identify consumer frustrations with existing phones, which led to the development of a user-friendly interface and a touch screen that set the industry standard. Apple's pricing strategy also played a crucial role, positioning the iPhone as a premium product and subsequently adjusting prices to capture a broader market share. The go-to-market strategy was carefully executed with massive advertising campaigns and key partnerships, notably with AT&T as the exclusive carrier, which helped secure a strong market entry.
Product Planning	Tesla's approach to product planning is particularly evident in its development of the Model S. Tesla planned the Model S as a premium sedan that would redefine electric vehicles. The roadmap included significant milestones like the innovative use of battery technology and autopilot features. Tesla's market requirements were meticulously aligned with its long-term strategic goals, prioritizing sustainability and cutting-edge technology. The iterative nature of Tesla's product planning allows for continuous enhancement based on user feedback and technological advancements, thereby maintaining its competitive edge.

(Continued)

TABLE 7.1 (Continued)

Process Groups	Company and Key Activities
Product Development	Spotify's Agile product development process is a textbook example of modern digital practices. The company's development teams operate in 'squads' that function autonomously, allowing for rapid testing and adaptation of features based on real-time user data. Spotify employs continuous delivery mechanisms to ensure that updates are smoothly rolled out to users without disrupting the user experience. This approach has enabled Spotify to stay ahead of consumer preferences in the highly competitive music streaming industry.
Product Launch	Dropbox's referral program was a groundbreaking marketing strategy that significantly contributed to its launch and subsequent viral growth. By incentivizing current users with extra storage space for every new user they brought on board, Dropbox effectively used its existing customer base to reach a wider audience. This marketing strategy was highly successful due to its simplicity and the immediate value it provided to users, helping Dropbox scale rapidly without the corresponding marketing expenditures typically seen in such growth phases.
Product Support	Adobe has transformed its customer support strategy by leveraging a comprehensive digital infrastructure that includes an extensive knowledge base, community forums, and direct support channels. This structure allows users to resolve many issues independently, reducing the burden on support teams and improving customer satisfaction. Adobe's focus on continuous product maintenance and updates ensures that customer feedback and emerging issues are promptly addressed, enhancing the overall user experience and product reliability.

7.4 Product Case Scenario: An Assistive Listening Product

This Product Case Scenario contains essential information about **MobileLinQ's** new product, **MobileListen**, an assistive listening technology for lecture theatres. This product will be used throughout the book to illustrate key concepts around managing digital products and services.

7.4.1   Introduction

MobileLinQ, a Singapore-based innovator in assistive technology, is gearing up to transform the learning experience for students with auditory disabilities through its latest product, **MobileListen**. This new assistive listening technology aims to address the limitations of current auditory assistance solutions in universities and capitalize on the ongoing digital transformation in higher education. Figure 7.2 shows the visual map of how **MobileLinQ's** assistive technology works on a typical campus learning environment. With **MobileLinQ's** product, lectures are transmitted over **WiFi** in real-time and in high quality to mobile devices. To access a live stream, students simply download and install the free **MobileListen** App and connect to their university's **WiFi**. The simple combination of the mobile device, the app, and the classroom's **WiFi**, allows students to receive audio content that they would otherwise be unable to hear. This high-quality audio is transmitted throughout the lecture theatre, meaning students who want to make use of the product may sit absolutely anywhere in the room.

7.4.2   Background

With the rising number of students with auditory disabilities attending universities worldwide, there is a pressing need for more effective assistive listening technologies. Traditional solutions often require dedicated seating or specific hardware receivers, which can segregate or stigmatize students needing assistance. **MobileLinQ's MobileListen** intends to remove these barriers by utilizing a **'Bring Your Own Device'** (**BYOD**) approach, leveraging existing technology and infrastructure to offer a more inclusive and cost-effective solution.

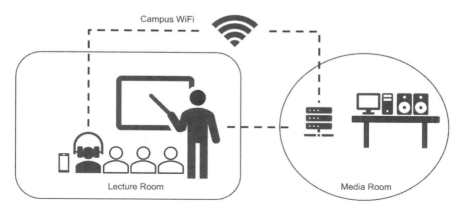

FIGURE 7.2   Product case scenario: An assistive listening product

7.4.3 Challenges in Current Assistive Listening Technologies

Existing assistive listening devices in universities are generally restricted to specific zones within a lecture hall, requiring students with hearing impairments to sit in designated areas. These systems depend heavily on specialized hardware, which not only increases the cost but also highlights the differences among students, potentially leading to stigmatization.

7.4.4 MobileListen's Innovative Approach

MobileListen is designed to deliver high-quality, live audio directly to students' mobile devices via **WiFi,** allowing them to hear lectures clearly from anywhere in the room. This approach not only fosters inclusivity but also enhances the overall learning experience for students with auditory disabilities. The key features of **MobileListen** include:

1 **BYOD Compatibility: MobileListen** supports a wide array of devices and personal hearing solutions like headphones and hearing aids, empowering students to use their own devices without extra expenses.
2 **Customizable User Experience:** The technology allows adjustments in volume and audio quality, ensuring that the needs of students with various types of auditory impairments are met.
3 **Low Total Cost of Ownership:** By leveraging existing **WiFi** infrastructure, MobileListen minimizes the need for additional hardware and reduces the costs associated with installation and maintenance. This not only eases the financial burden on educational institutions but also simplifies operations, enhancing deployment speed and reducing the workload on **IT** and **AV** staff.

7.4.5 Strategic Implementation

To implement **MobileListen** effectively, **MobileLinQ** plans to engage closely with university **IT** departments to integrate the technology seamlessly with existing network frameworks. This collaboration will ensure that the setup is optimized for audio quality and accessibility, while also maintaining security and privacy standards.

7.4.6 Future Prospects

Looking ahead, **MobileListen** has the potential to set new standards in educational technology by providing a scalable, user-friendly solution that can be adapted for various educational settings beyond universities, such as conferences and public lectures. **MobileLinQ** is also exploring enhancements such as AI-driven audio optimizations and real-time transcription services to further enrich the usability of **MobileListen.**

7.4.7   MobileLinQ's Conclusion

MobileLinQ's **MobileListen** product represents a significant step forward in creating a more inclusive academic environment. Through innovative use of existing technologies and a strong focus on user needs, **MobileLinQ** is poised to make a substantial impact on the way educational content is accessed by students with auditory disabilities, paving the way for broader applications in any auditory-challenged environment.

7.5   Product Case Scenario: A Mobile Car-Sharing Platform

This Product Case Scenario contains essential information about **QuikDrive's** car-sharing service to car owners and car renters which operates in shopping malls, residential estates, office buildings, bus and rail stations, hotels and airports in Singapore. This product will be used throughout the book to illustrate key concepts around managing digital products and services.

7.5.1   Introduction

With the rising costs of car ownership in Singapore, more citizens are turning to car-sharing platforms as a flexible, cost-effective alternative. **QuikDrive**, a Singapore-based company, offers a car-sharing solution through its mobile app and website, connecting car owners with renters and managing the rental process. This case study explores **QuikDrive's** innovative approach to car-sharing, its implementation, and its future potential to transform the transportation landscape in Singapore. Figure 7.3 shows the **QuikDrive** platform in the form of a website and mobile app, that brings car owners and renters together, manages rental bookings and collects payment.

QuikDrive

A platform which brings car owners and renters together, manages rental bookings and collects payment.

Offers a pay-per-use service to renters

Operates in shopping malls, residential estates, office buildings, bus and rail stations, hotels and airports.

FIGURE 7.3   Case scenario: A mobile car-sharing platform

7.5.2 Background

Car ownership in Singapore is prohibitively expensive due to the high cost of obtaining a **Certificate of Entitlement (COE)**, which is required to own a car. With an average sedan costing more than **S$100,000**, many Singaporeans are seeking alternatives to ownership. Car-sharing has emerged as a popular solution, providing individuals with the flexibility and convenience of driving without the long-term financial burden of owning a vehicle.

QuikDrive entered the market with a platform designed to empower car owners to monetize their unused vehicles and provide renters with an affordable, convenient car-sharing option. By offering both a website and mobile app, **QuikDrive** simplifies the process for both owners and renters, facilitating vehicle rentals, payments, and insurance coverage.

7.5.3 Challenges in Current Market

Car-sharing platforms are not without their challenges. Current offerings often face issues such as:

- **Complicated user interfaces,** which make the process of renting or leasing cars cumbersome.
- **Unclear rental terms** that leave both car owners and renters uncertain about their rights and obligations.
- **Limited rental options and locations,** which can reduce the convenience of accessing vehicles for renters.
- **Lack of trust between owners and renters,** leading to concerns over the condition of the car and payment security.
- **High subscription fees** for some platforms, which can deter potential users, particularly renters who only occasionally need access to a car.

These issues have highlighted the need for a more streamlined, flexible, and user-friendly approach, which **QuikDrive** aims to address through its new platform.

7.5.4 Product Innovative Approach

QuikDrive differentiates itself from other car-sharing platforms with a variety of innovative features designed to enhance both the car owner and renter experiences.

For Car Owners

1 **Convenient Lease Scheduling:** Car owners can easily plan when renters can use their vehicles through a flexible scheduling system.

2 **Car Return Location Selection**: Owners can set specific return locations, adding convenience and control over where the car will be dropped off.

3 **Renter Profile Verification**: Car owners can verify renters' identities and driving credentials, building trust and reducing risks.

4 **Insurance Coverage**: QuikDrive simplifies the process of insuring cars against damages while in use by renters.

5 **Late Return Compensation**: Owners receive compensation if renters return cars late, offering peace of mind and ensuring fairness.

For Renters

1 **Multiple Rental Options**: Renters can choose from various vehicle types based on their needs.

2 **Accessible Rental Locations**: Convenient pick-up and drop-off locations ensure that renters can access cars easily across Singapore.

3 **Digital Key**: Renters can lock and unlock cars via their smartphones, eliminating the need to exchange physical keys.

4 **Virtual Cash Cards**: The platform integrates virtual cash cards, making payments seamless for road tolls and other charges.

5 **No Subscription Fees**: QuikDrive removes the barrier of membership fees, making car-sharing more accessible for casual users.

These features allow **QuikDrive** to stand out by addressing both the logistical and psychological concerns of car owners and renters, ensuring a smooth and secure experience for all parties involved.

7.5.5 Strategic Implementation

QuikDrive's strategic implementation focuses on three core objectives:

1 **Improving the Customer Experience:**

- The platform's integration of both web and mobile technologies simplifies the car-sharing process, providing users with a seamless experience. Renters can quickly book cars and manage their rentals on the go through the mobile app, while car owners can manage availability, view bookings, and communicate with renters easily.

2 **Increasing Adoption Rates:**

- By eliminating membership subscription fees and automating the sign-up process, **QuikDrive** reduces the friction of entry for new users. The streamlined onboarding process includes automatic driver's license and credit card verification, making it faster and easier for users to begin renting or leasing vehicles.

3 **Leveraging Data Analytics and Machine Learning:**

- **QuikDrive** plans to implement data analytics and machine learning to monitor real-time operations, predict user preferences, and optimize vehicle availability. By analysing user behaviour and demand patterns, **QuikDrive** can ensure that cars are available when and where they are most needed, improving operational efficiency and reducing downtime for owners.

7.5.6 Future Prospects

As Singapore continues to focus on sustainability and reducing the environmental impact of vehicle ownership, car-sharing platforms like **QuikDrive** are positioned for growth. By offering a cost-effective, convenient alternative to owning a car, **QuikDrive** has the potential to expand its user base and transform urban mobility in Singapore.

Key future prospects include

1 **Expansion into New Markets: QuikDrive** can scale its platform to other densely populated urban areas across Southeast Asia, where similar car ownership challenges exist.
2 **Integration with Public Transportation:** Collaborating with public transportation systems could provide users with a multi-modal transport solution, allowing them to seamlessly switch between public and private transport based on their needs.
3 **Electric Vehicle Integration:** As Singapore shifts towards more sustainable transportation solutions, **QuikDrive** can integrate electric vehicles (**EVs**) into its platform, catering to eco-conscious users and supporting the government's goal of reducing carbon emissions.

By continuing to innovate and adapt to the needs of its users, **QuikDrive** is well-positioned to grow and evolve, driving forward the future of car-sharing in Singapore and beyond.

7.5.7 QuikDrive's Conclusion

QuikDrive represents a forward-thinking solution to the challenges of car ownership in Singapore. By offering a flexible, convenient platform for both car owners and renters, the company has created an innovative model that simplifies car-sharing and enhances user trust. Through its strategic implementation of technology, **QuikDrive** is poised to disrupt the traditional car rental market and expand its reach, transforming urban mobility in Singapore. The future of **QuikDrive** looks promising as it explores new opportunities for growth, integration, and sustainability.

7.6 Conclusion

The **Digital Product Management Framework** outlined in this chapter provides a comprehensive approach to managing digital products through strategic planning, Agile development, effective marketing, and continuous support. By adhering to this framework, organizations can ensure that their digital products are not only successful in the short term but also sustainable and competitive in the long run. This chapter sets the foundation for the detailed exploration of each process group in the subsequent chapters, equipping digital product managers with the tools and insights necessary for excellence in the digital era.

8
DEFINING A PRODUCT STRATEGY

8.1 Introduction

Creating a clear and impactful product vision is foundational for guiding a product's development and ensuring its market success. This initial phase is about setting a solid foundation by defining the long-term goals and the roadmap for achieving them. It involves understanding who the product will serve and the unique value it aims to provide. A well-articulated product vision aligns the efforts of various teams, ensuring that every step taken is in service of a coherent end goal. In this section, we explore the critical components that make up a product vision, dissecting how these elements combine to form a robust framework for guiding product decisions and market entry.

8.2 Product Vision

8.2.1 Product Vision Overview

A well-defined product vision serves as the north star for product managers, guiding the strategic planning and development processes. It identifies the target market and users, articulates the problem statement, and clarifies the pain points that the product aims to resolve. The vision not only details the benefits and gains customers experience by using the product but also underscores the product's unique value proposition – what sets it apart from competitors.

8.2.2 Developing a Product Vision

Developing a strong product vision is pivotal as it encapsulates the core of what a product aims to deliver, informed by thorough market data, customer

DOI: 10.1201/9781003484295-8

> A value proposition is a clear statement of the tangible results a customer gets from using your products or services.

'iPod.

1,000 songs in your pocket'.

Steve Jobs

FIGURE 8.1 iPod: Example of a product vision

insights, and a sharp competitive analysis. This vision translates into a value proposition statement that not only guides strategic and operational decisions but also clearly communicates the product's unique benefits to the target market. Taking the example of the **iPod**, Steve Jobs effectively used a compelling value proposition to differentiate the **iPod** from other music players. The vision of the **iPod** was articulated as putting '**1,000 songs in your pocket**', as shown in Figure 8.1. This simple yet powerful statement captured the essence of the **iPod's** offer: immense storage capacity, portability, and instant access to a vast music library, all in one sleek device.

This value proposition did more than describe the product; it connected emotionally with consumers by highlighting the iPod's ability to integrate seamlessly into daily life, suggesting a new lifestyle of convenience and accessibility to music anytime, anywhere. It addressed the customer's need for a practical, stylish, and user-friendly music player, setting the iPod apart in a crowded market dominated by larger, less efficient devices. Such a clear, resonant value proposition is crucial because it helps potential customers immediately grasp the unique selling point of the product without needing to delve into technical details. It frames the product not just as an object but as an essential tool that enriches the user's life, thereby driving higher market adoption and customer loyalty.

8.2.3   Key Elements in a Product Vision

Figure 8.2 shows the four key elements in a product vision that are essential for guiding the development and marketing of a product. They help define the product's purpose and its unique value to customers. Here's a breakdown of these elements:

1 **Target Customer:** The foundation of a product vision is a deep understanding of who the customers are. A clear picture of the target customer

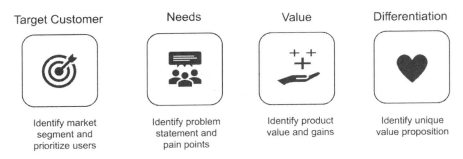

Target Customer	Needs	Value	Differentiation
Identify market segment and prioritize users	Identify problem statement and pain points	Identify product value and gains	Identify unique value proposition

FIGURE 8.2 Four key elements in a product vision

helps in tailoring product features and marketing strategies directly to the needs of this group. This requires comprehensive market research to define customer demographics, behaviours, and preferences.

2 **Customer Needs:** Identifying and prioritizing customer needs is crucial. This involves understanding the challenges customers face and how the product can solve these problems. Effective tools like customer interviews, surveys, and feedback mechanisms are instrumental in gathering this insight.

3 **Value Proposition:** The value proposition outlines the benefits the product offers to its customers. It goes beyond the features of the product to express the real gains customers will experience. Whether it's saving time, reducing costs, or enhancing enjoyment, the value proposition connects the product's capabilities to customer desires.

4 **Differentiation:** Lastly, differentiation highlights how the product stands out from its competitors. This could be through innovation, superior performance, additional features, cost-effectiveness, or better customer service. Differentiation is what makes a product unique in a crowded marketplace and is often what attracts customers to one product over another.

These elements collectively form the foundation of a product vision, helping to steer the strategic direction and development efforts towards creating a product that is both meaningful and successful in the market. They are crucial for aligning the product development team and stakeholders with a common understanding of what the product aims to achieve and for whom.

8.2.4 Product Vision in Assistive Listening Product Case Scenario

We can better understand the four key elements of a product vision through the product case scenario of the **MobileLinQ's** assistive listening product depicted in Figure 8.3.

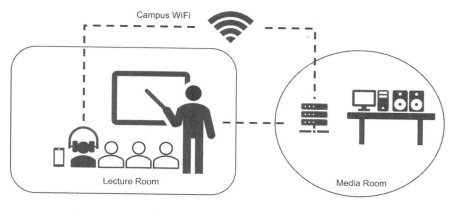

FIGURE 8.3   Case scenario: An assistive listening product

In the Product Case Scenario, we are introduced to **MobileLinQ**, a company based in Singapore, which is developing an assistive listening technology called **MobileListen**, specifically designed for university students with auditory disabilities. This technology aims to transform the learning experience for these students by utilizing a '**Bring Your Own Device**' approach, where high-quality lecture audio is transmitted live via **WiFi** to students' personal mobile devices through a free app. This solution allows students the freedom to sit anywhere in the lecture hall without the need for specialized hardware or designated seating, which are common in existing assistive listening devices. By leveraging existing **WiFi** infrastructure, **MobileListen** not only minimizes costs but also simplifies implementation and maintenance, thus enhancing operational efficiency and promoting inclusivity. This approach addresses the critical needs for customization and flexibility in auditory assistance, providing a seamless and enriched educational experience for students with auditory disabilities.

Here's an example of **MobileLinQ's** high-level product vision for their new assistive listening technology:

MobileLinQ's PRODUCT VISION

'Imagine a world, where all students with auditory disabilities, who are often excluded from hearing lectures properly, can now benefit from barrier-free listening. This is possible with MobileListen - an inclusive assistive listening solution for the university campus. Unlike existing products, MobileListen allows students to sit anywhere in the room, and hear high quality audio'.

The product vision guides product managers in identifying the target market and users. It helps define the problem statement and pain points faced by customers. It outlines the benefits and gains experienced by customers who use the product. And, it describes the unique value proposition the product offers, which others don't.

Here is the application of the four key elements of a product vision for **MobileLinQ's MobileListen**:

1 Target Customer

Definition: Identifying the specific group of customers for whom the product is designed.

Application: **MobileLinQ's** target customers are university students with auditory disabilities. Thousands of university-going students include those with hearing disabilities. Broadly speaking, this describes the target market.

The universities themselves are **MobileLinQ's** customers, but the actual users are lecturers, and of course: students with auditory disabilities, who will benefit directly from the **MobileListen** product. This clear focus helps tailor the product's design and features to meet the unique needs of this group, ensuring that the assistive listening technology is both relevant and beneficial.

2 Customer Needs

Definition: Understanding the specific needs and problems faced by the target customers that the product aims to solve.

Application: The primary need of **MobileLinQ's** customers is to access and understand lecture content easily without being confined to specific seating or special equipment. Determining the specific needs of both customers and users requires product managers to articulate a problem statement and define pain points.

Let's first take a look at users and the challenges faced the hearing-impaired students. In this case, the problem might be described as follows:

'Many university students with auditory disabilities require assistance in hearing the content of lectures'.

There is a need to overcome the audio challenges of poor acoustics in lecture theatres, the distance from the lecturer, and background noise in the lecture room environment.

An example of a pain point for users would be this:

'Some students with hearing disabilities face anxiety and stigmatization from other students, and even lecturers'.

Another paint point for them would be this:

'Many of these students struggle with both comprehension, and interaction in class'.

Next, let's take a look at customers such as universities that are attended by these hearing-impaired students. A pain point for the customers might be as follows:

'Universities consistently fail to provide adequate, inclusive support to their students with auditory disabilities'.

Product managers at **MobileLinQ** can design and build **MobileListen** so that it can meet these needs, or solve these pain points for their customers and users. This product addresses these needs by providing a flexible and inclusive solution that allows students to listen to lectures from anywhere in the classroom through their own devices.

3 Value Proposition

Definition: The benefits or gains that the product promises to deliver to its customers.

Application: Determining the value that a product will deliver, entails identifying the specific gains that customers and users will benefit from by using the product.

For one, students with hearing disabilities will have full access to high-quality, live lecture content. They can gain access to content that they might otherwise not do so using other means. They benefit from reduced anxiety about whether or not they'll be able to hear in class. They gain increased levels of engagement with the material and the class. The lecturers also benefit from knowing that their content is reaching everyone in the class, and the knowledge that all students can participate.

MobileListen's value proposition lies in enhancing the educational experience by offering high-quality, customizable, and accessible auditory assistance. This technology enables students to engage with academic content delivered by professors in a way that suits their individual needs, thereby fostering a better learning environment and promoting inclusivity.

4 Differentiation

Definition: How the product stands out from existing solutions in the market.

Application: To complete the product vision, a product manager must be able to understand, and then articulate: what differentiates their proposed product, from that of their direct, and indirect competitors.

This can also be described as determining your product's **unique selling proposition,** or **USP.** This is a common way of explaining what makes your product better than your competitors.

In the case of **MobileLinQ's** new product, they start by looking at any existing products that try to meet the same needs, or address the same problem.

What they find is that existing assistive listening solutions rely on dedicated seating zones, which, for various technological reasons, require students to sit in the front two rows. **MobileLinQ** also discovers that existing solutions require students to use specific hardware receivers, like headphones.

So, the two ways that **MobileLinQ** can differentiate its product are by providing a solution that lets students sit anywhere in the lecture theatre, and by letting students use any hardware – even their mobile devices.

Unlike traditional assistive listening devices that require fixed seating and specialized receivers, **MobileListen** differentiates itself with its **'Bring Your Own Device'** model and reliance on existing **WiFi** infrastructure. This approach not only reduces costs and logistical barriers but also empowers students by integrating seamlessly into their current lifestyle and technology usage.

MobileLinQ can propose to a potential university to use its existing campus WiFi network and audio-visual systems to provide a plug-and-play solution that lets students sit anywhere in the room, and receive the same level of high-quality audio content. It also leverages technology to allow students to use their mobile devices, hearing aids, personal headphones, and other hardware, to connect to the assistive listening system, thereby differentiating itself from the existing products on the market.

By focusing on these four elements, **MobileLinQ** can effectively communicate its product vision, ensuring that all stakeholders, from developers to end-users, understand and support the product's goals and benefits. This alignment is crucial for successful product development and market acceptance.

A complete and successful product vision has four elements: target customer, needs, value, and differentiation. It helps the product manager and the product team understand who a product is for, what needs it serves, what value it delivers, and how it differs from other products.

8.2.5 Crafting an Effective Elevator Pitch

An elevator pitch condenses the product vision into a compelling and succinct statement that can be communicated quickly. Figure 8.4 shows a template of an elevator pitch.

An elevator pitch is a short, 1–3 sentence statement that explains what makes your product unique.

FOR [TARGET CUSTOMER]
WHO HAS [CUSTOMER NEED],
[PRODUCT NAME] **IS** A [MARKET CATEGORY]
THAT [KEY BENEFIT].
UNLIKE [COMPETITION],
THE **PRODUCT** [KEY DIFFERENTIATOR].

FIGURE 8.4   An elevator pitch template

FOR the business user

WHO needs to be productive in the office and on the go,

The Surface **IS** a convertible laptop, tablet, and sketchpad, all in one

THAT is easy to carry and gives you full computing productivity no matter where you are.

UNLIKE laptops,

The **Surface** serves your on-the-go needs without having to carry an extra device.

FIGURE 8.5   Microsoft Surface: Example of an elevator pitch

For instance, **Microsoft Surface's** pitch might focus on its versatility as a device that replaces your laptop, tablet, and sketchpad, all in one. This not only communicates the product's key features but also highlights its unique positioning as a multi-functional device. Figure 8.5 shows the elevator pitch for Microsoft Surface.

8.2.6   Elevator Pitch for a New Revolutionary Product

Let us take a look at how an elevator pitch can be made for a new revolutionary product unveiled by **Goodyear** in an article published on

3 March 2020. Below is an extract of the article, 'The Goodyear reCharge Concept – Making Tire Changing Easy with Customized Capsules that Renew your Tires':

GOODYEAR'S reCharge CONCEPT

BRUSSELS, 3 March 2020 – The Goodyear reCharge is a revolutionary self-regenerating concept tire that can adapt and change to meet individual mobility needs.

'Goodyear wants the tire to be an even more powerful contributor to answering consumers' specific mobility needs', said Mike Rytokoski, Vice-President and Chief Marketing Officer, Goodyear Europe, 'It was with that ambition that we set out to create a concept tire primed for the future of personalized and convenient electric mobility'.

The reCharge concept includes a number of innovative features that are built around three pillars:

1   Personalized
    At the core of the reCharge concept is a reloadable and biodegradable tread compound that can be recharged with individual capsules, radically simplifying the process of replacing your tires. Filled with a customized liquid compound, these capsules allow the tread to regenerate and the tire to adapt over time to climatic circumstances, road conditions, or simply how you want to travel. Thanks to artificial intelligence a driver profile would be created around which the liquid compound would be customized, generating a compound blend tailored to each individual.
2   Sustainable
    The compound itself would be made from a biological material and would be reinforced with fibres inspired by one of the toughest natural materials in the world – spider silk. This would make it both extremely durable and 100% biodegradable.
3   Hassle-Free
    In addition to radically simplifying the process of replacing your tires with rechargeable capsules, the tread would be supported by a light-weight, non-pneumatic frame and tall-and-narrow shape. This is a thin, robust low-maintenance construction that would eliminate the need for pressure maintenance or downtime related to punctures.

'The Goodyear reCharge is a concept tire without compromise, supporting personalized, sustainable and hassle-free electric mobility', concluded Sebastien Fontaine, Lead Designer at the Goodyear Innovation Centre in Luxembourg.

The following is one example of an elevator pitch for the Goodyear reCharge:

GOODYEAR'S ELEVATOR PITCH FOR reCharge:

FOR the radical car owners
WHO want a customizable way to replace worn tyres,
Our solution **IS A** cheaper and effortless way to replace tyres
THAT works with AI to regrow the tyre threads by using a special liquid capsule,
UNLIKE the manual and labour-intensive process of swapping old tyres for new ones,
Our **PRODUCT** can create a compound unique to each driver and adjusts itself based on road conditions and the weather.

A strong product vision serves as the compass for all product-related activities, ensuring that the product remains aligned with the target market's needs and the company's broader business goals. By clearly defining the target customer, understanding their needs, articulating a compelling value proposition, and establishing clear differentiation in the market, companies can create products that not only meet but exceed market expectations. This section has laid the groundwork for understanding how these strategic elements are crucial in crafting a product roadmap that is not only realistic but also aspirational, guiding the product from conception through to launch and beyond, ensuring sustained success in the competitive marketplace.

By integrating these elements, the product vision section becomes a cornerstone document that directs all downstream activities, ensuring that every team member is aligned and moving towards a common goal.

8.2.7 The Value Proposition Canvas

Figure 8.6 shows the **Value Proposition Canvas** which is a strategic tool used in product management and marketing to help businesses identify and articulate the value that their products or services offer to customers. Developed by Alexander Osterwalder as part of the broader **Business Model Canvas**, the **Value Proposition Canvas** focuses specifically on ensuring a fit between the product and market by detailing customer needs and product features.

Figure 8.6 also shows how a product manager achieves a product-solution fit when the value map matches the customer profile map (left to right). Correspondingly, a product-market fit is achieved when the market validates this match (right to left).

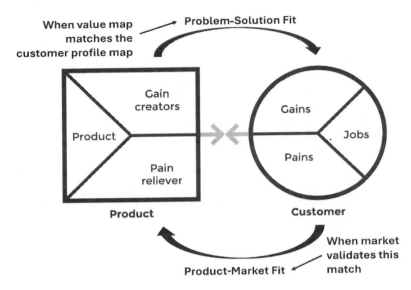

FIGURE 8.6   The Value Proposition Canvas

Purpose of the Value Proposition Canvas:

- **Customer Understanding:** It helps businesses deeply understand their customers' needs, wants, and pain points. This part of the canvas is called the **Customer Profile**, where businesses detail what jobs their customers are trying to get done, the pains they experience while trying to accomplish these jobs, and the gains they perceive from the solutions available.

- **Product Fit:** On the other side of the canvas is the **Value Map**. Here, businesses list the products and services their value proposition consists of, how these relieve pain points, and how they create gains for customers. This helps in aligning the product features directly with customer desires and requirements.

- **Communication:** It serves as a foundation to more effectively communicate the value of a product to potential customers, ensuring that marketing and sales strategies resonate more effectively with the target audience.

- **Innovation:** By clearly understanding customer needs and directly linking them to the product's features, businesses can identify areas of innovation and improvement. This can lead to the development of new features, adjustments to existing products, or even entirely new products.

The **Value Proposition Canvas** is an excellent tool for ensuring that a product's offerings are aligned with customer expectations. By mapping out

TABLE 8.1 Pains + pain relievers and gains + gain creators for Uber customers

Customer Pains	Pain Relievers
Hassle to hail or call for a taxi	Easy app-based booking system
Uncertainty and long waiting times	Real-time tracking and estimated arrival time
Inaccessibility in less serviced areas	Wide availability across varied locations
Customer Gains	Gain Creators
Getting around without driving	Convenient and reliable rides at any time
24/7 availability, any day	Constant service availability
Multiple service options	Variety of car choices to suit different needs

customer profiles and the product's features side-by-side, teams can visualize how well the product meets the needs of its intended users. For example, **Uber's** value proposition of offering a reliable, efficient, and cost-effective transportation solution clearly addresses the specific needs and pains of urban commuters.

Table 8.1 summarizes how Uber addresses the specific needs and challenges faced by its customers while enhancing their overall experience.

This strategic tool is essential not just in planning stages but also throughout the lifecycle of a product, as it ensures that the company remains tightly aligned with the evolving needs and contexts of its customers, thereby increasing the product's market success. Businesses use the **Value Proposition Canvas** to ensure that there is a clear customer-product fit before they invest heavily in product development or marketing campaigns. It is particularly useful in iterative product development processes, such as **Agile** methodologies, where understanding and meeting customer needs is a priority. The canvas can be revisited and revised as more customer feedback is gathered, making it a dynamic tool that evolves with the product and the market.

8.2.8   An Example of the Value Proposition Canvas

Let's try out to fill up the **Value Proposition Canvas** through a product case scenario of a car-sharing platform offered by the product case scenario company **QuikDrive**, where you are hired as a product manager. Car-sharing is a model of car rental where people rent cars for short periods of time, often by the hour. They are attractive to customers who make only occasional use of a vehicle, as well as others who would like occasional access to a vehicle of a different type than they use day-to-day. In Figure 8.7, we see that **QuikDrive** is offering the car-sharing service to renters which operates in shopping malls, residential estates, office buildings,

QuikDrive

A platform which brings car owners and renters together, manages rental bookings and collects payment.

Offers a pay-per-use service to renters

Operates in shopping malls, residential estates, office buildings, bus and rail stations, hotels and airports.

FIGURE 8.7 Case scenario: A mobile car-sharing platform

bus and rail stations, hotels and airports in Singapore. It uses the one-way car-sharing model, which enables members to begin and end their trip at different locations through free floating zones or station-based models with designated parking locations.

Your company wants to improve the car-sharing experience of your customers by employing mobile technology. Your project team has been asked to develop a mobile application to provide **QuikDrive** users with a smooth and user-friendly way to rent cars from your company. The mobile application will simplify the process and improve the experience of renting cars. The application is expected to help car renters go through the entire car rental process in a smoother and easier way. Like all existing car rental applications, your application should include comprehensive information of all the car rental locations across the island and their stocks, and should also allow users to filter and compare all the available options until they find the ones that best fit their needs. Furthermore, to differentiate your product from the others, you decide to endow the application with the capability of managing car rental activities such as reservations, check-ins, and returns for the users, though this will require some physical setups to make things function well. All in all, you want to make the onsite car renting experience occur mostly between the renters and the cars.

A market survey has been conducted to determine the product functionalities desired by and the problems faced by car renters. You proceed to list the findings under two sets of tables: Value Map and Customer Profile, as shown in Figure 8.8.

Creating a **Value Proposition Canvas** for a car-sharing platform like **Quik-Drive** can help clarify how the service addresses the needs of its users and

Desires:

1	Low environment impact
2	Finds fastest route
3	Choice and availability of vehicles
4	Comfortable and private
5	Flexible and sharable
6	Smartphone enabled
7	Productive travel time
8	Pay-per-use (lower overall cost)

Problems:

1	Arrive in shortest time
2	Difficulty in navigation
3	Go whenever and wherever I want
4	High cost of ownership
5	Travel comfortably and privately
6	Go green
7	Limited resources
8	Not environment-friendly

QuikDrive

VALUE MAP

CUSTOMER PROFILE

FIGURE 8.8   QuikDrive's market survey on desires and problems

differentiate it from competitors. Here's how to fill out the canvas using the car-sharing platform as an example:

1 **Customer Profile**

Customer Jobs (What customers are trying to achieve)

- Travel efficiently to their destinations at their convenience.
- Minimize environmental impact while traveling.

Pains (Challenges or frustrations faced by the customer):

- Long travel times and difficulties with navigation.
- High cost of owning a car, along with environmental concerns.
- Need for a comfortable, private, and safe travel experience.
- Constraints related to vehicle availability and resource efficiency.

Gains (Benefits the customer seeks or expects):

- Access to an environmentally friendly mode of transport.
- Quick and efficient travel using the fastest routes.
- Flexible use of different vehicle models suitable for various needs.
- Enjoyment of a comfortable, private space, and smart features to enhance productivity during travel.

2 **Value Map**

Products and Services (How your products relieve pain and create gains):

- A diverse fleet of eco-friendly cars easily accessible via an app.
- Advanced route optimization features within the app to ensure the fastest travel times.

Pain Relievers (How you address customer pains):

- Provide a user-friendly app with GPS and route optimization to assist in navigation and reduce travel time.
- Offer a variety of vehicles, including premium options for comfort and standard models for cost efficiency.
- Ensure cars are well-maintained and cleaned, adhering to high safety and hygiene standards.

Gain Creators (How you enhance customer gains):

- Include hybrid and electric vehicles to support environmental sustainability.
- Implement a flexible pricing model such as pay-per-use to lower the cost compared to car ownership.
- Enable car sharing and scheduled bookings to maximize resource use and reduce environmental impact.

Figure 8.9 shows a sample of **QuikDrive's Value Proposition Canvas** for car renters.

Here's how you might apply the **Value Proposition Canvas** for **QuikDrive**:

- **Customer Jobs**: Users want a quick, convenient, and eco-friendly travel option.
- **Pains**: Users are frustrated by the inefficiencies and environmental impact of traditional car travel.
- **Gains**: Users value flexibility, comfort, and the ability to travel on their terms without harming the environment.

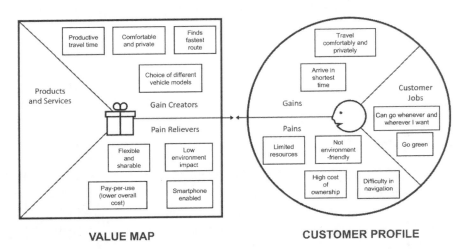

FIGURE 8.9   QuikDrive's Value Proposition Canvas for car renters

- **Products and Services:** QuikDrive offers a wide range of vehicles through an easy-to-use app, featuring cars that are eco-friendly and equipped with the latest navigation technology.
- **Pain Relievers:** QuikDrive uses real-time data to ensure vehicle availability and optimal routing to minimize travel time and environmental impact.
- **Gain Creators:** QuikDrive's vehicles are selected for their low environmental impact and are available in various models to suit different preferences and needs, all bookable via a smartphone app.

This canvas helps **QuikDrive** focus on what is most valuable to their customers, ensuring the service design and operations align with user expectations and needs.

8.3 Conclusion

A strong product strategy grounded in a clear product vision serves as the compass for all product-related activities, ensuring that the product remains aligned with the target market's needs and the company's broader business goals. By clearly defining the target customer, understanding their needs, articulating a compelling value proposition, and establishing clear differentiation in the market, companies can create products that not only meet but exceed market expectations. This section has laid the groundwork for understanding how these strategic elements are crucial in subsequent product planning where crafting a product roadmap that is not only realistic but also aspirational can effectively guide the product from conception through to launch and beyond, ensuring sustained success in the competitive marketplace.

9

EXPLORING MARKET DYNAMICS

9.1 Introduction

Understanding and identifying market opportunities is fundamental for digital product managers aiming to achieve sustained success in competitive environments. This chapter delves into the complex and ever-evolving landscape of market dynamics within the digital product management realm. As markets continuously shift due to technological innovations, regulatory changes, and varying consumer demands, understanding these dynamics becomes crucial for product managers. We will explore key factors that influence market behaviour and trends, such as economic conditions, competitive actions, and technological advancements. Through real-world examples and analytical insights, this chapter aims to equip product managers with the necessary tools to navigate and leverage market dynamics effectively, ensuring their products can thrive in a competitive digital environment.

9.2 Market Dynamics

This section offers a comprehensive approach to understanding market dynamics by integrating innovation strategies and **PESTEL** analysis. It discusses disruptive innovation, sustaining innovation, under-served customers, blue and red ocean strategies, and evaluates the broader external environment that affects market opportunities.

9.2.1 Disruptive Innovation

Disruptive innovation introduces products or services that eventually shift the market by creating a new segment or displacing established competitors.

DOI: 10.1201/9781003484295-9

This segment outlines how to identify potential disruptions by looking at under-served customer needs and technological advancements, with examples from industries such as entertainment where streaming services have shifted consumption habits.

Disruptive innovation, a term coined by Clayton Christensen, describes a process where a smaller company with fewer resources is able to challenge established incumbent businesses. Typically, these disruptors start by successfully targeting those overlooked segments, gaining a foothold by delivering more-suitable functionality – frequently at a lower price. Incumbents, focusing on improving their products for the most demanding and high-end customers, may overlook the needs of others. As the disruptors improve their products and services, they eventually move upmarket and begin taking customers from those established businesses.

Disruptive innovation is generally segmented into two types:

1 **Low-End Disruption**

This occurs when the disruptor targets the lower end of the market, where the incumbent's mainstream customers may find the disruptors' offerings sufficient. These customers typically seek more affordable, less complex solutions. A quintessential example of low-end disruption is **Airbnb**. It began in 2007 when founders Brian Chesky and Joe Gebbia rented out air mattresses in their apartment to guests attending a local conference. Despite the modest accommodations, it provided a 'good enough' solution at a much lower cost compared to hotels. Over time, **Airbnb** evolved from offering basic lodging options to providing over seven million unique accommodations and 50,000 experiences globally, thereby reshaping the traditional hotel industry.

Another example of low-end disruption is the rise of budget airlines like **Southwest** or **Ryanair,** which entered the market with lower-cost flights that were good enough for cost-conscious travellers, fundamentally changing the airline industry by serving an underserved market.

2 **New-Market Disruption**

This form of disruption targets non-consumption; the disruptor offers a product or service that the incumbents have overlooked. This new market finds the offer attractive because it transforms a product that was historically too expensive or complicated into something affordable and accessible. A quintessential example of new-market disruption is the introduction of the transistor radio in 1954 by **Texas Instruments**. Prior to this innovation, the radio market was dominated by bulky, expensive stereo systems placed in living rooms, catering primarily to affluent families who appreciated their superior sound quality. In stark contrast, the transistor radio, characterized by its portability and affordability, albeit with inferior sound quality, opened the market to entirely new demographics. Teenagers, the less affluent, and mobile workers who previously had limited access to radio technology found value in these new devices. The transistor radio, therefore, created a new segment within the broader radio market by prioritizing accessibility and convenience over audio quality. The established radio manufacturers found little economic rationale to compete in this lower-margin segment. Consequently, they ceded this emerging market to **Texas Instruments**, which capitalized on the unaddressed needs of these new consumer groups. Over time, the evolution of portable audio devices continued, with advancements such as the **Sony Walkman**, **MP3** players, and eventually digital devices like the **Apple iPod** and smartphones, further eroding the demand for traditional, high-end radio consoles. This narrative of the transistor radio exemplifies how new-market disruptions can redefine industries by tapping into previously unmet consumer needs, reshaping market landscapes and progressively marginalizing established incumbents who fail to adapt to evolving consumer preferences. Another example is the personal computer, which, at its inception, brought computing to a mass audience that had not been able to afford or use the mainframe computers which were previously only accessible to large businesses and universities.

Each type of disruption has its pathway but shares a common theme: they redefine the landscape of their markets, often setting a new standard and expectation level for products or services. This dynamic can reshape entire industries, making it crucial for businesses to understand and anticipate potential disruptions in their sectors.

9.2.2 Sustaining Innovation

Focusing on improvements to existing products, sustaining innovation helps existing market leaders maintain their competitive edge. This subsection explores how companies can leverage continuous improvements to meet the evolving demands of their current customer base, using case studies from the technology sector, such as ongoing upgrades in smartphone capabilities. In addition, sustaining innovation is characterized by its ability to foster economic growth and create new industries and jobs without causing social harm or negatively impacting existing markets. This type of innovation supports both business and societal progress, allowing them to flourish together.

1 **Continuous Improvements to Meet Evolving Customer Needs**
Sustaining innovation within the technology sector is exemplified by the continuous improvements in smartphone capabilities by leading companies like **Apple** and **Samsung**. These companies leverage technological

advancements not only to meet the evolving demands of their current customer base but also to maintain a competitive edge in the highly dynamic tech market.

Apple regularly updates its **iPhone** series with enhanced features like improved camera systems, faster processors, and advanced software capabilities. These incremental innovations help **Apple** retain existing customers and attract new ones by staying at the forefront of smartphone technology.

Samsung's introduction of foldable screens with its **Galaxy Fold** series represents a significant sustaining innovation. By enhancing the functionality and design of smartphones, **Samsung** meets the growing consumer demand for larger screens and more versatile devices, thereby strengthening its market position and continuing to appeal to tech-savvy consumers.

Other examples in the tech sector that showcase sustaining innovation include software companies like **Adobe** and **Microsoft**. **Adobe's** continuous development of its **Creative Cloud** suite exemplifies sustaining innovation. Regular updates to tools like **Photoshop, Illustrator,** and **Premiere Pro** enhance features such as user interface, processing speed, and integration capabilities. These improvements ensure Adobe remains essential for creative professionals, maintaining its dominance in the digital content creation market. **Microsoft's** ongoing updates to its Windows operating system and Office suite represent another clear example of sustaining innovation. By consistently integrating new features, enhancing security measures, and improving user experience, **Microsoft** maintains its relevance and competitive edge in both consumer and enterprise markets, ensuring that their large existing user base remains committed and satisfied.

2 **Fostering Economic Growth in Support of Business and Societal Progress**
Sustaining innovation is characterized by its ability to foster economic growth and create new industries and jobs without causing social harm or negatively impacting existing markets. This type of innovation supports both business and societal progress, allowing them to flourish together. For instance, the invention of sanitary napkins introduced a significant advancement in personal hygiene which opened new market opportunities while improving quality of life.

Similarly, Dr. Muhammad Yunus's initiative to establish microfinance through **Grameen Bank** in Bangladesh catalysed economic empowerment by providing small loans to the underserved, thus fostering the creation of many micro-enterprises.

Kickstarter is another excellent example of sustaining innovation, serving as a crowdfunding platform that enables creators to bring their ideas to life with community support. According to a **University of Pennsylvania** study, **Kickstarter** has generated $4.3 billion for projects, supported over 160,000 ideas, and contributed to the creation of 8,800 new companies and nonprofits. This platform has also helped create more than 300,000 part-time and full-time jobs, adding over $5.3 billion of economic value. This illustrates how sustaining innovation can drive substantial economic and social benefits, making it a powerful model for progress without detrimental side effects.

9.2.3 Identifying Under-Served Customers

This sub-section highlights the importance of recognizing and targeting under-served or niche markets that present new growth opportunities. It suggests methods for market segmentation and analysis to discover these opportunities, illustrated by examples like financial technologies that cater to previously unbanked populations.

Have you ever wondered how a company could double its annual revenue, within just two years of implementing a new product strategy?

Here's an example drawn from the following article published by Harvard Business Review entitled 'Turn Customer Input Into Innovation' that is written by Antony W. Ulwick based on his work with Cordis Corporation (now a division of Johnson & Johnson): Turn Customer Input into Innovation (hbr.org)

9.2.3.1 Turn Customer Input into Innovation:

Cordis Corporation, a medical device manufacturer in Florida, approached a leading growth strategy and innovation consulting firm called **Strategyn,** to help them identify a market opportunity for angioplasty balloons. These balloons prevent arterial blockage from recurring in patients with cardiovascular disease.

This segment reveals the guidance **Strategyn** provided to **Cordis Corporation,** helping them to successfully identify a market opportunity, resulting in a gain of at least 5% in market share.

Using a methodology developed by **Strategyn, Cordis** conducted outcomes-based interviews with cardiologists and nurses. The interviews focused on the results that these users wanted to achieve when performing surgery on patients.

The interview data helped to drive the new product strategy for **Cordis,** addressing both important and unsatisfied needs in the market, ultimately leading **Cordis** to achieve rapid growth in revenue and market share.

Cordis used the interviews to identify new product opportunities, by focusing on the desired outcomes that are important to cardiologists and nurses but are not satisfied by the existing products.

Cordis applied a simple formula, which they called the 'opportunity algorithm', to the interview data. Figure 9.1 illustrates how the formula works. **Strategyn** suggested doing so as a means to identify new market opportunities.

Desired Outcome Segment 1: Interventional Cardiologists	Importance	Satisfaction	Opportunity
1. Minimize restenosis (or the recurrence of a blockage)	9.5	3.2	15.8
2. Minimize the amount of force required to cross the lesion with the balloon	8.3	4.2	12.4
3. Minimize the amount of damage (dissection) that is inadvertently caused to any vessel when putting the guide wire in place	9.5	7.5	11.5
4. Minimize the time it takes to place the balloon across the lesion	9.1	8.4	9.8
5. Minimize the time it takes to complete the procedure	5.1	1.0	9.2
6. Minimize the time it takes to move the balloon through a winding vessel	7.7	6.6	8.8

Formula : Opportunity = Importance + (Importance – Satisfaction)

FIGURE 9.1 The opportunity algorithm

The opportunity algorithm states that **Opportunity** can be determined by looking at the **Importance** of outcomes compared with the **Satisfaction** of users in relation to those outcomes.

> Opportunity is calculated as follows:
>
> [Importance + (Importance – Satisfaction) = Opportunity]

The survey asks participants to rate each outcome. First, in terms of its importance. And then, in terms of satisfaction, which is the degree to which the outcome is being met by current products. These ratings are then fed into the 'opportunity algorithm', to compute the relative attractiveness of each opportunity.

For example, the scores from **Cordis'** user survey were inserted into the 'opportunity algorithm'. For outcome 1, participants gave a score of 9.5 for Importance, and a low score of 3.2 for Satisfaction, which resulted in an Opportunity score of 15.8.

$$\big[\text{Importance} + (\text{Importance} - \text{Satisfaction}) = \text{Opportunity}\big]$$
$$\big[9.5 + (9.5 - 3.2) = 15.8\big]$$

For outcome 3, participants gave the same score of 9.5 for Importance, but a high score of 7.5 for Satisfaction, which resulted in a much lower

Opportunity score of 11.5 for outcome 3, when compared to a score of 15.8 for outcome 1.

Outcome 1	Outcome 3
15.8	11.5

Using this formula, or algorithm, to compute the relative attractiveness of each opportunity, **Cordis** was able to successfully channel its Research and Development efforts, focusing on those opportunities with the highest scores.

You've now seen how outcome-based interviews, and the **opportunity algorithm**, can be used to shape a new product strategy aimed at addressing both important, and unsatisfied, user needs. Using this approach helped **Cordis** to identify new market opportunities that afforded them rapid growth in both revenue and market share. **Cordis Corporation's** interviews were carefully designed to determine stakeholders' desired outcomes, in terms of the importance, and the degree to which each outcome is satisfied.

9.2.4 Blue Ocean vs. Red Ocean Strategies

How do companies uncover and prioritize the most promising new market opportunities for products and services?

The best opportunities arise from understanding what outcomes customers desire, particularly those customers who aren't satisfied by existing products or services.

In this segment, let's explore three approaches to identifying market opportunities: observing market trends, analysing market problems, and uncovering a gap in the market.

1 **Observing Market Trends**

Keeping pace with market trends is never easy. A good way to stay ahead of the curve and avoid competitors passing you by is to make use of the blue and red ocean strategies.

A blue ocean is used to describe an unknown market that is untainted by competition. Whilst red ocean denotes a market where cutthroat competition turns the ocean bloody red.

In a blue ocean, you'll need to listen to your customers to gain insight on their behaviours and needs, so as to create new demand for your product and make competition irrelevant.

While it's good to avoid a red ocean where possible, sometimes you may not have the choice. If you find yourself in a red ocean, you'll need to capture more of the existing demand through product differentiation. You'll also need to proactively look out for emerging trends and beat the competition to it.

Cirque du Soleil: Reinventing the Circus

Cirque du Soleil, founded by street performers Guy Laliberté and Gilles Ste-Croix, transformed the traditional circus into a global theatrical phenomenon. By removing costly and low-value elements like three-ring structures and trained animals, they focused on a sophisticated blend of theatre and classic circus drama. This shift not only differentiated them from traditional circuses but also enabled them to tap into a new market of theatregoers seeking novel entertainment experiences. The company's innovative approach has led to performances in over 271 countries and annual revenues exceeding $900 million.

Nintendo Wii: Revolutionizing Gaming with Motion Control

The **Nintendo Wii,** introduced in 2006, exemplified value innovation – a core principle of the Blue Ocean Strategy. By simultaneously pursuing cost reduction and differentiation, **Nintendo** eschewed conventional features like hard disks and DVD functionality and minimized processing quality and graphics. This strategy significantly lowered costs while differentiating its product through a unique wireless motion control stick. These innovations enabled **Nintendo** to captivate non-traditional gaming demographics, including non-gamers, the elderly, and families, thereby creating a new market space and avoiding direct competition with giants like **PlayStation** and **Xbox** in the saturated gaming market.

MobileLinQ's Market Trends

Now, let's look at the market trends for the assistive listening product, which provide a market opportunity for **MobileLinQ:**

1 The market for assistive listening over **WiFi** is projected to expand.
2 University lecture rooms are likely to have modern settings, ideal for assistive listening over **WiFi**.
3 Enrolment of students with auditory disabilities has risen in recent decades.

New players have entered the assistive listening market, including Sonova, Sennheiser, WS Audiology, William Demant, and many more.

Source: https://www.businessresearchinsights.com/market-reports/assistive-listening-devices-alds-market-103502

2 **Analysing Market Problems**

Another way to identify a market opportunity is to analyse market problems. This means identifying an existing market problem to solve, which could include inefficiencies, poor workflows, bad design, and so on.

To identify a market problem, begin by talking to potential users in your target market. Conduct interviews, surveys, and facilitated workshops to gather a variety of data points. Then, derive recognizable patterns across the data.

Next, use a set of market criteria to perform an evaluation, of whether the problem identified presents a good or bad opportunity. Such market criteria include urgency, market size, pricing potential, among others. Based on your findings, decide whether or not to pursue the opportunity.

Let's refer to the assistive listening case. **MobileLinQ** identified a market opportunity, by examining data points which describe the market problems faced by universities:

- Many of the university students who have auditory disabilities require assistance to hear the content of their lectures.
- Thus, the market problem to overcome involves the audio challenges of poor acoustics, distance, and background noise in a lecture room environment.
- Another market problem associated with legacy-assistive listening systems is that university faculty and staff face operational difficulties, cost inefficiencies, and the exclusion of certain students.

MobileLinQ identified that they can solve these market problems, by offering assistive listening technology which provides quality audio in any size lecture room, despite the room's natural acoustics, and, at a lower overall cost.

MobileLinQ's product also offers professors peace of mind, in that all students in attendance will hear critical lesson points and be able to join group discussions.

3 **Identifying a Gap in the Market**

The third way to identify a market opportunity is to identify a gap in the market, which is a market segment that existing products are not yet serving.

The best opportunities arise from paying attention to outcomes that are important to consumers but are not yet satisfied by existing products and services. Prioritizing consumers' unmet needs will cause your products to practically sell themselves. Plus, you'll avoid diving into a market that is already oversaturated, like that of a red ocean.

Now, let's look at the '**gap in the market**' for the assistive listening product. Examining where existing assistive listening products fall short will help determine **MobileLinQ's** market opportunity:

- Traditional assistive listening technology uses induction loops, infrared transmission systems, and FM systems which have a limited range, and are easily disrupted.
- Some existing assistive listening solutions rely on dedicated seating zones and hardware receiver devices, which require students to sit in certain places or wear noticeable hardware devices.

MobileLinQ exploited these gaps in the market by leveraging assistive listening over campus **WIFI** and **AV** systems. The result is that students can access quality audio, anywhere in a lecture room, with little disruption and no seating restrictions.

In this segment, you learned about three approaches to identify market opportunities:

- Observing market trends involves applying the blue ocean strategy of listening to customers, to get insight on their behaviours and needs. Or, using the red ocean strategy, which promotes product differentiation, whilst proactively keeping an eye on emerging trends.
- Analysing market problems uses customer interviews, surveys, and workshops to identify a set of common problems that require solving. A set of criteria are then used to evaluate the market opportunity presented by addressing the problem.
- Lastly, finding a gap in the market involves focusing on outcomes that are important to customers, but are not yet satisfied by existing products and services.

9.2.5 PESTEL Analysis

Incorporating **PESTEL** analysis, this subsection extends the market evaluation by considering external factors that influence market dynamics. **PESTEL** is an acronym for Political, Economic, Social, Technological, Environmental, and Legal. This is illustrated in Figure 9.2. This tool guides product managers on how to better understand the macro-environmental contexts that impact strategic decision-making. For instance, regulatory changes in digital privacy can significantly affect product strategies in the technology sector, such as market growth or decline, business position, potential, and direction.

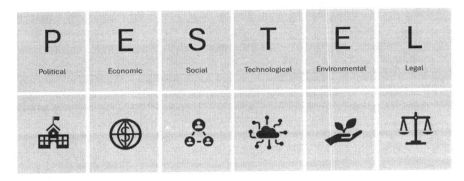

FIGURE 9.2 PESTEL Model

9.2.5.1 Smart Home Security Example:

Let's apply a **PESTEL** analysis to a digital product like a smart home security system to understand the various external factors that can influence its market dynamics:

- **Political**
  - **Regulation on Data Privacy:** Smart home devices often collect a lot of personal data, which is subject to data protection laws like the **GDPR** in Europe or the **CCPA** in California. These regulations dictate how data must be handled and can affect product functionality and customer trust.
  - **Government Incentives:** Some governments may provide incentives for products that contribute to safety and energy efficiency, which could benefit smart home security systems.

- **Economic**
  - **Economic Fluctuations:** In times of economic downturn, consumers may prioritize essential spending and cut back on perceived luxuries like advanced home security systems. Conversely, in a booming economy, discretionary spending increases.
  - **Interest Rates:** Low interest rates may encourage consumers to invest in home improvements, including security upgrades.

- **Social**
  - **Consumer Attitudes Towards Privacy:** Growing concerns about privacy and data security can influence consumer willingness to adopt smart home technologies that monitor personal spaces.
  - **Aging Population:** Older demographics might seek enhanced security features that offer safety and monitoring without the need for physical exertion.

- Technological

    - **Advancements in IoT:** Improvements in **Internet of Things (IoT)** technologies can enhance how smart home security systems integrate with other devices, offering better service and new features.
    - **Cybersecurity Risks:** As technology advances, so do the techniques of hackers. Ensuring robust cybersecurity measures is crucial for maintaining consumer trust and compliance with regulatory standards.

- Environmental

    - **Energy Consumption:** Consumers and regulators are increasingly aware of the environmental impact of electronic products. Energy-efficient security systems that minimize power usage could be more attractive to eco-conscious buyers.
    - **Sustainability Practices:** The environmental impact of producing and disposing of tech products can affect brand reputation and consumer choices.

- Legal

    - **Compliance with Building Codes:** Installation of security systems must often comply with local building codes and regulations, which can vary significantly by region.
    - **Lawsuits and Liabilities:** There is potential for legal action if security systems fail to prevent security breaches or if they intrude on privacy without consent.

9.3 Conclusion

This chapter provides a comprehensive overview of market dynamics essential for digital product management. We've delved into the distinctions between disruptive and sustaining innovations and how these forces shape industries. The **opportunity algorithm** was introduced to help identify underserved customer segments effectively. Strategies like blue and red ocean tactics have been discussed to illustrate competitive positioning in saturated versus untapped markets. Additionally, the **PESTEL** analysis was highlighted as a crucial tool for assessing external factors that influence market conditions. Understanding these dynamics equips product managers with the insights needed to navigate complex markets, ensuring strategic alignment with evolving consumer and technological trends. This foundation is critical for developing products that not only meet current market demands but also anticipate future needs.

10

NAVIGATING MARKET OPPORTUNITIES

10.1 Introduction

In the digital era, identifying and capitalizing on market opportunities is crucial for the sustained success of any product. This chapter provides a structured approach to understanding the depths of market opportunities through the application of analytical models and strategic frameworks. It equips product managers with the necessary tools to assess the size, segmentation, growth, and competitive dynamics of their target markets. With a focus on actionable insights, this chapter guides readers through the process of transforming market analysis into strategic opportunities, thereby driving product success in diverse markets.

10.2 Market Sizing

Market sizing is the process of estimating the potential of a market, quantifying the number of potential customers or the value of a market segment. It is crucial for determining the viability of entering a new market, understanding the potential for revenue and growth, and guiding strategic planning. It also aids in resource allocation, ensuring that investments align with the potential returns from a market. Knowing how to calculate a total addressable market is just as important for those looking to launch a product in a new market as it is for startups.

If you're familiar with market size formulas you've probably heard of **TAM, SAM,** and **SOM.** These calculations are used in business and marketing

DOI: 10.1201/9781003484295-10

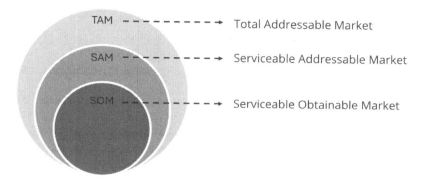

FIGURE 10.1   TAM SAM SOM model

to estimate the potential market size for a product or service. This model is illustrated in Figure 10.1.

1   **Total Addressable Market (TAM):** **TAM** represents the entire revenue opportunity available for a product or service, assuming 100% market share. It is the broadest metric, providing an upper limit for market potential, assuming there are no limitations on factors such as geography, price, or distribution.

2   **Serviceable Addressable Market (SAM):** The segment of the **TAM** targeted by your products and services which is within your geographical reach or service delivery capabilities.

3   **Serviceable Obtainable Market (SOM):** The portion of **SAM** that you can capture. This is a realistic forecast of your market share considering competition, market readiness, and other limiting factors such as the company's marketing and sales capabilities, competition, and market saturation.

Let's explore how to use **TAM SAM SOM** to calculate the size of a market, thereby determining the actual, serviceable, and obtainable market for a product like **MobileLinQ's** assistive listening technology.

Not every student who needs audio assistance in lecture rooms is counted in the market that is available to **MobileLinQ**. Some customers may fall outside of their operable territory, while others may simply prefer the competition's products.

MobileLinQ's analysis of industry data indicates that global revenue in the assistive listening segment is projected to reach $150 million. In addition, the **Average Revenue Per User**, or ARPU, is expected to amount to $300.

To calculate the **Total Addressable Market**, or **TAM**, the total revenue is divided by the **ARPU**. In the **MobileLinQ** case, $150 million is divided by

$300, which gives an estimated 500,000 users in the market for assistive listening technology.

TAM = Total Revenue/ARPU
TAM = $150M/$300
TAM = 500,000

The **Serviceable Addressable Market, or SAM,** narrows down the **Total Addressable Market, TAM,** to the portion of the market that the company is looking to target with its specific product.

So, to calculate **SAM,** first segmentize customers, to decrease the original market size indicated by **TAM.** Segments can be based on geographic locations, or demographic representation, for instance.

Thereafter, multiply **TAM** by the percentage of users who fall within the chosen segment.

In the **MobileLinQ** case, a 50% ballpark is estimated for the chosen segment. So, we can multiply 500,000 by 50%, which predicts that 250,000 users are in the market for assistive listening technology.

SAM = TAM × segment of users (%)
SAM = 500,000 × 50%
SAM = 250,000

The final step in calculating the size of a market is, determining the **Serviceable Obtainable Market, or SOM. SOM** indicates the market size that a company will realistically target within the short term, based on available manpower and infrastructure.

Therefore, to calculate **SOM,** first look through historic performance and projection forecasts, to establish an assumption about what percentage of the market can realistically be served, with the organization's current infrastructure and manpower.

Thereafter, multiply **SAM** by the percentage assumption of the market that can be served. In the **MobileLinQ** case, being a relatively small company, let's assume a 2% of the **SAM** will be achievable, based on its manpower and infrastructure. So, we multiply 250,000 by 2%, which predicts that 5,000 users are in the market for assistive listening technology.

SOM = SAM × assumption (%)
SOM = 250,000 × 2%
SOM = 5,000

In this segment, you have seen how to use **TAM SAM SOM** to calculate the size of a market to determine the actual, serviceable, and obtainable market for a product. A quick and easy way of finding **TAM** is to reference professional data that has already been collected in industry reports by **Gartner, Forrester,** and **IDC.**

Since it's unlikely for your business to have **SAM** equal to **TAM,** you should start with a population and then logically apply demographic, geographic, and economic assumptions to eliminate irrelevant segments.

Finally, to reach a realistic **SOM,** look through historic performance and projection forecasts to predict the actual, serviceable, and obtainable market for a product.

Now that you've seen how to calculate the actual, serviceable, and obtainable market for the case product, begin thinking about the market size for a product of your choice.

What geographical factors might limit the total available market? Are there any other factors – such as competition – that might reduce that market size further?

10.3   Market Segmentation

A 'one-size-fits-all' approach in sales and marketing often results in missed opportunities and excess inventory. By segmenting your customer base and tailoring your offerings to the specific needs of each segment, you can significantly enhance your revenue and improve customer retention.

10.3.1   Understanding Customer Segments

Think about the various types of people you interact with daily, typically categorized as family, friends, or colleagues, each with distinct needs and roles. Similarly, customer segmentation allows businesses to address the diverse needs and preferences of their client base effectively.

10.3.2   Segmentation Strategies

Demographic, geographic, psychographic, and behavioral segmentation are four common strategies used by companies to categorize their customers and choose the best mix for their products and advertising, as illustrated in Figure 10.2.

1   **Demographic Segmentation:** Involves grouping customers based on measurable statistics such as age, income, education, and occupation. This method helps in identifying who your customers are.

WHO	WHERE	WHY	HOW
	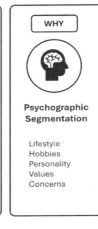		
Demographic Segmentation	**Geographic Segmentation**	**Psychographic Segmentation**	**Behavioural Segmentation**
Age Gender Income Education Occupation	Country City Language Climate Population	Lifestyle Hobbies Personality Values Concerns	Purchase Usage Engagement Intent Occasion

FIGURE 10.2 Market segmentation strategies

2 **Geographic Segmentation**: Customers are segmented based on their location. This can range from broad segments like countries or cities to more specific areas like neighbourhoods. This type is crucial for businesses whose products or services vary in relevance and appeal across different regions.
3 **Psychographic Segmentation**: Goes deeper by examining customers' lifestyles, values, interests, and attitudes. It is particularly useful for crafting compelling marketing messages that resonate on a personal level.
4 **Behavioural Segmentation**: Focuses on how customers interact with your brand, including their purchase behaviours, loyalty, and product usage. This segmentation helps in understanding why customers make their purchasing decisions.

10.3.3 Effective Communication and Segmentation

By clearly identifying and communicating with these segments, companies can make more strategic decisions about product offerings, marketing strategies, and customer engagement, leading to a direct impact on the bottom line. This tailored approach ensures that marketing efforts are concentrated on the most receptive audiences, maximizing both customer satisfaction and profitability.

10.3.4 Application of Segmentation

Let's explore the use of market segmentation for the **MobileLinQ** assistive listening technology.

1 **Demographic Segmentation**
   Product managers can use demographic segmentation to segment their target market into age, gender, income, education, occupation, or other

similar groupings. To do so, product managers ask: **WHO** is the target market?

So, for example, when **MobileLinQ** breaks down its target market audience into a group of students with hearing disabilities, that is demographic segmentation. This helps narrow the focus of **MobileLinQ's** product development, as well as its marketing strategies.

Another example, and one that you might be familiar with, is **Coca-Cola's** segmentation strategy. When **Diet Coke** was launched, only women took to the new drink. **Coca-Cola** had difficulty in convincing men to drink it. Later, another new drink **Coke Zero** was launched as a celebrator of guy enjoyment. This strategy worked! While men had avoided **Diet Coke** because of its association with women, they flocked to **Coke Zero**. We see how **Coca-Cola** positioned two different drinks for two different target market audiences, divided along what we'd call demographic segmentation lines. In **Coca-Cola's** case, each segment leads to a different product and different marketing associated with that product.

2 **Geographic Segmentation**

Product managers can use geographic segmentation to break down their target market into smaller, more manageable groups, based on geographic location.

To do so, they ask: **WHERE** is the target market based?

Geographic segmentation strategies help product managers focus on specific countries, cities, regions, languages, and other geographically based criteria.

For **MobileLinQ**, they are focusing on universities in Singapore, not elsewhere in Malaysia, or Thailand.

Later, when their product has proved successful in Singapore, they will use it as a springboard to expand to other universities in the broader southeast Asia region.

3 **Psychographic Segmentation**

Product managers can use psychographic segmentation to group their target market according to shared psychological characteristics, beliefs, or motivations. For example certain lifestyle choices, hobbies, cultures, values, or concerns.

To determine a psychographic segment, product managers ask: **WHY** someone would use their product.

So, **MobileLinQ** might ask themselves why students with disabilities would use their assistive listening technology. Other than the primary need, to hear the lecture content properly, students may be motivated to use the product for different psychological reasons.

Why would students with auditory disabilities use the product?

Well, some students may be motivated by a need or want to engage in the classroom discussions and participate in the classroom interactions in a more equal way.

Others may be motivated by the desire to feel included, or may be concerned about stigmatization, and therefore are motivated to use this product because it promises to help address stigma.

4 **Behavioural Segmentation**

Behavioural segmentation is perhaps the most useful strategy for product managers because it hinges on understanding customer behaviour and can therefore inform how the product might actually be used by customers.

This strategy breaks the target market audience down into smaller groups, depending on their spending habits, brand loyalty, levels of engagement, frequency of use, and other behavioural, or usage patterns.

For this strategy, product managers should ask themselves: **HOW** will their product be used?

If **MobileLinQ** were to segment their target market according to behavioural patterns, they could draw on data on universities that have adopted some of the other, existing assistive listening solutions.

By understanding how their target market audience uses, or responds to the existing products, they can establish smaller, targeted groups.

For example, students who use existing listening technology solutions, but not frequently because they're dissatisfied. Or, professors who have the option to use an existing product, but choose not to, because they find that students don't want to use it, or they have great difficulty in using it.

Another example is universities that could be using one of the existing products but had abandoned it because of high maintenance cost.

10.3.5 Challenges in Market Segmentation

1 **Identifying Relevant Variables**

One of the main challenges in market segmentation is selecting the appropriate variables that truly distinguish consumer behaviour or needs. Companies must sift through vast amounts of data to identify those characteristics – demographic, psychographic, geographic, or behavioural – that best define distinct and actionable segments.

2 **Achieving Segment Accessibility**

After identifying potential market segments, the next challenge is reaching them effectively. Each segment may require different marketing strategies or channels, which can complicate execution and increase costs.

3 **Ensuring Segment Substantiality**

Segments must be large and profitable enough to serve. A common pitfall is targeting niches that are too small to generate meaningful returns, which can lead to wasted resources and efforts.

4 **Maintaining Stability Over Time**

Markets evolve, and what might be a viable segment today could change due to shifts in consumer preferences, technology, or competitive landscapes. Ensuring that segments remain relevant over time requires ongoing research and adaptability.

5 **Ethical and Legal Considerations**

Segmentation strategies must also navigate ethical and legal constraints, ensuring that targeting practices do not lead to discrimination or violate privacy laws. This becomes particularly complex in global markets with varying regulations.

These challenges necessitate a robust analytical approach and strategic foresight to ensure that segmentation contributes positively to a company's market strategy.

10.3.6 *Expansion through Segmentation Strategy*

Segmenting the market is a fundamental step in understanding the diverse needs and preferences within a potential customer base. It allows businesses to identify specific groups of customers based on distinct characteristics and tailor their products or services accordingly. An effective segmentation strategy can lead to the expansion of a product line, offering a broader range of options that cater to a wider audience. This approach not only helps in addressing the varied needs within a market but also enhances customer satisfaction and loyalty by providing options that resonate more closely with different user groups.

For example, a tech company might segment its market based on user technical expertise: beginners, intermediate users, and tech-savvy customers. This segmentation allows the company to develop products with different levels of functionality and complexity, thereby widening its market reach and appealing to a larger customer base through a more nuanced and targeted product line.

When a company considers expanding its product line to serve a broader audience, there are both advantages as well as disadvantages, as shown in Table 10.1.

These factors should be carefully weighed to determine if expanding a product line aligns with the company's strategic goals and capabilities. Addressing these challenges requires a careful balance of strategy, clear communication, and efficient operations to ensure that the benefits of market segmentation outweigh the potential downsides.

In this segment, you've learned about the four different types of marketing segmentation that can help you define your target market, so that you can prompt and sell your product more effectively. Your customers' decisions will be influenced by whether the product meets their needs and delivers the promised results. Market segmentation allows you to recognize these needs and better target the right customers. The behavioural segmentation strategy is the most useful as it involves having a good understanding of customer behaviour, such as spending habits, loyalty to brand, product feedback, and

TABLE 10.1 Advantages and disadvantages of product line expansion

Advantages:	Serving Multiple Segments	By targeting different market segments, a company can cater to varied customer needs more precisely, enhancing customer satisfaction and loyalty.
	Increased Shelf Presence	Occupying more shelf space in distributors' venues can lead to higher visibility and market penetration.
	Comprehensive Product Offerings	Offering a diverse range of products can satisfy a broader array of customer preferences and needs, making the brand a one-stop shop.
	Preempting Competition	By covering more market segments, a company can block competitors and protect its market share.
	Enhanced Customer Loyalty	Offering more variety can meet the diverse needs of existing customers, increasing their loyalty.
	Improved Brand Image	A larger product range can enhance the perception of the brand as versatile and customer-focused.
	Economies of Scale	With more products, a company can achieve cost savings in production and marketing.
	Risk Diversification	Spreading out over multiple products can reduce the financial risk associated with market fluctuations affecting a single product.
Disadvantages	Cannibalism	When a company introduces multiple similar products targeting the same market, these products can eat into each other's sales rather than capturing new demand, diluting overall profitability.
	Increased Complexity	Managing a broader product range can complicate manufacturing and logistics, increasing operational costs and the potential for errors.
	Resource Intensification	More products mean more inventory, requiring additional resources for management and potentially leading to increased waste if demand estimation is inaccurate.

(Continued)

TABLE 10.1 (Continued)

Market Confusion	A wide range of similar products can confuse customers and distributors, making it harder for them to make purchasing decisions. This could dilute the brand's impact and effectiveness in the marketplace.
Higher Costs	Initial costs for development, marketing, and distribution may increase.
Diluted Brand Identity	Too diverse a product line might weaken a brand's identity, confusing customers.

so on. This segmentation strategy helps you to deliver relevant and targeted marketing campaigns with the right product positioning and value messaging.

10.4 Competitive Analysis

You may have heard this famous quote from Sun Tzu, the Chinese military strategist, in his book *The Art of War*: 'If you know the enemy and know yourself, you need not fear the result of a hundred battles'.

As a product manager, if you know your enemy and yourself, you can use that knowledge to win battles in todays' competitive marketplace.

One of the best ways to understand your competitors in the marketplace is to conduct a competitive analysis. By doing so, you'll determine who your competitors are, exactly what products or services they offer, and how they compare with your products or services.

Competitive analysis is a crucial step in navigating market opportunities. It allows digital product managers to understand their competitors, assess their market position, and identify both threats and opportunities within the industry. By conducting a thorough competitive analysis, product managers can make informed decisions about product differentiation, positioning, and growth strategies.

10.4.1 SWOT Analysis

One of the most widely used frameworks for competitive analysis is **SWOT analysis,** which examines a company's **Strengths, Weaknesses, Opportunities,** and **Threats,** as shown in Figure 10.3.

1 **Strengths**
   Strengths refer to the internal factors that give a company an advantage over its competitors. This could include factors like a strong brand

STRENGTHS
- Brand Reputation
- Proprietary Technology
- Established Customer Base

WEAKNESSES
- Product Limitations
- Poor Customer Service
- Single Revenue Stream

OPPORTUNITIES
- Changes in Market
- Technology Advancements
- Emerging Customer Needs

THREATS
- Increased Competition
- Economic Downturns
- Changes in Regulations

FIGURE 10.3 SWOT analysis

reputation, proprietary technology, unique products, or an established customer base.

Example

Apple is a prime example of a company with significant strengths in the competitive landscape. **Apple's** strong brand loyalty and premium product positioning (e.g., the **iPhone** and **MacBook**) give it a competitive edge in the tech market. Its vertically integrated ecosystem (iOS, App Store, iCloud) further strengthens customer retention, as users often find it difficult to switch to competing platforms without losing some of the convenience and synergy Apple's ecosystem provides.

Lesson for Product Managers

Understanding a company's core strengths allows product managers to capitalize on these assets. For example, **Apple** continues to innovate around its core ecosystem, ensuring each product release reinforces its strengths while adding value to the customer experience.

2 **Weaknesses**

Weaknesses are internal factors that may hinder a company's success compared to its competitors. This could include issues like a limited product range, poor customer service, or reliance on a single revenue stream.

Example

In the case of **BlackBerry**, its failure to innovate in user interface design, particularly the adoption of touchscreens, was a key weakness that led to its decline in the smartphone market. While competitors like **Apple** and **Samsung** were developing sleek, touch-based smartphones, **BlackBerry** continued to rely on its physical keyboard, which became outdated as consumer preferences shifted.

Lesson for Product Managers

Recognizing and addressing weaknesses early is essential. If **BlackBerry** had adapted to the touchscreen trend earlier, it might have maintained its competitive position. Product managers must continuously assess product feedback and market trends to prevent becoming outdated or irrelevant.

3 **Opportunities**

Opportunities are external factors that a company can leverage for growth or competitive advantage. These can arise from changes in the market, technology advancements, or emerging customer needs.

Example:

Netflix capitalized on the opportunity of streaming media at a time when traditional cable television was dominant. Recognizing the shift towards online consumption, **Netflix** pivoted from its original DVD rental model to streaming video on-demand, making it a leader in the entertainment industry. As internet speeds increased and consumer preferences shifted to convenience, **Netflix** scaled quickly, acquiring millions of subscribers worldwide.

Lesson for Product Managers:

Seizing market opportunities is about being proactive. Product managers must stay ahead of industry trends and anticipate shifts in consumer behaviours, just as **Netflix** identified the streaming market and led the charge into the digital age. This proactive approach ensures that companies can lead rather than follow.

4 **Threats**

Threats are external factors that can negatively impact a company's growth or position in the market. These threats can include increased competition, economic downturns, changes in regulations, or shifts in consumer behaviour.

Example:

Facebook (now **Meta**) faces ongoing threats from privacy regulations and consumer mistrust regarding data privacy. Increasing regulatory scrutiny, such as the **General Data Protection Regulation (GDPR)** in Europe, has forced **Facebook** to alter its data practices and policies. Additionally, emerging competitors like **TikTok** are drawing younger users away from **Facebook**, creating competition for user attention and engagement.

Lesson for Product Managers:

Being aware of external threats allows product managers to develop mitigation strategies, whether that's improving product features, complying with new regulations, or adjusting marketing approaches. **Facebook's** response to data privacy concerns, for instance, included implementing stronger privacy controls and transparency measures to address regulatory threats.

10.4.2 Using SWOT for Competitive Positioning

By analysing competitors through the **SWOT** framework, product managers gain a clearer understanding of where their company stands in relation to others in the market. This strategic insight helps in multiple ways:

1 **Identifying Competitive Differentiation:**
   What are your company's unique strengths, and how do they differentiate you from competitors? For example, **Apple's** emphasis on user experience and ecosystem is a significant differentiator from Android's more fragmented approach.
2 **Improving Product Positioning:**
   If weaknesses are found, how can they be addressed through product development or marketing? For example, recognizing customer complaints about customer support can lead to process improvements or additional product features to reduce customer pain points.
3 **Spotting Untapped Opportunities:**
   Are there growing trends or market gaps that your competitors have missed? **Netflix's** pivot to streaming from DVDs came from recognizing consumer behaviour shifts that **Blockbuster** ignored, securing **Netflix's** place as a dominant force in digital entertainment.
4 **Preparing for Future Threats:**
   Threats can be turned into opportunities if addressed early enough. **Facebook's** response to data privacy concerns with proactive policy changes illustrates how companies can adapt to regulatory threats while protecting their market position.

10.4.3 Tools for Competitive Analysis

Beyond **SWOT**, there are additional tools that product managers can use to strengthen their competitive analysis:

1 **Porter's Five Forces:** This model helps assess the competitive intensity and profitability of a market by examining forces such as industry rivalry, supplier power, and the threat of new entrants.

2 **Benchmarking**: Comparing **key performance indicators** (**KPIs**) of your product against competitors helps identify gaps and areas for improvement.
3 **Market Surveys and Customer Feedback**: Directly obtaining customer feedback and analysing how competitors are serving (or not serving) customer needs can reveal opportunities for differentiation.

10.4.4 Conclusion of Competitive Analysis

Competitive analysis is a cornerstone of navigating market opportunities. Whether you're using **SWOT** analysis to identify strengths, weaknesses, opportunities, and threats or leveraging additional tools like **Porter's Five Forces**, these frameworks provide digital product managers with the insights needed to build and maintain competitive advantages. Real-world examples like **Apple, BlackBerry, Netflix,** and **Facebook** illustrate the importance of understanding the market landscape, being proactive in innovation, and continuously assessing both internal capabilities and external challenges.

By conducting thorough and ongoing competitive analysis, product managers can position their products strategically, seize opportunities, and mitigate risks in an increasingly competitive digital landscape.

10.5 Market Growth

In business, market growth strategies are essential for driving a company's success. These strategies help businesses expand their reach, improve their offerings, and stay competitive in dynamic markets. Several tools can be used to formulate and assess market growth strategies, including the **Growth Share Matrix** (**BCG Matrix**), the **Ansoff Matrix**, and **CAGR** (**Compound Annual Growth Rate**). These tools provide a structured approach to understanding the market and identifying opportunities for growth, helping companies make informed decisions on resource allocation, product development, and market expansion.

10.5.1 Growth Share Matrix (BCG Matrix)

Typically, the creation of a new product, or modification of an existing one, is a business decision that is taken after assessing the marketplace performance of the company's product portfolio. Therefore, product managers need to know the strengths and weaknesses of their existing products, so that they can determine whether a new product, or a change to a product, will be successful in the market.

To understand how the products in your portfolio perform, you can use the **Boston Consulting Group's Growth Share Matrix**, which allows you to make strategic investment decisions for each of your products.

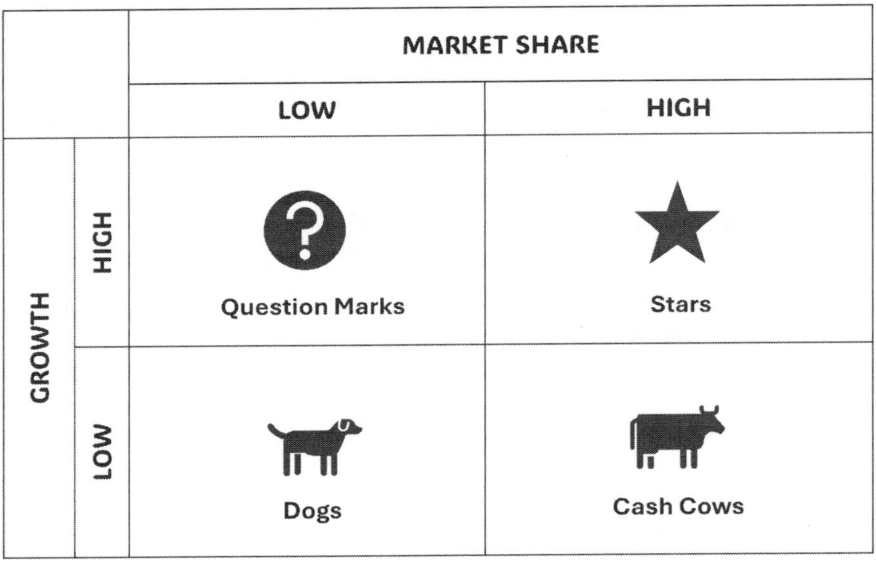

		MARKET SHARE	
		LOW	**HIGH**
GROWTH	**HIGH**	Question Marks	Stars
	LOW	Dogs	Cash Cows

FIGURE 10.4   BCG Matrix

The **BCG Matrix** shown in Figure 10.4 labels products according to their market share and growth potential, categorizing products as stars, cash cows, pets, or question marks. Each category helps companies decide where to invest resources and how to prioritize growth initiatives.

Question Marks: These represent products or business units in a high-growth market but with a low market share. They have potential but require significant investment to become market leaders. The strategy here is to assess whether to invest to gain market share or divest if growth prospects are weak.

Stars: Stars are products in a high-growth market with a high market share. They are market leaders and require continuous investment to sustain growth and defend against competitors. The goal is to turn Stars into future Cash Cows as the market matures.

Cash Cows: Cash Cows have a high market share in a low-growth market. These products generate consistent profits with minimal investment. Companies typically use profits from Cash Cows to fund other strategic areas, such as new product development or market expansion.

Dogs: Dogs are products with low market share in a low-growth market. These products do not generate significant profits, and companies often choose to divest or discontinue them to free up resources.

Using the **BCG Matrix** enables companies to balance their portfolio by investing in high-growth areas (Stars and Question Marks) while leveraging profits from mature products (Cash Cows). It also helps them make decisions about exiting less profitable markets (Dogs), aligning resources with long-term growth opportunities.

10.5.2 Ansoff Matrix

How do you think the **Virgin Group** moved from music production, to travel, and then to mobile phones? How did **Disney** move from producing animated movies, to building theme parks and holiday resorts? And how do you think **Canon** diversified, expanding from a camera-making company, to one that manufactures a wide range of office equipment?

Each of these companies understood the relationship between their new and existing products, as well as the new and existing markets. As a result, they could see the potential for market growth and could develop strategies to unlock that potential. The **Ansoff Matrix** can be used to accomplish this.

The **Ansoff Matrix**, as shown in Figure 10.5, helps product managers grow their companies, by identifying product-market growth, examining the relationship between new and existing products, as well as new and existing markets. Product managers then leverage these relationships to develop strategies for market growth.

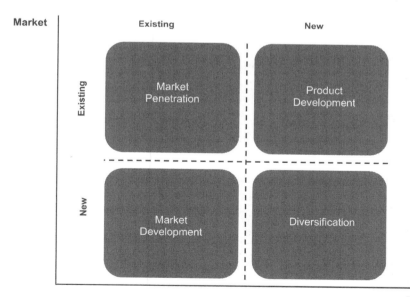

FIGURE 10.5   Ansoff Matrix

The **Ansoff Matrix** outlines four growth strategies based on two key variables: existing vs. new markets and existing vs. new products. These four strategies are:

1 **Market Penetration**: This strategy focuses on growing the market share of existing products in existing markets. It involves increasing sales to current customers or acquiring competitors' customers. Common tactics include aggressive marketing, pricing strategies, and product enhancements. This is a low-risk strategy as the company is working in a familiar market with established products.
2 **Product Development**: Product development involves introducing new products to existing markets. Companies use this strategy to meet changing customer needs or leverage technological advancements. This can involve updating existing products or launching entirely new offerings. It's a moderate-risk strategy as the market is known, but the product is new.
3 **Market Development**: Market development focuses on entering new markets with existing products. This could involve geographic expansion, targeting new customer segments, or finding new uses for current products. It's a moderate-risk strategy, as while the product is familiar, the market is new and potentially unpredictable.
4 **Diversification**: This is the riskiest growth strategy, involving the development of new products for new markets. It is often pursued when growth opportunities are limited in the existing market. Diversification can be related (new products that align with the company's current offerings) or unrelated (entirely new ventures). Although it carries high risk, diversification can offer significant rewards if successful.

The **Ansoff Matrix** helps companies identify and evaluate potential growth strategies based on their risk tolerance and available resources. It encourages businesses to think critically about where they should focus their efforts, whether in existing markets or by venturing into new ones.

10.5.3 CAGR (Compound Annual Growth Rate)

The **Compound Annual Growth Rate** (CAGR) is a measure that helps companies analyse market growth over time. It represents the annual growth rate of an investment, revenue, or market size, assuming consistent year-over-year growth. **CAGR** is used to smooth out the volatility of short-term fluctuations and provide a clear picture of long-term growth trends.

The formula for calculating **CAGR** is:

$$\text{CAGR} = \left(\frac{\text{Ending Value}}{\text{Beginning Value}}\right)^{\frac{1}{\text{Number of Years}}} - 1$$

For example, if a company's revenue grew from $50 million to $100 million over five years, the **CAGR** would indicate the average annual growth rate over that period. This metric is useful for tracking performance across different time frames and comparing growth rates across products, industries, or markets. In the above example, the calculated **CAGR** is approximately 14.87% per year.

Using **CAGR** in market growth strategies allows companies to:

1 **Assess past performance:** Evaluate how well a product or market has grown over time.
2 **Set realistic growth targets:** Use historical CAGR data to set achievable growth goals for the future.
3 **Compare growth opportunities:** Analyse the relative growth rates of different markets or products to determine where to allocate resources for maximum impact.

The benchmarks for **CAGR** vary based on the company's size, age, and market maturity. Understanding these benchmarks helps gauge whether a company's growth rate aligns with industry standards and expectations. Below are typical **CAGR** benchmarks for three different types of companies:

1 **Established Companies (10+ Years)**
For companies with a history of over 10 years, a **CAGR** benchmark typically falls in the range of 5% to 10%. These companies are often operating in mature markets with steady demand and well-established customer bases. Their growth is more incremental, focused on maintaining market share and optimizing operations. While their growth rates are lower than younger or smaller companies, they tend to generate reliable, consistent returns with fewer risks.

- Benchmark: 5%–10% CAGR
- Key Focus: Incremental growth, market stabilization, operational efficiency

2 **Smaller Companies (Mid-Sized, Growth Stage)**
Smaller, mid-sized companies in a growth phase often exhibit higher **CAGR**, typically between 10% and 20%. These companies are expanding their market share, introducing new products, and exploring additional markets. Since they still have room to scale, their growth is driven by a combination of market penetration and innovation. While their growth rates are higher, they also face more risks as they try to scale their operations and compete with larger players.

- Benchmark: 10%–20% CAGR
- Key Focus: Market expansion, scaling operations, product diversification

3 **Startups (Early Stage Companies)**
Startups, especially those in emerging industries, often aim for significantly higher **CAGRs** of 20% or more. These companies are in the early stages of rapid growth, developing innovative products, disrupting markets, and gaining initial traction. While the potential for high returns is attractive, the volatility and risk of failure are much greater. For startups, high growth rates are essential for gaining venture capital funding and positioning themselves for future exits or expansions.

- Benchmark: 20%+ CAGR
- Key Focus: Rapid scaling, product-market fit, attracting investment, market disruption

The appropriate **CAGR** benchmark varies depending on the company's stage and market maturity. Established companies prioritize steady, sustainable growth, while smaller and startup companies focus on scaling quickly. Product managers and investors can use these benchmarks to evaluate whether a company's growth rate aligns with industry norms, ensuring realistic and strategic growth expectations.

CAGR is particularly valuable when combined with tools like the **BCG Matrix** and **Ansoff Matrix**. For example, businesses can use **CAGR** to track the growth of their Stars or Question Marks in the **BCG Matrix** or to measure the success of market penetration or product development strategies from the **Ansoff Matrix**.

10.5.4 Integrating the Tools for Market Growth

Each of these tools – the **BCG Matrix,** the **Ansoff Matrix,** and CAGR – plays a critical role in shaping a comprehensive market growth strategy. When used together, they provide a holistic approach to strategic planning:

1 The **BCG Matrix** helps classify products and prioritize investments based on current market share and growth potential.
2 The **Ansoff Matrix** outlines specific strategies for expanding market presence or introducing new products.
3 **CAGR** tracks long-term growth performance, allowing companies to measure the success of their strategies and refine them over time.

By combining these tools, companies can develop well-rounded growth strategies that balance short-term gains with long-term sustainability. They can identify where to invest, which markets to enter, and how to build products that meet evolving customer needs, all while monitoring growth trends over time.

Market growth is a multifaceted challenge that requires a strategic and informed approach. Tools like the **BCG Matrix**, the **Ansoff Matrix**, and **CAGR** offer powerful frameworks to classify opportunities, devise growth strategies, and track performance over time. Companies that master the use of these tools can position themselves for long-term success by identifying and pursuing the most promising avenues for growth.

10.6 Conclusion

In conclusion, this chapter has equipped product managers with essential tools and frameworks for identifying and analysing market opportunities, a cornerstone for successful digital product management. By leveraging comprehensive market evaluation methods such as **TAM, SAM**, and **SOM**, product managers can accurately define their market size and segment the most promising opportunities. The systematic approach to market segmentation– considering who the target audience is, where they are located, why they are appealing, and how to capture them – ensures a targeted and strategic market entry.

Furthermore, conducting thorough competitive analysis using tools like **SWOT** allows product managers to identify key differentiators, understand competitive pressures, and recognize potential barriers to success. This insight is crucial for positioning the product uniquely in the market.

Market growth strategies, including the **BCG Growth Share Matrix**, **Ansoff Matrix**, and **CAGR**, offer dynamic frameworks for guiding resource allocation, product development, and long-term growth planning. By understanding these growth pathways and tracking performance over time, product managers can make informed, data-driven decisions that align with both short-term objectives and long-term business goals.

Altogether, these methodologies provide a robust and comprehensive toolkit for navigating the complexities of market dynamics, enabling product managers to capture new opportunities with confidence and foresight. The strategic insights gained from this chapter empower product teams to craft sustainable growth strategies that drive product success in competitive markets.

11

BUILDING A BUSINESS CASE

11.1 Introduction

In this chapter, we explore the critical components involved in constructing a robust business case to justify the launch of a new product or a strategic change to an existing one. A well-formulated business case serves as a foundation for decision-making, addressing a range of factors including business goals, market opportunity, strategic alignment, problem identification, proposed solutions, projected benefits, product roadmap, and various assumptions and constraints. Each of these factors plays an essential role in supporting the overall product strategy and helping stakeholders understand the value of the initiative.

However, two of the most significant considerations are financial assessment and risk assessment, which this chapter delves into in greater depth. Financial assessment provides a quantitative basis for evaluating the economic viability of the product, considering key metrics such as costs, revenue forecasts, **ROI**, and break-even analysis. Risk assessment, on the other hand, addresses potential uncertainties that could impact the product's success, using a structured approach with a Risk Impact-Probability Matrix to identify, rate, prioritize, and mitigate risks. By focusing on these two critical dimensions, this chapter equips product managers with the necessary tools to create compelling, data-driven business cases that align with organizational goals while managing potential risks effectively.

11.2 Conducting a Financial Assessment

A well-constructed financial assessment is critical to determining whether a new product or strategic change is economically viable. It provides

DOI: 10.1201/9781003484295-11

stakeholders with clear, data-driven insights into the financial implications of a proposal, ensuring informed decision-making. In this section, we will explore the key components of a financial assessment and outline the methodologies used to evaluate the financial health and potential profitability of a product initiative.

1 **Cost Estimation**
   The first step in financial assessment is estimating the total cost associated with the development, launch, and ongoing maintenance of the product. These costs can be categorized into:

   • **Development Costs:** This includes the costs of research, design, engineering, testing, and any third-party services required to bring the product to market. It is essential to account for both direct labour costs and the necessary tooling, software, or other development resources.
   • **Operational Costs:** Post-launch, operational costs cover customer support, product maintenance, server or infrastructure costs (for digital products), and marketing efforts to drive adoption.
   • **Marketing and Sales Costs:** A portion of the budget should be allocated to marketing and sales activities, such as advertising, sales team commissions, promotions, and public relations efforts that will be crucial for product awareness and customer acquisition.

2 **Revenue Projections**
   After estimating costs, the next step is to forecast revenue. Revenue projections depend on several factors, including market size, pricing strategy, and anticipated sales volume. Here are the key elements of revenue forecasting:

   • **Sales Volume Estimation:** Predicting the number of units (or subscriptions for digital products) you expect to sell over time. This can be based on market analysis, historical sales data (for existing products), or competitive benchmarking.
   • **Pricing Strategy:** The price point directly impacts revenue. Careful consideration should be given to the pricing model, whether it's value-based pricing, premium pricing, or subscription-based pricing. A well-defined pricing strategy must align with the target market's willingness to pay.
   • **Market Penetration Rates:** To achieve realistic market penetration rates, product managers use three key market-sizing concepts: **Total Addressable Market (TAM)**, **Serviceable Addressable Market (SAM)**, and **Serviceable Obtainable Market (SOM)**. **TAM** represents the total market demand if there were no constraints, while **SAM** narrows

this down to the segment your product can realistically serve based on specific features, geographic reach, or demographic focus. **SOM** further refines **SAM** to reflect the portion of the market your product can capture in the near term, considering competition, resources, and operational capacity. This tiered approach ensures accurate revenue forecasts, realistic sales targets, and informed strategic planning, helping to avoid overestimations and guiding effective market penetration strategies.

3 **Profitability Analysis**

Once costs and revenue projections are established, the next step is to determine profitability. The following financial metrics are commonly used to assess whether the product will generate sufficient returns:

- **Gross Margin:** This measures the difference between revenue and the cost of goods sold (**COGS**), indicating how profitable the product is before operational expenses are deducted.
- **Net Present Value (NPV):** **NPV** calculates the current value of future cash flows, considering the time value of money. A positive **NPV** indicates that the project is expected to generate more value than its cost, while a negative **NPV** suggests the opposite.
- **Internal Rate of Return (IRR):** This metric evaluates the rate of return expected on the invested capital. The higher the **IRR,** the more attractive the product is from a financial perspective.
- **Break-Even Analysis:** This identifies the point at which total revenue equals total costs. Understanding the break-even point helps in determining how many units need to be sold or how much market penetration is required to cover all costs.

4 **Scenario and Sensitivity Analysis**

Financial assessment should also consider different scenarios to account for uncertainty. Scenario analysis explores how changes in key variables (e.g., pricing, costs, sales volume) can impact the product's financial outlook. This ensures that the product can withstand fluctuations in the market or changes in customer behaviour.

- **Best-Case, Worst-Case, and Most Likely Case:** By creating multiple scenarios, product managers can prepare for a range of outcomes, from highly optimistic to conservative projections.
- **Sensitivity Analysis:** This helps in identifying which variables have the most impact on profitability. For example, if a slight increase in operational costs drastically reduces profits, this variable should be closely monitored and managed.

5 **Return on Investment (ROI)**

Finally, product managers need to calculate the **ROI**, which measures the overall gain or loss generated by the product relative to its cost. **ROI** is calculated using the formula:

$$ROI = (Gross\ Return - Cost\ of\ Investment) \div Cost\ of\ Investment$$

Where:

- Net Return = Gross Return – Cost of Investment

The difference between the gross return and the cost of investment is the net return.

For purposes of comparability, the return on investment metric is typically expressed in percentage form, so the resulting value from the above formula must then be multiplied by 100.

A high **ROI** indicates that the product will likely yield significant returns relative to the investment made. This metric is often a deciding factor for executives or investors when determining whether to proceed with a product proposal.

For example, suppose a new product proposal is considering an investment, where the expected gross return is $1M while the total cost incurred is $800K.

The net return on the investment is anticipated to be $200K.

- Gross Return = $1M
- Initial Cost = $800K
- Net Return = $200K

With that said, the **ROI** ratio can be calculated by dividing the $200K net return by the cost of $800K, which comes out to 25%.

- Expected Return on Investment (ROI) = $200K ÷ $800K = 0.25, or 25%

By conducting a thorough financial assessment, product managers can build a strong case for their product, grounded in quantifiable data. This section has covered the essential elements of cost estimation, revenue projections, profitability analysis, scenario planning, and **ROI** calculation, which together offer a comprehensive view of the financial viability of a product.

Next, we will explore risk assessment and how it complements financial assessment by identifying potential uncertainties that could influence the product's success.

11.3 Conducting a Risk Assessment

Risk assessment is a vital part of building a business case, ensuring that potential uncertainties and challenges are identified and managed before they negatively impact a product's success. By systematically evaluating risks, product managers can create mitigation strategies that minimize the impact of potential issues. In this section, we explore the use of a **Risk Impact-Probability Matrix** and outline the four key steps in conducting a risk assessment: identifying, rating, prioritizing, and mitigation planning, as illustrated in Figure 11.1.

1 **Identify Risks**

   The first step in any risk assessment is identifying potential risks that could affect the product's development, launch, or post-launch performance. Risks can stem from various sources, including:

   - **Market Risks:** Changes in market demand, customer preferences, or new competitive threats that can affect product viability.
   - **Technical Risks:** Challenges related to technology development, such as delays in production, integration issues, or software bugs.
   - **Financial Risks:** Budget overruns, unanticipated costs, or lower-than-expected revenue.
   - **Operational Risks:** Risks related to the ability to deliver or support the product, including supply chain disruptions, customer service capacity, or scaling issues.

   Product managers should work closely with cross-functional teams to brainstorm and document all potential risks, regardless of their perceived likelihood or impact at this stage.

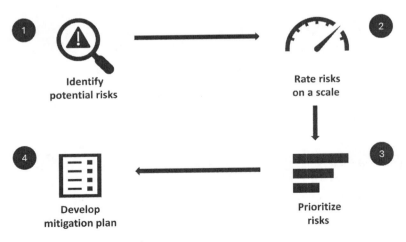

FIGURE 11.1 Four steps in risk assessment

2 **Rate Risks (Impact and Probability)**

Once potential risks are identified, the next step is to rate each risk based on two key factors: impact and probability.

- **Impact:** This measures the severity of the risk if it were to occur. Impacts can range from minor (small delays or cost increases) to catastrophic (complete product failure or significant financial losses). Impacts can be assessed both qualitatively (low, medium, high) or quantitatively (assigning a numerical value, such as a score from 1 to 5).
- **Probability:** This measures the likelihood that a risk will occur. Some risks may be very likely (e.g., a well-known technical challenge), while others may have a low probability (e.g., a sudden shift in regulatory requirements). Similar to impact, probability can be assessed qualitatively or quantitatively.

Using a **Risk Impact-Probability Matrix** as shown in Figure 11.2, product managers can visualize and categorize risks by assigning a score to each risk's impact and probability. This matrix helps create a clear picture of which risks are most critical and require immediate attention.

3 **Prioritize Risks**

After rating the risks, the next step is to prioritize them. Not all risks are equal, so focusing on those that have the greatest potential to disrupt the product is essential. High-impact, high-probability risks should be addressed first, while lower-priority risks can be monitored and managed as needed.

- **Urgent Risks:** High-impact, high-probability risks that need immediate mitigation planning.
- **Moderate Risks:** Risks that may have either a high probability with low impact or a high impact with low probability. These should be carefully monitored, with contingency plans in place.

		Probability				
		Very High [5]	High [4]	Medium [3]	Low [2]	Very Low [1]
Impact	Catastrophic [4]	20	16	12	8	4
	Critical [3]	15	12	9	6	3
	Marginal [2]	10	8	6	4	2
	Negligible [1]	5	4	3	2	1

Risk Factor
= 3 x 3 = 9

FIGURE 11.2 Risk Impact-Probability Matrix

- **Low-Priority Risks**: Low-impact, low-probability risks that can be documented and reassessed periodically but may not require immediate action.

By prioritizing risks, product managers can allocate resources efficiently and focus on resolving the most significant threats to the product's success.

4 **Mitigation Planning**

The final step is developing strategies to mitigate or manage prioritized risks. Mitigation planning involves defining actions to reduce the likelihood or impact of each risk, ensuring that even if the risk occurs, its effects on the product are minimized.

Common mitigation strategies as illustrated in Table 11.1 include:

- **Risk Avoidance**: Taking steps to eliminate the risk altogether, such as changing product features or timelines to avoid potential issues.
- **Risk Transferring**: Transferring some or all of the risk to a third party, such as through partnerships, outsourcing, or insurance.
- **Risk Reduction**: Implementing safeguards to reduce the likelihood or impact of a risk. For example, adding redundancy to technical systems to mitigate downtime risks.
- **Risk Acceptance**: Accepting, in some cases, risks with low impact or probability that require no action beyond monitoring the situation.

Mitigation plans should be documented and communicated to all stakeholders, ensuring that everyone is aware of the potential risks and the steps being taken to address them.

By conducting a thorough risk assessment, product managers can proactively manage uncertainties that could hinder a product's success. The use of a **Risk Impact-Probability Matrix** provides a structured approach to rating and prioritizing risks, while mitigation planning ensures that these risks are addressed before they can cause significant disruption. When paired with

TABLE 11.1 Risk mitigation techniques

Technique	Definition	Examples
Avoid	Eliminate cause of risk	Extend schedule, reduce scope, etc.
Transfer	Have third party take on responsibility for risk	Insurance, warranties, etc.
Reduce	Reduce probability or impact of risk	Adopt less complex processes, conduct more tests, etc.
Accept	Contingency plans for risk	No action, or have a contingency reserve

financial assessment, risk assessment forms the backbone of a strong business case, providing stakeholders with confidence in the product's strategic and financial viability.

In the next section, we will explore how to combine both financial and risk assessments to build a comprehensive and compelling business case.

11.4 Combining Financial and Risk Assessments

After conducting both financial and risk assessments, the next step is to synthesize these analyses into a comprehensive business case. The goal of this section is to demonstrate how integrating financial metrics with risk management strategies creates a holistic view of the product's potential success and challenges. A well-rounded business case enables product managers to present a balanced perspective, showing both the upside of pursuing the product and the contingencies in place to manage potential risks.

11.4.1 Linking Financial Outcomes to Risk Factors

One of the primary objectives in merging financial and risk assessments is to understand how various risk factors might influence financial outcomes. A good business case highlights potential disruptions to revenue, cost overruns, or delays and ties these risks back to the financial projections.

- **Scenario-Based Financial Forecasting**: Using insights from risk assessment, product managers can build multiple financial scenarios (e.g., best case, worst case, and most likely case). For example, if technical risks increase the likelihood of delayed product launch, this will reduce revenue forecasts and increase operational costs in the worst-case scenario. Scenario analysis allows stakeholders to understand the financial implications of these risks and prepares the organization for possible variations in the outcomes.
- **Mitigated vs. Unmitigated Financial Projections**: Another useful approach is to provide two sets of financial projections – one based on mitigated risks and one without risk mitigation. This helps to visualize the potential value of implementing risk management strategies. For example, if a mitigation plan successfully reduces the likelihood of a significant operational disruption, the financial assessment will reflect more stable cash flows and a lower likelihood of incurring additional costs.

11.4.2 Balancing ROI with Risk Exposure

In the decision-making process, stakeholders must weigh the expected **ROI** against the risks the product poses. While a high **ROI** is desirable, excessive risk exposure can deter investment and undermine the product's long-term viability. The business case should clearly outline this balance by providing:

- **Risk-Adjusted ROI:** Adjust ROI calculations by factoring in the likelihood and impact of identified risks. This can provide a more realistic picture of what returns the organization might expect once all potential risks are accounted for.
- **Risk vs. Reward:** Some risks, especially those related to market dynamics or competition, may have a high probability but are necessary for capturing significant market share. The business case should argue why taking on these risks might be worthwhile, especially if the potential rewards outweigh the associated risk exposure.

11.4.3 Developing a Contingency Plan

While risk assessment includes mitigation strategies, the business case should also propose a broader contingency plan that outlines the steps the organization will take in the event of major risk events. This contingency plan will demonstrate preparedness and increase stakeholder confidence in the product's risk management.

Key elements of the contingency plan include:

- **Emergency Funding or Budget Adjustments:** In cases where financial projections are significantly impacted by risk events, having a reserve budget or access to additional funding sources is crucial for avoiding project failure. The contingency plan should specify how much reserve budget is necessary and how it will be accessed.
- **Alternative Strategies:** If the product encounters severe market or technical challenges, alternative paths should be identified. This could involve altering the product's features, changing the target market, or delaying the launch. By preparing for these alternatives, the business case conveys adaptability in the face of unforeseen obstacles.

11.4.4 Communicating Risk Management to Stakeholders

Effectively communicating the integration of financial and risk assessments is essential for gaining stakeholder approval. This involves:

- **Presenting the Risk Impact-Probability Matrix:** Share the matrix with stakeholders to visually demonstrate which risks are being prioritized and how they will be addressed. This visual aid helps explain why certain risks are being emphasized and how mitigation efforts will affect the product's overall risk profile.

- **Highlighting Key Financial Metrics:** Use financial metrics such as payback period, break-even point, and risk-adjusted ROI to show stakeholders the product's financial potential in the context of its risk exposure. Providing these numbers gives a clear and concise view of both short-term and long-term outcomes.
- **Transparent Risk Reporting:** Be upfront about high-impact risks that cannot be fully mitigated and clearly outline the steps being taken to manage them. Transparency builds trust and ensures that stakeholders are aware of both the challenges and opportunities the product presents.

By integrating financial and risk assessments, product managers can present a well-rounded business case that goes beyond simple revenue projections. This combined approach offers a clear view of how risks can impact the product's financial success, while also demonstrating preparedness and adaptability. In this way, the business case becomes a powerful tool for decision-making, ensuring that stakeholders understand both the rewards and challenges of bringing the product to market.

In the following section, we will look at how this combined approach can be translated into a product roadmap and strategy, aligning financial goals and risk management efforts with long-term product development and market success.

11.5 Conclusion

Building a compelling business case is an essential skill for product managers, as it serves as the foundation for justifying new product initiatives or strategic changes. In this chapter, we've explored the many factors involved in constructing a solid business case, focusing particularly on financial and risk assessments, which are critical for determining the product's viability and ensuring long-term success.

A thorough **financial assessment** provides a clear picture of the economic potential of the product, incorporating cost estimation, revenue projections, profitability analysis, payback period, and break-even analysis. These financial metrics offer stakeholders the data they need to make informed decisions about whether to invest in the product. By understanding the financial returns and resource commitments required, product managers can align their proposals with the company's strategic goals.

Equally important is conducting a comprehensive **risk assessment**, which identifies potential threats to the product's success and outlines mitigation strategies to address them. By using tools like the Risk Impact-Probability Matrix and following a structured approach – identifying, rating, prioritizing, and mitigation planning – product managers can anticipate challenges and develop contingency plans to minimize their impact.

Combining these two critical assessments ensures that the business case presents a balanced view of the product's potential. It helps stakeholders understand not only the financial upside but also the risks involved, along with the strategies in place to mitigate those risks. Ultimately, this comprehensive approach enhances decision-making, increases confidence in the product's feasibility, and sets the foundation for a successful product launch and sustained market performance.

This chapter equips product managers with the tools and methodologies needed to build a strong, data-driven business case, ensuring that both the financial potential and risk exposure of a product are thoroughly evaluated and effectively communicated to stakeholders.

12

DEVELOPING A PRODUCT POSITIONING

12.1 Introduction

Product positioning is one of the most critical aspects of product management, shaping how customers perceive and connect with a product in the marketplace. In a world where consumers are faced with a myriad of choices, the way a product is positioned can be the difference between success and failure. Effective product positioning helps establish a distinct and desirable identity in the minds of customers, making it clear why they should choose your product over others.

At the core of product positioning is the ability to communicate the unique value and benefits your product offers, addressing key questions such as: what problem does the product solve? Who is the target customer? How does it stand out from competitors? A well-crafted positioning strategy answers these questions, guiding everything from marketing messages to sales tactics, and ensuring that customers understand the relevance of your product to their needs.

This chapter explores two critical tools for developing strong product positioning: customer perception mapping and the six core positioning strategies – price, quality, demographics, category, differentiation, and competition. We will also introduce the concept of finding the 'sweet spot' in competitive positioning by aligning 3 Cs: **Customer** needs, company **Competencies**, and gaps where **Competitors** fail to meet those needs. By doing so, product managers can create a positioning strategy that is both competitive and sustainable.

Through these frameworks, you will gain a deeper understanding of how to shape the way your product is perceived in the marketplace and create a clear, differentiated product identity that resonates with customers and drives business success.

DOI: 10.1201/9781003484295-12

12.2 The Importance of Product Positioning

Product positioning is critical because it defines how customers perceive and differentiate your product from competitors. In today's saturated markets, where consumers are faced with countless options, a well-executed product positioning strategy helps your product stand out, establishes a unique identity, and resonates with the target audience. By positioning your product correctly, you ensure that customers not only understand what your product offers but also recognize its value in addressing their specific needs.

12.2.1 Why Is Product Positioning Important?

1 **Creates a Clear Identity in the Market:** Without clear positioning, a product may struggle to stand out, leading to confusion among potential customers about what it offers and why it's valuable. Strong positioning highlights the product's strengths and differentiators, providing a clear identity that customers can associate with specific benefits. This is especially important in competitive industries where multiple products offer similar features or benefits.

2 **Builds Emotional Connections:** Product positioning is not just about functionality – it also involves creating an emotional connection with the customer. Products that successfully position themselves as solutions to customer pain points are more likely to foster brand loyalty. This emotional connection can transform customers into brand advocates, helping to drive both sales and long-term brand equity.

3 **Influences Customer Decision-Making:** Effective positioning plays a key role in influencing the customer's buying decisions. By clearly communicating the product's value and benefits, product managers can shift customers' perceptions and guide them towards making a purchase. If customers can easily understand why your product is the best choice for them, they are more likely to choose it over competing products.

4 **Supports Marketing and Sales Efforts:** A clearly defined product positioning strategy provides a foundation for marketing campaigns, sales tactics, and overall brand communication. When a product's unique value is consistently communicated across all customer touchpoints, it reinforces the brand's message and ensures that everyone from marketing to sales is aligned. Without this consistency, the product's message can become fragmented, diluting its impact.

12.2.2 Real-World Examples of Good Product Positioning

- **Apple (iPhone):** Apple's **iPhone** is a prime example of excellent product positioning. **Apple** has positioned the **iPhone** as a premium, high-quality, innovative device that offers a seamless user experience. It focuses on cutting-edge technology combined with elegant design, marketing the phone not just as a device but as a lifestyle product. This positioning has allowed **Apple** to build a loyal customer base willing to pay a premium, despite the availability of lower-priced alternatives. **Apple's** marketing consistently reinforces this positioning, creating strong brand loyalty and differentiation from competitors like **Samsung** and **Google**.

- **Tesla (Electric Vehicles)**: **Tesla** has positioned itself as a leader in electric vehicles (EVs) by focusing on sustainability, cutting-edge technology, and high performance. **Tesla's** positioning taps into the growing demand for environmentally friendly solutions while also emphasizing the luxury and performance aspects of its vehicles. This dual focus allows **Tesla** to appeal to eco-conscious consumers and car enthusiasts alike, solidifying its position as a dominant player in the **EV** market.

- **Nike (Athletic Wear)**: **Nike** has mastered emotional branding by positioning itself not just as a manufacturer of athletic wear but as an enabler of personal achievement and athletic excellence. Its famous slogan, '**Just Do It**', and its collaborations with top athletes reinforce this positioning. **Nike's** ability to associate its products with motivation, success, and empowerment has driven strong brand loyalty, making it a global leader in the sportswear industry.

12.2.3 *Examples of Poor Product Positioning*

- **Pepsi (Pepsi AM)**: **Pepsi** attempted to launch **Pepsi AM**, a soda specifically marketed as a breakfast beverage. This product failed because it was poorly positioned – consumers were not ready to replace their traditional morning coffee or juice with a soda. The positioning clashed with established breakfast routines, and **Pepsi AM** was quickly pulled from the market. This failure highlights the importance of aligning product positioning with customer expectations and behaviours.

- **Colgate (Frozen Dinners)**: **Colgate**, a company best known for oral hygiene products, once ventured into the frozen food market with its line of **Colgate**-branded frozen dinners. This was a classic case of poor brand extension and positioning, as consumers found it difficult to associate a toothpaste brand with food. The mismatched brand positioning led to the product's swift failure, proving that even strong brands can fail if the positioning does not make sense in the context of consumer perception.

- **Microsoft (Zune)**: **Microsoft's Zune** was intended to compete with the **Apple iPod** in the portable music player market. However, its positioning was unclear. While **Apple** had already established itself as the go-to brand for sleek, innovative, and user-friendly devices, **Microsoft** struggled to differentiate **Zune** from the **iPod**. The marketing efforts were inconsistent, and the product lacked a unique value proposition, leading to **Zune's** inability to capture significant market share.

12.2.4 Importance of Effective Product Positioning

The success of products like the **iPhone, Tesla,** and **Nike** shows that effective positioning is about more than just price or features – it's about creating a product identity that resonates with consumers on both rational and emotional levels. On the other hand, failures like **Pepsi AM** and **Colgate's** frozen dinners demonstrate the risks of poor positioning, such as misaligning with customer expectations or creating confusing brand messages.

In summary, strong product positioning is critical to:

- Establishing a clear, differentiated market identity.
- Building emotional connections with customers that foster brand loyalty.
- Supporting consistent and effective marketing and sales strategies.
- Ensuring that customers understand the value of the product and are motivated to choose it over competitors.

As you continue through this chapter, you will learn how to use strategic positioning tools like customer perception mapping and competitive positioning to develop a positioning strategy that will make your product stand out and resonate with your target audience.

12.3 Understanding Customer Perception Mapping

Customer perception mapping is a crucial tool for product managers to visualize how customers perceive their product relative to competitors across various attributes, such as price, quality, innovation, and features. By capturing how your product is positioned in the minds of customers, perception maps offer invaluable insights into how your product stands in the competitive landscape and where opportunities for differentiation might lie. They also help in refining your brand messaging and ensuring that the product is aligned with customer needs and preferences.

12.3.1 What Is Customer Perception Mapping?

Customer perception mapping involves creating a visual representation of customer opinions about your product compared to others. These maps typically use two key dimensions – such as **price** and **quality** – to plot how customers view different products in a given market. This visualization allows you to identify where your product sits in the competitive space, which products are perceived as direct competitors, and whether there are gaps in the market that your product could fill.

12.3.2   Steps to Create a Customer Perception Map

1 **Identify Key Attributes**: Start by identifying the most relevant attributes that define your product and its competitors. These could include dimensions like price, quality, innovation, ease of use, customer service, or sustainability. It's important to choose attributes that are significant to your target customers and that differentiate the products in your market.
2 **Gather Customer Data**: Next, gather data on how customers perceive your product and your competitors. These data can be collected through customer surveys, focus groups, reviews, or market research reports. Ask customers to rate products based on the key attributes identified or use available customer feedback and market analysis.
3 **Plot the Data**: Once you have the data, plot the products on a two-dimensional grid, with each axis representing a key attribute. For example, if you're mapping based on **price** and **quality**, you would place low-cost, low-quality products in the bottom-left corner and high-cost, high-quality products in the top-right corner. This will create a visual representation of how customers perceive each product in the competitive landscape.
4 **Analyse the Map**: After plotting the products, analyse the perception map to identify clusters, gaps, or outliers. Clusters indicate areas where multiple products compete closely, while gaps may reveal opportunities where customer needs are unmet. Outliers could represent products that stand out due to unique features or poorly defined positioning.

12.3.3   Example of Customer Perception Mapping

A classic example of customer perception mapping can be seen in the automotive industry. Car manufacturers such as **Toyota, BMW,** and **Tesla** use perception maps to understand how customers view their products across dimensions like **performance, luxury, fuel efficiency,** and **price.** Figure 12.1 shows a perception map using price and quality.

If we were to create a customer perception map for automakers with the dimensions of price and quality, several well-known automakers could be placed on the map according to their perceived strengths in these areas. Here's how some automakers might be positioned:

• **BMW and Audi** are often plotted in the high-performance, luxury segment, appealing to customers seeking premium quality and superior driving experiences.
• **Toyota** is often positioned in the affordable, high-reliability section of the perception map, appealing to cost-conscious customers who value dependability.
• **KIA** would typically be positioned as **moderate-to-low price** and **moderate-to-high quality.**

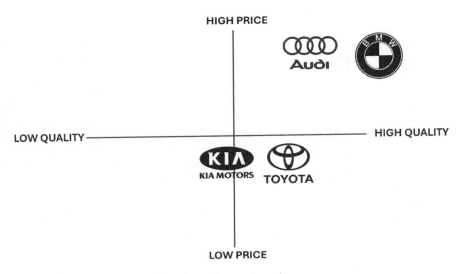

FIGURE 12.1 Perception map using price and quality

Figure 12.2 shows a perception map using innovation and sustainability.

If we were to create a customer perception map for automakers with the dimensions of innovation and sustainability, here's how some automakers might be positioned:

- **BYD and Tesla** occupy the innovation-performance corner, being perceived as a high-end, eco-friendly option with advanced technology.

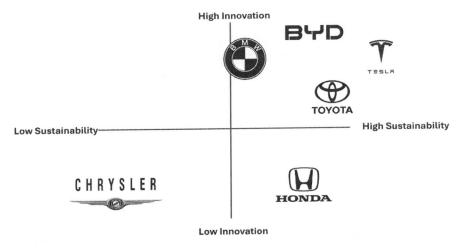

FIGURE 12.2 Perception map using innovation and sustainability

- **Toyota**: Toyota was a pioneer in hybrid vehicles with the Prius and has been a leader in fuel-efficient and environmentally friendly vehicles. However, its EV lineup is not as developed as some competitors, so it would be ranked high on sustainability but more moderate on innovation.
- **Honda**: Honda has focused more on hybrid vehicles and fuel efficiency over full EV innovation. While it has strong environmental credentials, especially in the hybrid space, it's slower in rolling out fully electric and highly innovative vehicles compared to companies like Tesla or BYD.
- **Fiat Chrysler** (now known as **Stellantis North America**) has historically lagged in both innovation and sustainability, with a limited focus on EVs and sustainability. However, recent commitments to electrify its lineup through Stellantis are slowly improving its positioning.

These mappings allow these companies to adjust their marketing, refine their product lines, and even launch new products that fill gaps in the market. For instance, if Tesla noticed a gap in the lower-price, high-innovation segment, they might consider introducing a more affordable electric vehicle with high-tech features.

12.3.4 How Product Managers Use Customer Perception Mapping

Customer perception maps are powerful tools for product managers because they provide a snapshot of the competitive landscape and help guide strategic decision-making. Here are some of the ways product managers can use perception mapping:

1 **Gauging Perceived Competition:**

- **Identify Competitors**: By plotting your product alongside others, you can see which competitors are closest to you in customers' minds. This helps in defining who your true competitors are and understanding their strengths and weaknesses.
- **Differentiate from Competitors**: Once you know how customers perceive your product relative to competitors, you can adjust your positioning to better differentiate your product. If your product is perceived too similarly to a competitor, you may need to shift focus to unique attributes.

Example: In the smartphone industry, **Samsung** uses perception mapping to gauge how customers perceive its **Galaxy** phones relative to the **iPhone**. **Samsung** can then adjust its messaging to highlight features like display quality, battery life, or innovative design to differentiate itself from **Apple**.

2 **Identifying Market Gaps or Open Spaces:**

- **Spotting Opportunities:** Perception maps reveal areas where customer needs are not fully met by existing products. These gaps present opportunities for your product to move into a less competitive space, offering features or benefits that other products don't.
- **Filling Market Voids:** If your perception map shows a gap for high-quality, mid-priced products, and customer feedback supports demand for such a product, you can refine your product to target that specific market void.

Example: In the fashion industry, brands like **Zara** have identified a gap between high-fashion luxury and fast fashion. By positioning itself as a brand offering affordable, stylish clothing that mimics luxury designs, **Zara** has successfully filled this gap, gaining a competitive edge in the global market.

3 **Refining Brand Messaging:**

- **Aligning Messaging with Perceptions:** If customers perceive your product as high-quality but expensive, your marketing should reinforce the premium value they are receiving for the price. Conversely, if the perception doesn't match your intended message, you may need to adjust your communications to clarify your product's value proposition.
- **Reinforcing Brand Identity:** Perception maps can guide how you consistently communicate your brand across advertising, sales pitches, and product packaging. The goal is to ensure that customers consistently understand your product's position and value.

Example: Patagonia, known for sustainability and outdoor gear, leverages perception mapping to ensure their brand messaging aligns with their core value of environmental responsibility. They highlight this in their marketing to reinforce their position as a leader in eco-conscious outdoor wear, a clear distinction from other brands in the market.

4 **Clarifying Product Positioning:**

- **Simplifying Your Message:** Mapping allows you to see where there might be overlap with competitors and whether your message is clear enough to stand out. If too many competitors are in the same space with similar messaging, you can refine your positioning to offer a simpler, more distinct message to customers.
- **Building a Stronger Identity:** Understanding how customers view your product helps you emphasize your product's strengths in areas that competitors cannot match.

Example: Red Bull has positioned itself not just as an energy drink but as a brand that promotes extreme sports and high-performance lifestyles. This positioning sets it apart from other energy drinks, and customer perception maps would likely show Red Bull dominating this high-energy, adventure-driven segment of the market.

5 **Adjusting Positioning Strategy Over Time:**

- **Evolving with Market Trends:** As customer preferences shift and new competitors enter the market, perception mapping helps you adapt your product positioning. By regularly updating your perception maps, you can see if customer views are changing and adjust your strategy to stay relevant.
- **Course-Correcting:** If your product is not where you want it to be on the perception map, you can use the insights to tweak aspects such as pricing, features, or marketing to better align with your target customers.

Example: Uber initially positioned itself as a premium alternative to traditional taxis with **UberBLACK,** but as customer preferences shifted towards affordability, **Uber** adjusted its positioning by introducing **UberX,** which targets budget-conscious customers. This shift helped Uber capture a much larger market share, making it the leader in ride-hailing.

12.3.5 *Conclusion: The Power of Customer Perception Mapping*

Customer perception mapping offers product managers a dynamic, visual tool to understand how their product is viewed in the marketplace, how it compares to competitors, and where opportunities lie. It helps define a product's competitive advantage, sharpen brand messaging, and ensure that the product resonates with customers. By continuously using and updating perception maps, product managers can stay ahead of market trends, identify new opportunities, and position their products effectively for long-term success.

12.4 Six Key Product Positioning Strategies

Product positioning plays a critical role in defining how customers perceive your product relative to competitors. By leveraging six key product positioning strategies – **price, quality, demographics, category, differentiation, and competition** – product managers can effectively communicate their product's value to the market. Let's explore how these strategies work, using real-world examples from global multi-national companies and Singapore-based companies across various industries like food and beverage (F&B), e-commerce, fashion, and digital services.

12.4.1 *Price Positioning*

Price positioning defines where your product sits in the pricing spectrum – either as a budget-friendly option or a premium, high-value product.

- **Premium Pricing Example (F&B): Lindt** chocolate positions itself as a high-end, premium brand, focusing on quality ingredients and luxurious packaging. Similarly, **Haagen-Dazs** ice cream positions itself as a premium brand by using rich, high-quality ingredients and offering an indulgent experience. Both brands use high price points to signal superior quality, appealing to customers who are willing to pay more for a premium product. **Janice Wong Singapore**, known for its artisanal desserts and chocolates, positions itself as a premium brand with sophisticated, high-quality products. The brand emphasizes artistry and innovation, which justifies its higher price point. **Janice Wong's** pricing appeals to customers seeking a luxurious, exclusive experience, particularly for gifts and special occasions.
- **Budget Pricing Example (E-commerce): Shopee** is an example of a brand that effectively uses budget pricing to dominate the Southeast Asian e-commerce market. **Shopee** offers a wide variety of products at competitive prices, along with frequent promotions and discounts. This pricing strategy appeals to price-sensitive consumers in Singapore and across the region, making **Shopee** a go-to platform for affordable online shopping.

12.4.2 *Quality Positioning*

Quality positioning is centred around the superior craftsmanship, durability, or performance of the product. It focuses on delivering high value for the cost, which often appeals to discerning consumers willing to invest in long-lasting or high-performing products.

- **High-Quality Example (Clothing): Benjamin Barker**, a homegrown Singapore menswear brand, is positioned as a provider of high-quality, tailored clothing. With a focus on craftsmanship and premium fabrics, the brand appeals to professionals who value both style and durability. The higher price reflects its emphasis on quality and personal service, positioning **Benjamin Barker** as a sophisticated choice for corporate wear and formal events.
- **Moderate Quality Example (Home Furnishings/Clothing): Castlery**, a Singapore-based furniture retailer, positions itself as an affordable yet high-quality option for modern home furnishings. **Castlery** offers stylish, durable furniture at reasonable prices, appealing to customers who seek

quality but are not looking to pay top-tier prices like they would at premium outlets. The brand's combination of quality and affordability has helped it expand locally and internationally. In the clothing and home furnishings sectors, brands like **H&M** and **IKEA** leverage budget pricing to appeal to price-sensitive consumers. **H&M** offers trendy clothing at affordable prices, making it accessible to a wide demographic. **IKEA**, on the other hand, provides stylish yet inexpensive furniture, appealing to customers looking for functional, well-designed products at a lower cost. Both brands excel at delivering perceived value for the price, making them popular choices in the mass market.

12.4.3 Demographics Positioning

Demographics-based positioning tailors a product to meet the needs and preferences of a specific audience segment, such as age, gender, or lifestyle.

- **Targeting Young Professionals Example (Fashion): Love, Bonito** is a Singapore-based fashion brand that caters specifically to modern, fashion-forward women. The brand is positioned to meet the needs of young professionals and millennials who seek stylish yet affordable clothing for work, social events, and everyday wear. By understanding the preferences of this demographic, **Love, Bonito** tailors its designs, marketing, and retail experience to create a strong brand connection with its target audience.
- **Targeting Families Example (E-commerce): RedMart**, Singapore's leading online grocery delivery service (acquired by **Lazada**), positions itself as a convenient solution for busy families. **RedMart** appeals to households with children by offering a wide range of groceries, household essentials, and fresh produce with same-day delivery. This demographic positioning focuses on time-saving convenience for families who value quick, hassle-free shopping.

12.4.4 Category Positioning

Category positioning defines how a product stands out within its broader market category – either as an innovator, leader, or disruptor.

- **Category Leader Example (F&B/Streaming): Tiger Beer**, a product of Singapore's Asia Pacific Breweries, is positioned as a category leader in the local and international beer market. Known for its heritage and quality, **Tiger Beer** emphasizes its roots as a Singaporean brand with a global reach. This strong category positioning has helped it maintain dominance as one of Singapore's most iconic beer brands, both domestically and abroad. **Netflix** has successfully positioned itself as the category leader in the streaming industry by offering a vast library of original and licensed content and continuously innovating with features like personalized recommendations. **Netflix** transformed the category of digital streaming by focusing on convenience and instant access, making it the go-to platform for customers seeking diverse content without advertisements.

- **New Entrant Example (Digital Services): Grab,** which started as a ride-hailing service, has evolved into a multi-service app, positioning itself as a disruptor in the digital services category. **Grab** now offers food delivery (**GrabFood**), digital payments (**GrabPay**), and financial services (**GrabFinance**), positioning itself as a one-stop solution for daily services. Grab's category positioning as a comprehensive digital service provider has helped it differentiate from traditional competitors in each sector.

12.4.5   Differentiation Positioning

Differentiation focuses on what makes your product unique compared to competitors. This could be in terms of features, benefits, customer experience, or brand ethos.

- **Unique Feature Example (E-commerce): Carousell,** a Singapore-based online marketplace, differentiates itself by being a **peer-to-peer (P2P)** platform where users can buy and sell pre-loved items. Unlike other e-commerce platforms, **Carousell** emphasizes sustainability through reusing and recycling goods, which resonates with environmentally conscious consumers. This unique value proposition sets **Carousell** apart from more traditional e-commerce sites like **Lazada** and **Shopee**, giving it a distinct competitive edge.
- **Unique Value Example (Ice Cream): Ben & Jerry's** ice cream has differentiated itself from competitors by focusing on quirky flavours, creative packaging, and a commitment to social causes. This positioning appeals to customers who not only care about taste but also value brands that stand for ethical and environmental sustainability. **Ben & Jerry's** is known for its fun, high-quality products with a social mission, making it stand out from traditional ice cream brands. **Udders Ice Cream** stands out in the highly competitive F&B industry by offering unique and bold flavours inspired by local Singaporean tastes. Udders incorporates flavours such as Mao Shan Wang durian and Chendol into its ice creams, differentiating it from more conventional ice cream brands. By leveraging local flavours, **Udders** appeals to customers seeking a fun, adventurous, and uniquely Singaporean dessert experience.

12.4.6 Competition Positioning

Competition-based positioning highlights your product's advantages compared to a direct competitor, often through feature comparisons or service differentiation.

- **Direct Competition Example (Ride-Hailing):** In Singapore's competitive ride-hailing market, **TADA** positions itself directly against **Grab** by emphasizing no commission fees for drivers, which translates into more affordable rides for customers. By differentiating itself as a fairer, driver-friendly alternative to **Grab**, **TADA** has been able to attract both drivers and cost-conscious passengers looking for a better deal in the ride-hailing space.
- **Market Challenger Example (Telecommunications):** Circles.Life, a Singapore-based **mobile virtual network operator (MVNO)**, positions itself as a challenger to traditional telecom giants like **Singtel** and **StarHub**. Circles.Life differentiates itself by offering fully digital mobile plans with flexible data options and no-contract plans, appealing to tech-savvy consumers who want more control over their mobile services. This competitive positioning has allowed **Circles.Life** to carve out a niche in the highly competitive telco industry by addressing customer frustrations with rigid contracts and poor flexibility from traditional carriers.

12.4.7 Leveraging These Strategies to Build Strong Positioning

By applying these six key product positioning strategies, product managers can craft a product identity that resonates with their target customers. Each strategy provides a unique way to define how a product is perceived, whether by emphasizing its affordability, quality, demographic appeal, category leadership, unique features, or advantages over competitors.

For example, Singapore's **Love, Bonito** successfully combines demographics, quality, and differentiation positioning by catering to young professional women with stylish, high-quality clothing that fits their lifestyle and budget. Similarly, **Grab** utilizes category positioning and differentiation by expanding its range of services and becoming a leader in the digital services space.

By selecting and combining one or more of these strategies, product managers can clarify their product's market position and develop a compelling value proposition that meets the specific needs of their audience.

In the next section, we will explore how product managers can refine their competitive positioning by identifying market gaps and open spaces where customer needs are unmet and how to communicate these strategies effectively to both internal and external stakeholders.

12.5 Finding the Sweet Spot in Competitive Positioning

In competitive markets, finding the **sweet spot** in positioning is essential to ensure your product stands out while addressing unmet customer needs. The sweet spot in competitive positioning occurs where three key factors align:

1 **Customer Needs:** What the customer desires or values.
2 **Company Competencies:** The unique strengths and capabilities your company possesses.
3 **Competitor Gaps:** Areas where competitors cannot or do not effectively meet customer needs.

By identifying where your product can fulfil customer needs with competencies that competitors lack, you create a unique value proposition that is difficult to replicate. This positioning sweet spot not only differentiates your product but also increases its relevance to the target audience, giving it a strong competitive advantage.

Key Components of the Sweet Spot

1 **Understanding Customer Needs:** To find the sweet spot, you must first understand what your target customers are looking for – whether it's in terms of price, quality, convenience, or specific features. Customer research, surveys, focus groups, and feedback can help identify the critical pain points and desires that customers have, which competitors may not fully address.
2 **Leveraging Company Competencies:** Your company's competencies are the unique strengths or capabilities that set you apart from competitors. These can include proprietary technology, superior customer service, operational efficiency, or innovative product design. A successful product positioning strategy must leverage these core competencies to deliver value to customers in a way that competitors cannot easily replicate.
3 **Identifying Competitor Gaps:** Competitor analysis is a vital step in finding the sweet spot. You need to identify where competitors are falling short in meeting customer needs. This could be in the form of poor customer service, outdated technology, or lack of innovation. The goal is to find areas where your product can exceed customer expectations and outperform competitors.

Finding the Sweet Spot: Examples

Let's explore how companies across various industries have successfully found the sweet spot in their competitive positioning by aligning **customer needs, company competencies,** and **competitor gaps.**

1 **Grab (Ride-Hailing and Super App)**

   Customer Needs: Convenience, all-in-one service, seamless integration of multiple services (transportation, food delivery, payments).

Company Competencies: Grab initially excelled in ride-hailing but expanded its competencies by building an ecosystem of services (**Grab-Food, GrabPay, GrabFinance**), all within one app. **Grab's** ability to integrate transportation, food delivery, and financial services into a seamless platform is a core strength.

Competitor Gaps: Competitors like **Uber** focused primarily on ride-hailing without expanding into adjacent services. This left a gap for an all-in-one app solution that could meet the diverse needs of Southeast Asian customers who preferred integrated services.

Sweet Spot: Grab found its sweet spot by addressing the demand for convenience and a super-app experience. By leveraging its ride-hailing expertise and expanding into new services like food delivery and digital payments, **Grab** filled a gap in the market that competitors hadn't fully explored. This strategy differentiated **Grab** from other ride-hailing platforms and allowed it to become the dominant player in Southeast Asia's digital economy.

2 Razer (Gaming Hardware and Accessories)

Customer Needs: Gamers need high-performance, durable, and aesthetically appealing gaming hardware that enhances their gaming experience.

Company Competencies: Razer is known for its cutting-edge technology and product innovation, particularly in gaming hardware such as laptops, mice, keyboards, and headsets. Its focus on performance, sleek design, and customization options for gamers is a major strength.

Competitor Gaps: While competitors like **Logitech** and **Corsair** offer quality gaming accessories, they don't always focus on the aesthetics and lifestyle appeal that Razer does. Many competitors offer functional products but lack the 'cool factor' and community-building that **Razer** has cultivated among gamers.

Sweet Spot: Razer identified its sweet spot by focusing on high-performance gaming hardware combined with sleek, customizable designs that appeal to serious gamers. Its unique positioning as a lifestyle brand for gamers – rather than just a hardware manufacturer – allowed it to dominate the gaming market. **Razer** tapped into the gap where competitors offered solid products but lacked brand identity and design appeal, which **Razer** turned into a competitive advantage.

3 Circles.Life (Telecommunications)

Customer Needs: Consumers in Singapore and the region want flexible, no-contract mobile plans that offer affordable data and customization options.

Company Competencies: Circles.Life's strength is in its digital-first approach. By operating as a **mobile virtual network operator** (**MVNO**), it avoids the overhead costs of running a physical network and passes

184 Digital Product Management

these savings on to customers. Its digital platform allows for easy plan customization and data add-ons, which appeals to customers who prioritize flexibility.

Competitor Gaps: Traditional telecom providers like **Singtel** and **StarHub** often require long-term contracts, offer rigid pricing plans, and have limited flexibility. This leaves a gap for a mobile service provider that offers greater control and customization at a lower cost.

Sweet Spot: Circles.Life identified its sweet spot by offering no-contract, flexible data plans with a customer-centric digital platform. It filled a gap left by traditional telecom providers, meeting the needs of tech-savvy consumers who want greater control over their mobile plans without being locked into lengthy contracts. This competitive positioning has helped **Circles.Life** differentiate itself and grow rapidly in Singapore and beyond.

Key Takeaways: How to Find the Sweet Spot

1 **Start with the Customer:** Understand what your target customers value most – whether it's convenience, quality, customization, or affordability.
2 **Leverage Your Strengths:** Identify your company's unique competencies – whether it's technology, local expertise, or operational efficiency – and use them to meet customer needs in a way that competitors cannot.
3 **Analyse Competitor Weaknesses:** Identify gaps in competitors' offerings. Where are they falling short in meeting customer expectations? Look for opportunities to differentiate your product by filling those gaps.
4 **Align All Three Factors:** The sweet spot is where your product perfectly aligns with customer needs, leverages your company's strengths, and outperforms competitors. This positioning will help you carve out a unique and defensible market position.

By focusing on these three factors, companies can create a unique competitive advantage and build lasting market leadership.

12.6   Crafting a Positioning Statement

A **positioning statement** is a concise declaration that communicates the unique value your product offers to its target customers. It serves as the foundation for all messaging and marketing efforts, ensuring consistency across various channels and touchpoints. A well-crafted positioning statement clearly articulates what makes your product different, who it serves, and why it's the best choice for that audience.

The **Elevator Pitch** format is a popular approach to crafting a positioning statement because it forces you to convey the essence of your product's value in a short, impactful way. This format is particularly useful for product managers, marketers, and sales teams when explaining the product to stakeholders, customers, or investors.

A good positioning statement generally answers the following questions:

- **Who** is the target customer?
- **What** is the customer's need or problem?
- **How** does the product solve this problem or meet this need?
- **What makes the product unique** compared to competitors?

12.6.1   The Elevator Pitch Format

The **Elevator Pitch** format helps you break down your positioning statement into a clear, easy-to-digest narrative. It often follows this structure:

1. **For (Target Customer):** Identify the specific group of customers you're targeting.
2. **Who (Customer Need):** Articulate the main problem or need that your target customer has.
3. **Our product (Product Name):** Introduce the product or service being positioned.
4. **Is a (Product Category):** Define the category your product falls into.
5. **That (Unique Benefit/Value):** Describe the primary benefit your product offers, how it solves the customer's problem, or meets their needs.
6. **Unlike (Competitor):** Mention the key differentiator that sets your product apart from competitors.
7. **Our product (Competitive Advantage):** Clearly state why your product is the best option for the target customer.

12.6.2   Crafting Positioning Statements

Let's look at how this format can be applied to real-world examples across different industries.

1. **Grab (Super App)**
   - **For:** Busy individuals in Southeast Asia
   - **Who:** Need a convenient, all-in-one platform to manage transportation, food delivery, and payments
   - **Our product:** Grab
   - **Is a:** Super app
   - **That:** Combines ride-hailing, food delivery, and digital payments into a single, seamless experience

- **Unlike:** Uber, which focuses primarily on ride-hailing
- **Our product:** Offers a complete ecosystem of services tailored to the needs of Southeast Asian consumers, providing unmatched convenience and integration

Positioning Statement: *For busy individuals in Southeast Asia who need a convenient, all-in-one platform to manage transportation, food delivery, and payments, Grab is a super app that combines ride-hailing, food delivery, and digital payments into one seamless experience. Unlike Uber, Grab offers a complete ecosystem of services tailored to Southeast Asia, providing unmatched convenience and integration.*

2 **Love, Bonito (Fashion)**

- **For:** Fashion-conscious Asian women
- **Who:** Struggle to find stylish, well-fitting clothing that caters to their body shapes and cultural preferences
- **Our product:** Love, Bonito
- **Is a:** Women's fashion brand
- **That:** Offers fashionable, affordable clothing specifically designed for Asian women's body shapes and styles
- **Unlike:** Global fast-fashion brands like Zara, which cater to a broad market
- **Our product:** Focuses on fit, style, and cultural relevance for Asian women, ensuring a better fit and design that resonates locally

Positioning Statement: *For fashion-conscious Asian women who struggle to find stylish, well-fitting clothing, Love, Bonito is a fashion brand that offers trendy, affordable pieces specifically designed for Asian body shapes and cultural preferences. Unlike global fast-fashion brands like Zara, Love, Bonito focuses on fit and style tailored to Asian women, ensuring a more personalized and relevant fashion experience.*

3 **Circles.Life (Telecommunications)**

- **For:** Tech-savvy, data-hungry mobile users
- **Who:** Want flexible, no-contract mobile plans with affordable data options
- **Our product:** Circles.Life
- **Is a:** Digital-first mobile network provider
- **That:** Offers customizable, no-contract mobile plans with unlimited data options
- **Unlike:** Traditional telecoms like Singtel and StarHub, which offer rigid contracts and limited flexibility
- **Our product:** Gives customers full control over their mobile plan with no hidden fees and the ability to easily customize data usage

Positioning Statement: *For tech-savvy, data-hungry mobile users who want flexible, no-contract mobile plans, Circles.Life is a digital-first mobile network provider that offers customizable plans with unlimited data options. Unlike traditional telecoms like Singtel and StarHub, Circles.Life gives customers full control over their plan with no hidden fees and easy customization options.*

4 **Carousell (Online Marketplace)**

- **For:** Environmentally conscious and budget-conscious consumers
- **Who:** Want to buy and sell second-hand goods easily and safely
- **Our product:** Carousell
- **Is a:** Peer-to-peer online marketplace
- **That:** Allows users to buy and sell pre-loved items, promoting sustainability and reducing waste
- **Unlike:** Traditional e-commerce platforms like Lazada or Shopee, which focus on new products
- **Our product:** Emphasizes community-driven commerce, where users can buy and sell directly with each other, reducing waste and supporting a circular economy

Positioning Statement: *For environmentally and budget-conscious consumers who want to buy and sell second-hand goods easily, Carousell is a peer-to-peer online marketplace that promotes sustainability by enabling users to sell pre-loved items. Unlike traditional e-commerce platforms like Lazada or Shopee, Carousell focuses on community-driven commerce and a circular economy, making it easier to reduce waste and support sustainable buying practices.*

5 **Udders (Ice Cream)**

- **For:** Ice cream lovers in Singapore
- **Who:** Crave adventurous, local flavours with high-quality ingredients
- **Our product:** Udders Ice Cream
- **Is a:** Premium ice cream brand
- **That:** Offers bold, adventurous flavours inspired by local tastes, such as Mao Shan Wang durian and Chendol
- **Unlike:** International ice cream brands that focus on conventional flavours
- **Our product:** Embraces Singapore's unique food culture, delivering innovative flavours made from the best ingredients to adventurous food lovers

Positioning Statement: *For ice cream lovers in Singapore who crave bold, adventurous flavours, Udders Ice Cream is a premium brand that offers innovative flavours inspired by local tastes like Mao Shan Wang durian and Chendol. Unlike international ice cream brands, Udders celebrates Singaporean food culture, providing high-quality, locally inspired ice cream to adventurous food lovers.*

12.6.3 Tips for Crafting a Strong Positioning Statement

1 **Be Clear and Specific:** Clearly define the target audience and the specific problem or need your product addresses. Avoid vague or broad statements.
2 **Focus on Value and Differentiation:** Highlight the unique value your product offers compared to competitors. What makes your product different, and why should customers choose it?
3 **Keep It Short and Impactful:** Your positioning statement should be concise – ideally, it should fit into an elevator pitch format. Aim for clarity and brevity to ensure it resonates quickly.
4 **Use Customer-Centric Language:** Frame your positioning statement from the perspective of the customer. Focus on how your product solves their problem or improves their experience.

By using the Elevator Pitch format to craft your positioning statement, you ensure that your product's unique value is communicated clearly, helping both internal teams and external audiences understand what sets your product apart in the marketplace.

12.7 Communicating Product Positioning

Once you have crafted a clear and compelling positioning statement, the next critical step is to communicate it effectively across all touchpoints – both internally and externally. A well-communicated positioning strategy ensures that your product's unique value is consistently understood by your target audience, from your marketing campaigns to sales teams and customer service interactions.

Product positioning is not just about what you say but how you say it, where you say it, and who says it. Whether it's through advertising, social media, product packaging, or customer service, all communication must reinforce the product's core value and differentiators.

12.7.1 Key Channels for Communicating Product Positioning

1 **Marketing Campaigns**
2 **Product Packaging and Design**
3 **Sales and Customer Service Teams**
4 **Digital Presence and Social Media**
5 **Internal Communication**

Let's look at each of these channels in more detail, along with real-world examples that show how successful brands have communicated their positioning effectively.

1 **Marketing Campaigns**

Marketing is often the first point of contact between your product and potential customers, so it is critical that your product positioning comes through clearly in your campaigns. Advertising should consistently highlight the key benefits, features, and values that differentiate your product from competitors.

- **Example: Tiger Beer (Singapore)** positions itself as a premium, homegrown beer brand that reflects Singapore's pride and tradition. Its marketing campaigns often emphasize local heritage and the quality of its brewing process. For instance, its 'Uncage' campaign highlighted **Tiger's** roots in Asia, showcasing the brand as a symbol of pride and resilience for the modern, urban Asian consumer. This reinforced the positioning of **Tiger Beer** as both a high-quality and culturally relevant choice for consumers who identify with its Asian origins.
- **Example: Grab** communicates its positioning as a comprehensive super app through its marketing campaigns, highlighting the convenience of using one platform for ride-hailing, food delivery, and payments. Campaigns like '**Everyday Everything**' emphasize that Grab is not just about transport but about integrating all daily needs into one seamless experience. This consistent message reinforces **Grab's** differentiation as a one-stop solution for a busy, digital-savvy Southeast Asian audience.

2 **Product Packaging and Design**

Product packaging and design play an essential role in communicating your product's positioning, especially for consumer goods. Packaging is often the first physical interaction a customer has with your product, and it needs to convey the right message about quality, value, and brand identity.

- **Example: Janice Wong (Singapore)**, a Singapore-based chocolatier and dessert artist, communicates her brand's premium positioning through elegant, artistic packaging that reflects the artistry of her creations. The packaging is not only beautiful but also evokes luxury and sophistication, reinforcing the brand's identity as a premium, high-end dessert brand. Each piece of packaging reflects **Janice Wong's** brand values of innovation, quality, and artistry.
- **Example: Udders Ice Cream** uses fun, quirky packaging to communicate its brand's adventurous and local flavour positioning. The packaging reflects the brand's bold and playful identity, with bright colours and humorous descriptions that resonate with young, adventurous consumers. This not only makes **Udders** stand out on the shelf but also reinforces its positioning as a fun and innovative brand that celebrates local flavours like durian and Chendol.

3   **Sales and Customer Service Teams**
Your sales and customer service teams play a crucial role in reinforcing your product's positioning, especially in industries where personalized service is critical. These teams must be well-versed in your product's unique value and be able to communicate it effectively to customers.

- **Example: Circles.Life,** a Singapore-based digital-first mobile network, positions itself as a customer-centric, flexible, and affordable option. Its customer service team reinforces this positioning by offering friendly, efficient service through digital channels like chatbots and apps, which align with the company's tech-savvy and customer-first brand. By ensuring that customers experience a hassle-free, responsive service, **Circles. Life** strengthens its brand promise of putting the customer in control of their mobile plan.
- **Example: Benjamin Barker,** a Singapore-based menswear brand, communicates its high-quality, tailored clothing positioning through personalized service in its stores. Sales associates are trained to provide styling advice and offer a tailored shopping experience, reinforcing the brand's premium image. This level of service ensures that customers not only purchase quality clothing but also feel they are receiving a personalized, high-end experience that matches the brand's positioning.

4   **Digital Presence and Social Media**
In today's digital world, your online presence – particularly on social media – is one of the most powerful tools for communicating your product positioning. Consistency across websites, social media platforms, and digital advertising is key to reinforcing your brand's unique identity.

- **Example: Love, Bonito,** a fashion brand targeting Asian women, effectively communicates its positioning across social media by highlighting how its clothing is specifically designed for the unique body shapes of Asian women. Through Instagram posts, influencer partnerships, and user-generated content, **Love, Bonito** showcases real women wearing their designs, reinforcing the message that their clothing is made for the modern Asian woman. Their digital campaigns consistently reflect their brand values of inclusivity, style, and cultural relevance.
- **Example: Carousell,** a Singapore-based peer-to-peer marketplace, uses social media to promote its core values of sustainability and community. Campaigns often feature stories of users who have successfully bought and sold pre-loved items, emphasizing the brand's positioning as a sustainable alternative to traditional e-commerce platforms. **Carousell's** use of user stories, sustainability tips, and community-focused content on platforms like Facebook and Instagram reinforces its value as a community-driven marketplace for environmentally conscious consumers.

5 **Internal Communication**
Before your positioning message reaches the public, it must be well-communicated internally to ensure alignment across all departments, from product development to marketing and sales. This helps ensure that every aspect of the product, including design, features, customer support, and marketing, reflects the same core message.

- **Example: Shopee**, as a major e-commerce player in Southeast Asia, positions itself as the most convenient and cost-effective online shopping platform. Internally, the company ensures that all teams – from logistics to customer support – are aligned with this positioning. By maintaining internal consistency around offering the best prices, frequent promotions, and a seamless shopping experience, **Shopee** ensures that its external communication reflects the same core values that guide its internal operations.
- Example: **Tiger Beer**'s internal communication reinforces its premium, local positioning by fostering a sense of pride in its heritage among employees. This includes internal campaigns and training that highlight the company's history and commitment to quality brewing. When employees fully understand and believe in the brand's core values, they are more effective at communicating these values to customers, whether in marketing materials or in interactions at events and promotions.

12.7.2 *Key Takeaways: Communicating Product Positioning*

1 **Consistency Across Channels**: Your product positioning should be consistently communicated across all channels – marketing, packaging, customer service, digital platforms, and internal communications. This ensures that customers receive the same message, reinforcing the brand identity and building trust.
2 **Tailored Messaging**: While the core positioning message should remain the same, it should be tailored to fit the medium. For example, social media messaging may be more casual and interactive, while in-store communications should be more personalized and service-oriented.
3 **Internal Alignment**: Ensuring that all internal teams understand and embrace the positioning is crucial. When internal teams are aligned with the brand's positioning, they can work together to deliver a cohesive and consistent customer experience.
4 **Storytelling and Authenticity**: Brands that effectively communicate their positioning often use storytelling to connect with their audience on an emotional level. Whether through user stories, heritage campaigns, or influencer partnerships, storytelling makes the brand's positioning feel more authentic and relatable.

By effectively communicating your product's positioning across all touch-points, you ensure that customers not only understand what makes your product unique but also trust that it consistently delivers on that promise. This consistency builds brand loyalty, drives customer engagement, and strengthens your market position.

12.8 Measuring the Effectiveness of Product Positioning

Once you've crafted and communicated your product positioning, it's essential to measure its effectiveness to ensure it resonates with your target market and differentiates your product from competitors. Product positioning is not static; it must be regularly evaluated and adjusted based on customer feedback, market changes, and competitive dynamics. By tracking **key performance indicators (KPIs)** and gathering customer insights, you can determine whether your positioning strategy is working and make data-driven decisions to refine it over time.

12.8.1 Key Metrics for Measuring Product Positioning Effectiveness

1 Customer Perception and Brand Awareness
2 Sales Performance and Market Share
3 Customer Satisfaction and Loyalty
4 Competitive Benchmarking
5 Brand Sentiment and Online Reviews
6 Market Research and Focus Groups

Let's explore how to use these metrics with real-world examples of brands that successfully measure and adjust their product positioning.

1 **Customer Perception and Brand Awareness**
   One of the most direct ways to measure the effectiveness of your product positioning is by tracking how customers perceive your brand. Surveys, polls, and brand tracking studies can help determine whether customers understand your product's unique value and whether their perception aligns with your intended positioning.

   • **Example: Love, Bonito (Fashion)** regularly conducts customer surveys and brand awareness studies to measure how well its positioning as a fashion brand designed specifically for Asian women resonates with its audience. By tracking customer feedback on fit, style, and cultural relevance, the company can gauge whether its positioning is hitting the mark. Based on survey results, **Love, Bonito** might adjust its marketing campaigns or product designs to better align with customer expectations and reinforce its brand message.

2   **Sales Performance and Market Share**
An increase in sales performance and market share is a key indicator that your product positioning is resonating with customers. By tracking product sales, revenue growth, and market penetration over time, you can measure how effectively your product is positioned in the market.

- **Example: Grab (Super App)** measures the success of its positioning as an all-in-one super app by tracking its share of the Southeast Asian market in categories like ride-hailing, food delivery, and digital payments. By analysing its market share growth in each category, **Grab** can determine whether its positioning as a one-stop solution for daily services is driving increased usage across the different verticals. For example, if **Grab** sees an uptick in food delivery and digital payment users, it can confirm that its integrated services are resonating with customers.

3   **Customer Satisfaction and Loyalty**
Customer satisfaction and loyalty are strong indicators of successful product positioning. If customers are satisfied with your product and continue to make repeat purchases, it shows that your product's positioning aligns with their needs and expectations. Customer loyalty programs, retention rates, and **Net Promoter Score (NPS)** are useful metrics to track.

- **Example: Tiger Beer (Beverages)** tracks customer satisfaction and loyalty through surveys and **NPS** to measure whether its premium positioning as a high-quality, homegrown beer resonates with consumers. A high **NPS** score and positive feedback from repeat customers indicate that **Tiger Beer's** focus on quality and local heritage is driving strong brand loyalty. If **Tiger Beer** notices declining satisfaction in certain markets, it can adjust its messaging or product offerings to better meet local tastes and preferences.

4   **Competitive Benchmarking**
Regularly comparing your product's performance to competitors helps you measure the effectiveness of your positioning strategy in the broader market. Competitive benchmarking involves tracking competitor pricing, market share, customer satisfaction, and marketing strategies to see how your product stacks up.

- **Example: Circles.Life (Telecommunications)** benchmarks its flexible, no-contract mobile plans against traditional telcos like **Singtel** and **StarHub** to see how well its positioning is resonating with tech-savvy, data-hungry consumers. By comparing its customer satisfaction scores, plan pricing, and market share against these larger competitors, **Circles.Life** can evaluate whether its positioning as a customer-centric, digital-first telco is successfully capturing market share. If competitors launch similar plans or features, **Circles.Life** may need to refine its positioning to stay ahead.

5 **Brand Sentiment and Online Reviews**
Tracking brand sentiment and customer reviews online gives you real-time feedback on how your product is perceived by the market. Social media listening tools, review sites, and user-generated content can provide valuable insights into customer experiences and whether your product positioning is translating into positive sentiment.

- **Example: Carousell (Online Marketplace)** uses social media monitoring and review platforms to measure brand sentiment and gather customer feedback on its positioning as a sustainable, community-driven marketplace for buying and selling pre-loved goods. Positive reviews that highlight the ease of use, community interaction, and eco-friendliness reinforce **Carousell's** positioning. If negative reviews or comments arise about user experiences, **Carousell** can address these concerns to ensure that its positioning remains strong and aligned with customer expectations.

6 **Market Research and Focus Groups**
Market research, such as focus groups or in-depth interviews, allows you to get direct feedback from customers about your product positioning. These insights can reveal whether customers understand your product's value and how they compare it to competitors.

- **Example: Udders Ice Cream (F&B)** regularly conducts focus groups to test new flavours and gauge customer perceptions of its adventurous, locally inspired ice cream offerings. By getting feedback on new flavours and understanding how customers perceive the brand's playful, bold identity, **Udders** can adjust its positioning to better meet the expectations of its adventurous consumer base. Focus groups also help **Udders** identify new trends in local tastes, allowing the brand to stay ahead of the competition by constantly refreshing its flavour lineup.

12.8.2 Refining Product Positioning Based on Insights

Once you've gathered data from these various sources, it's essential to analyse the insights and refine your positioning strategy if necessary. Here are some ways to adjust your positioning based on feedback:

1 **Adjust Messaging**: If customer surveys or focus groups reveal that customers don't fully understand your product's unique value, consider refining your messaging to make your positioning clearer and more compelling.

2 **Evolve Product Features:** If competitive benchmarking or market research shows that competitors are offering features that better meet customer needs, consider evolving your product's features to maintain your competitive edge.

3 **Reinforce Strengths:** If your product's positioning is resonating well with a particular audience segment, consider focusing more marketing efforts on that group to drive deeper engagement and loyalty.

4 **Respond to Trends:** If social media listening or online reviews indicate shifting consumer preferences, adjust your positioning to capitalize on emerging trends. This could mean repositioning your product to align with new consumer values, such as sustainability or technology.

12.8.3 *Key Takeaways: Measuring and Refining Product Positioning*

1 **Use Multiple Metrics:** Don't rely on just one source of data. Combine insights from sales performance, customer feedback, brand sentiment, and market research to get a comprehensive view of your product positioning's effectiveness.

2 **Track Progress Over Time:** Positioning effectiveness is not a one-time measurement. Regularly monitor key metrics to ensure your product's positioning stays relevant and resonates with the market.

3 **Be Ready to Pivot:** Markets change, competitors evolve, and customer preferences shift. Stay agile and be ready to refine your positioning strategy when these data indicate a need for change.

By continuously measuring and refining your product positioning, you can ensure that your product remains competitive, resonates with your target audience, and delivers on the promises made in your positioning statement.

12.9 Conclusion

This chapter has provided a comprehensive overview of how to develop a strong product positioning strategy, from understanding customer perceptions to applying positioning techniques that align with market opportunities. By leveraging the right strategy and finding the sweet spot where your product meets customer needs while outshining competitors, product managers can ensure that their product stands out and thrives in a competitive market.

13

SELECTING PRODUCT PRICING AND PACKAGING STRATEGIES

13.1 Introduction

Pricing and packaging strategies play a crucial role in how customers perceive the value of a product and in determining its success in the market. A well-thought-out pricing strategy ensures that the product is positioned correctly to meet customer expectations while maximizing revenue. Additionally, product packaging, both physical and digital, serves as a powerful tool for creating differentiation and driving purchasing decisions. In this chapter, we will explore various pricing models, including value-based, **ROI**, freemium, and psychological pricing, as well as strategies for using price, perception, and packaging to compete effectively in the market.

13.2 Value-Based and ROI Pricing

13.2.1 Value-Based Pricing

How can you, as a product manager, help your company avoid setting prices that are either too high for the customer, or lower than what they would be willing to pay if they knew the real value or benefits of using the product?

To help answer this question, and determine an appropriate pricing strategy, you can make use of two common pricing strategies: value-based pricing and Return on Investment, or **ROI**, pricing.

Value-based pricing is a strategy that sets prices based on the perceived value a product delivers to customers, rather than on production costs or market rates. This approach works especially well when your product offers

DOI: 10.1201/9781003484295-13

a clear and quantifiable benefit to customers, such as improved efficiency, cost savings, or emotional satisfaction.

How it works: The price of the product is set according to how much value the customer places on the product's benefits. This strategy requires a deep understanding of your customers' needs and what they are willing to pay for the specific value your product delivers.

- **Example**: **Apple** employs value-based pricing for its **iPhones** and **Mac-Books**. **Apple** justifies its premium pricing by offering a superior user experience, cutting-edge technology, and a strong brand image. Customers are willing to pay a higher price because they perceive the product as being of higher value compared to competitors.

What's essential to understand is that the perception of value changes over time.

Let's take a look at an interesting example of how the perception of value can change over time, and as a result impact price.

We'll do this by exploring the evolution of the perceived value of lobsters. Let's chart the lobster's journey from prison food to fine dining delicacy over the past four centuries using Figure 13.1.

In the 17th century, lobsters were so abundant that they weren't considered to be of much value. In fact, they were often fed to the prisoners and therefore, as you can imagine, they had a low perceived value by the public.

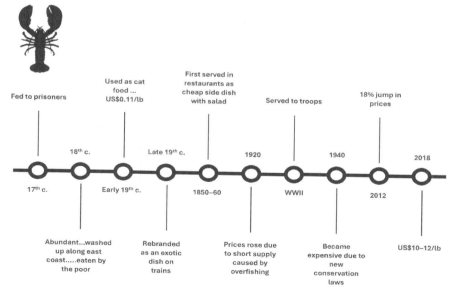

FIGURE 13.1   A lobster's journey

Similarly, in the 18th century, lobsters were so common that they were considered 'low class'. At the time they were mostly eaten by people who couldn't afford alternatives.

During the 19th century, however, some enterprising companies began canning and shipping lobster – across the sea from the United States to Europe and all over the United States, by rail. This contributed to an increase in demand, as customers bought canned lobster. Thus, the perceived value of lobster began to increase as it was traded as a canned good and bought and sold across the globe.

By the late 19th century, some business-savvy companies began serving lobster in dining cars on trains. They effectively managed to rebrand lobster as an exotic dish, served in luxury railway carriages, far from the coast. This further increased the perceived value of lobster.

Since then, lobster has more or less constantly climbed in value, while its stocks have been depleted, due to overfishing.

Today, due to their scarcity and high perceived value, lobster prices are extremely high. In the spring of 2018, lobsters sold for $10 to $12 a pound in the United States!

Today, the high price of lobster screams 'luxury', and lobsters are firmly entrenched as highly valuable in consumers' minds and culture.

Can you think of any other products, services, goods, or commodities that have undergone changes in perceived value?

Now, let's look at the value-based pricing strategy and how it could look for a typical new product to be sold by Company X, as shown in Figure 13.2.

To determine a value-based strategy for a product, you start with a cost-plus approach; this gets you to the starting price.

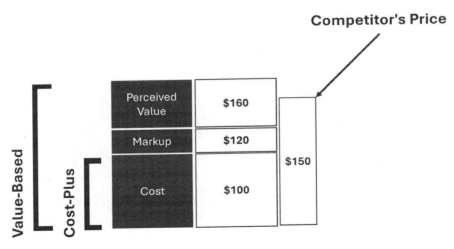

FIGURE 13.2 Value-based pricing

To do so, you add a percentage markup to the unit cost of the product. As a simple illustration, let's say the cost of developing the new product is $100 per unit.

To obtain a sustainable business model for the company, you require a 20% margin, which then sets the price at $120. This is your cost-plus starting price.

The next step in determining your value-based pricing strategy, is to align your price with what your customers would be willing to pay. This will be based on a detailed market analysis, which includes competitive analysis and customer perception mapping.

Assuming that the price of your closest competitor's product is $150, and customers perceive your product as a better-quality product, then you may set the price point of $160 or higher for your product.

Let's explore in the next section on another key consideration when setting a price for your product, which is the company's expected return on investment, or ROI.

13.2.2   ROI-Based Pricing

ROI (Return on Investment) pricing focuses on the financial returns that customers can achieve by using your product. This approach is particularly common in **B2B** markets where the product or service helps the customer generate more revenue or reduce costs.

How it works: The price is determined based on the expected **ROI** that the product will deliver to the customer. If a product significantly increases efficiency or revenue for a business, the price can be set higher because the customer's **ROI** justifies the cost.

- **Example: Salesforce** uses ROI-based pricing for its CRM software. The price is set based on the value it provides in terms of improving sales management, customer retention, and business growth. Since companies can see a measurable increase in sales and efficiency, they are willing to pay more for the platform.

A Simple Pricing Formula:

Below shows a simple pricing formula that Company X that is planning to sell a new product could use to set a price, using an **ROI** pricing strategy.

$$\text{Price} = (\text{ROI} \times \text{Investment Cost}) / \text{Units Sold} + \text{Unit Cost} = \text{Price}$$

Let's assume Company X wants to achieve an **ROI** of 30%. And, let's say it wants to make use of its in-house capability to build the product. To cover development costs as well as new hardware and software, building the product would cost them $500,000 – this is their investment cost.

To hit their mark of 30% **ROI**, they aim to sell 2,000 units. Remember earlier, we said the unit cost was $100. So, we place both numbers 2,000 and 100 into the formula.

So, according to the calculation, Company X would need to set their price at $175 per unit in order to achieve 30% **ROI**, by selling 2,000 units.

$$\text{Price} = \left(30\% \times \$500,000\right) / 2,000 + \$100 = \$175$$

It's important to note that pricing is not a decision you make once. In fact, you may need to test out different price points in the market, based on other factors, such as the demand for your product, or the number of buyers. Ultimately, you'll arrive at an optimal price.

A value-based pricing strategy helps product managers communicate to the market what they think a product is worth. One key challenge in communicating this value perception is making sure that your product stands out from your competition in the market. You can make informed pricing decisions by using market analysis, competitive analysis, and product positioning.

You also learned about **ROI** pricing, which is a popular profitability metric used to evaluate how well an investment has performed. If you use this method, remember to account for the time value of money!

13.3   Freemium Pricing

According to Phil Libin, the former CEO of **Evernote**, a free-to-use note-taking app, 'The easiest way to get one million people paying, is to get one billion people using'.

Evernote's business model typifies the freemium strategy, where customers are able to use a basic version of the product or service for free, but must pay to use additional, or premium features or services.

One of the key advantages of this model is that the free version attracts a large number of customers.

Freemium pricing is a popular model, particularly in the software and digital services industry, where users get basic features for free and must pay for premium features or additional functionality. The goal of freemium pricing is to attract a large user base with the free tier and then convert a portion of those users into paying customers.

How it works: The free version offers enough value to draw in users, but the premium version provides enhanced features that are worth paying for. This strategy works well when there is a clear differentiation between free and paid offerings, and when users can see the incremental benefits of upgrading.

Let's take a look at four examples of products that use the freemium model successfully: **Skype**, **Dropbox**, **Spotify**, and **LinkedIn**. When you hear the names **Skype**, **Dropbox**, and **Spotify**, what do you think? Probably: free phone calls, free storage space, and free music streaming. Well, you're not far off!

- **Skype,** a widely used communication platform, offers a freemium model where users can make voice and video calls to other **Skype** users for free. The free version of **Skype** allows users to conduct basic communication services, including group calls, screen sharing, and messaging. However, to access more advanced features – such as calling landlines and mobile phones, or sending SMS messages – users need to purchase **Skype** credits or subscribe to a premium plan. This differentiation between free and paid features drives users who require more versatile communication options to upgrade, creating a steady revenue stream.
- **Dropbox** also uses the freemium model, offering free cloud storage with limited space, while users can pay for additional storage and premium features. This allows **Dropbox** to acquire a large user base, some of whom convert to paid plans as their storage needs grow.
- **Spotify** uses a freemium model by offering a free version of its music streaming service with ads, while the premium version provides ad-free listening, offline downloads, and higher-quality audio. Many users are drawn to the free version initially, but a significant percentage upgrade to premium once they experience the limitations of the free tier.
- **LinkedIn,** the professional networking platform, uses a freemium pricing model by offering basic networking and job search functionality for free. Users can create profiles, connect with other professionals, and browse job postings without paying. However, **LinkedIn's** premium subscription (**LinkedIn Premium**) offers additional features such as access to more detailed insights on who viewed your profile, InMail messaging for contacting users outside your network, and advanced job search filters. The premium service also includes **LinkedIn Learning** for skill development. This freemium approach allows **LinkedIn** to attract millions of free users while converting some of them to paid members who see the value in upgrading for better networking and career opportunities.

The common goal that these four examples share is using the freemium strategy to show customers the value of the product and keep them wanting more. As they try out the free essential features, they learn just how useful the product is to them. And once they see that value, they will happily pay more for the premium features.

Another useful strategy often employed in a freemium model is to offer a free trial for a limited period of time. Then, nudge users to upgrade to the premium version. This is a good way to show freemium users what premium features they're missing out on, by not subscribing to the premium plan.

For example, in 2018 **Spotify** offered users a 60-day premium trial for free. During the trial period, users were given enough time to get accustomed to some of the premium features, such as unlimited skips, offline playlists, and the ability to play an album in its usual order – without the shuffle button firmly on lock.

Once accustomed to such experiences, the users of the free trial found it hard to go back to the free plan, which comes with annoying, unskippable advertisements.

You've seen how the freemium model allows a company to scale up and attract customers. By offering a free version to new users, you can show them the value of your product first, and then if they like it, they will tell others about it. Then, you can draw them to your premium package or plan, by offering a limited free trial to show them what else they're missing out on.

It's important to note that offering a service for free does not necessarily guarantee success every time, though! The free offer must appeal to NEW users. And, it must satisfy the needs of EXISTING, and POTENTIAL customers. More importantly, the target users must include those with buying potential.

You've seen how several successful products, like **Skype, Dropbox, Spotify**, and **LinkedIn**, all use the freemium pricing model successfully.

Can you think of any other products that you use, or know about, that use a freemium pricing strategy?

Imagine using this strategy for your product. How would you ensure that your customers see the value of your product as they interact with a free version? And then, how would you get them to upgrade to the paid premium plan, which offers them more value?

13.4 Psychological Pricing

Psychological pricing refers to strategies that leverage human psychology to make prices more attractive or encourage specific buying behaviours. These strategies can significantly influence how customers perceive the value of a product and their willingness to make a purchase.

Have you ever walked into a store to buy something, and walked out later to realize you just blew your budget? Or have you bought a big-ticket item and later had second thoughts about whether you made the right decision?

If you have, then maybe you'd feel better if I told you it wasn't your fault! Various psychological pricing strategies are used to encourage you to spend more than you intend on products or services.

In this section, you'll learn about two different ways of explaining how buyers make decisions: 'buying psychology', and 'buying rationale'. Then, I'll move on to explain some common pricing tactics that rely on understanding the psychology of buyers, using Figure 13.3.

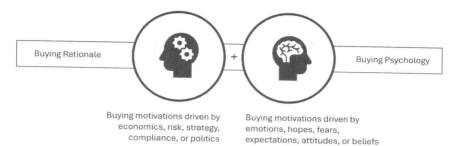

Buying Rationale + Buying Psychology

Buying motivations driven by economics, risk, strategy, compliance, or politics

Buying motivations driven by emotions, hopes, fears, expectations, attitudes, or beliefs

FIGURE 13.3   How people make buying decisions

Why do customers buy one product over another? And how do you get a customer to come back and buy again?

Well, there are many reasons, but a key to answering these questions lies in the subconscious part of the mind. Without always knowing it, people are driven by their emotions. This is no different when it comes to buying products and paying for services: people spend money for emotional reasons – often without realizing it.

People often make purchases based on emotion, and then find 'rational' reasons to justify their purchases. In fact, consumer surveys show that in most cases 20% of the decision to purchase something is logical or rational, while as much as 80% is emotional.

Different customers are motivated by different things. Some are motivated primarily by emotions, hopes, fears, expectations, attitudes, or beliefs. These motivations are termed 'buying psychology'.

On the other hand, motivations like economics, risk, and strategy are referred to as 'buying rationale'.

Whatever a customer's motivation for buying a product, your pricing and marketing should appeal to their motivations.

To illustrate this, let's consider a scenario. Two new customers, Carla and Jane, walk into a local gym to apply for a one-year membership. Carla opts for an annual payment plan of 1,200 dollars, while Jane goes for a monthly payment plan of 100 dollars a month. Who do you think is more likely to work out on a regular basis?

Rationally, you might think that both are equally likely to work out on a regular basis; after all they're both paying the same total amount for the same benefits. However, research done by a Harvard professor showed that Jane is actually more likely to exercise at the gym than Carla is.

You see, Carla initially feels the need to get her money's worth early in her membership, but that emotional drive actually decreases over the one-year period. Jane, on the other hand, will be constantly reminded of her monthly payment – every time it comes off her bank account – and so will continually feel the need to get her money's worth by exercising more regularly.

From the gym's point of view, Jane will also be more likely to renew her membership when the year is over.

You've seen how emotions play a significant role in influencing buyers' decisions. As such, product managers can leverage this 'buying psychology' to appeal to people's emotional motivations, thereby making better pricing decisions for their products and services.

Let's now look at some common pricing tactics that rely on buying psychology:

- **Charm Pricing**: This strategy involves pricing products slightly below a round number (e.g., $9.99 instead of $10). This small difference can make a product appear cheaper, even though the actual price difference is minimal. When people see 9 dollars and 99 cents, as opposed to 10 dollars, they perceive 9 dollars and 99 cents to be the cheaper option. This is because of 'left-digit bias'. Left-to-right readers are biassed towards the first digit that they read: in this case, the 9. So even though the difference between 9 dollars 99 cents and 10 dollars is tiny, the difference is perceived to be larger because we read the '9' and focus on that. In other words, our brains are telling us that the price is closer to 9, than it is to 10.

  - **Example: KFC** often prices its menu items using charm pricing, like $9.95 or $11.95 for a meal, to make the price seem more appealing.

- **Decoy Pricing**: Decoy pricing involves offering a third, less attractive option to make one of the other options seem more favourable by comparison. This tactic helps guide customers towards a higher-priced item that delivers better value.

  - **Example: The Straits Times**, a leading newspaper in Singapore, utilizes decoy pricing in its subscription plans to influence customer choices. In the face of declining physical newspaper sales and print advertising revenue, The Straits Times introduced the concept of 'Premium' articles in February 2018. Under this new system, articles with the Premium tag can only be accessed by paying subscribers. **There were** three subscription plans available: (1) Basic Digital for $14.90/month, (2) All-Digital for $29.90/month, and (3) All-Digital + Print for $29.90/month. The All-Digital option acted as a decoy, making the All-Digital + Print bundle appear as the best value. The decoy option increases the perceived value of the Print + All-Digital Bundle, leading more customers to choose that option, which aligns with the company's goal of increasing digital engagement. This strategic use of decoy pricing helps Straits Times nudge customers towards the more comprehensive plan without reducing the price of the premium bundle.

- **Anchoring**: Anchoring involves showing a higher-priced item first to make subsequent options seem more affordable by comparison. This technique influences customers' perception of value, as they are more likely to consider a lower-priced option after seeing a higher one.

  - **Example: Apple** anchors its pricing for new **iPhone** models by first showing the highest-priced version with all the bells and whistles, making the less expensive versions seem more reasonable in comparison.

13.5 Exotic Names

Another pricing tactic that relies on an understanding of buying psychology is the use of exotic names. This refers to a strategy where the product is given an apparently exotic, or rare name in order to increase its perceived value.

If a wine is hard to pronounce, is it worth more?

In a study at Brock University in Canada, researchers found that on average: people were willing to pay two dollars more for a wine because of the sound of its name!

Specifically, they tended to place more value on a hard-to-pronounce brand name, instead of one they could pronounce more easily.

In the study, three groups of participants were given the same wine, but for each group, the wine was given a different name. One had a somewhat Greek-sounding name: Titakis. The second sounded somewhat French, with the name Tselepou. And the third, which was the control group, had no name. Figure 13.4 shows the same wine served to three different groups of users that resulted in different prices that the users are willing to pay.

After the participants tasted the wine, they were asked three questions. How much do you like the wine? How keen would you be to buy it? And how much would you be willing to pay?

The results demonstrate the effects of an exotic name. The control group, where the wine had no name, valued the wine at 12 to 13 dollars a bottle. But, named 'Titakis', the wine was valued at 14 dollars a bottle. And when

| $14 | $16 | $12–13 |

| Titakis | Tselepou | No name |

FIGURE 13.4 Exotic = Value

it was named 'Tselepou', – even harder to pronounce – it was valued at 16 dollars a bottle!

The findings of this study suggest that unfamiliar, or exotic sounds imply scarcity, or rarity, and desirability. Thus, they command a higher price because they are perceived to be of more value.

Understanding that consumers are motivated by emotion and buying psychology when they make purchases, is key to using psychological pricing strategies. While some customers may think more rationally about their purchases than others do, and while some purchases may be rationally driven, very often people make purchases based on emotion and other reasons that they aren't always aware of.

In order to leverage psychological pricing strategies, you'll need to develop a thorough understanding of your target market, in terms of how they make decisions about the products they purchase.

You can also use tried-and-tested pricing tactics, like charm prices and exotic names to appeal to the ways in which people make decisions about the products they buy.

Now, think about the most recent product you purchased. How did you decide to buy that particular product? Do you think it was a rational decision? If not, what affected your choice and do you think there is anything you can learn from how the product was priced, packaged, labelled, or marketed?

13.6 Using Price, Perception, and Value to Compete in the Market

Many companies compete with each other by lowering their prices. In a price war, where competitors with similar products compete for customers by continually lowering prices, the only real winner is the customer. Always.

In today's digital world, where the availability of information has become the norm, customers make more informed choices when selecting from among the many competing products.

As a result, acquiring customers has become increasingly difficult for many companies. Often they resort to price wars in a bid to woo the customers. However, companies can make costly mistakes by choosing to compete on the basis of low prices.

In a competitive market, companies use different pricing strategies to win over customers, while fighting off competitors. Increasingly, price is the weapon of choice – and once it is used, it can often degenerate into a price war.

In this section you'll explore two examples that illustrate two different approaches to competing for customers. In one, two companies engage in a price war, and in the other two companies focus on other means of acquiring customers. Both illustrate the importance of understanding customer perception. Then, we will explore how to align price with perceived value and use it as a tool to position your product strategically in the market.

13.6.1 Xbox vs. PlayStation

Let's take a look at an example. When the original **Xbox** was released in 2001, it was **Microsoft's** first foray into the gaming console market. After the product was launched in the United States in November 2001, Microsoft launched it in Japan, Australia, and Europe in 2002.

However, due to poor sales, **Microsoft** lowered the price barely 4 weeks after the launch.

Then **Sony** – their biggest rival at the time – cut the prices of their new console, the **PlayStation 2**. In response to Sony's price cuts, **Microsoft** made a further price cut to its **Xbox**.

Instead of immediately attracting lots of customers, as **Microsoft** had expected, their additional price cut halted customer uptake. Customers decided to wait further in anticipation of further price cuts, hoping for an even better deal.

When competing on price alone, your customers will quickly realize that all they have to do is signify that another company's pricing is just a little bit better than yours, and wait for your price to drop.

So, if your competitor decides to undercut their prices to beat yours, you can choose not to play their game. Instead, by maintaining your prices and basing the pricing of your products on value, your company can still win.

Instead of engaging in price wars, product managers should focus on figuring out how to make their products different and worthwhile, showcasing that value to their customers. In other words, focus on customer perception, not on who has the cheapest product!

13.6.2 Apple vs. Samsung

Now, let's take a look at how **Samsung** and **Apple** compete in the smartphone market. Instead of engaging in price wars, both companies compete on improving customer experience, by fulfilling different needs.

You could say that **Samsung** competes in the market by aiming for breadth, while **Apple** competes by aiming for depth. In other words, **Samsung's** strategy is based on quantity, which is why it has such a wide range of smartphones. **Apple's** strategy, on the other hand, is based on quality, not quantity. Hence its strict mobile-app approval process.

Apple competes by building long-term relationships through value and customer experiences. Unlike **Apple**, **Samsung** wins over her customers through innovative products, with a broad range of phones in different shapes and sizes, offered at very attractive prices. Here, we see that pricing is only one element among a few in the competition between the two companies, each making use of her own core strengths to win in the smartphone market.

Customers will want to buy your products when they offer features, support, and services that the other companies cannot offer. You will avoid a costly price war by choosing to improve your customer's experience and fulfilling these needs.

Unlike the price war between **Sony** and **Microsoft**, when the two companies tried to undercut one another's prices for their respective gaming consoles, **Apple** and **Samsung** each uses a different way of competing in the market.

Instead of a price war, these two smartphone companies compete for market share by taking different approaches to value and customer experience. **Apple's** customers know the value of the **Apple** brand so they are willing to pay for a premium product. On the other hand, **Samsung** often offers consumers a wide range of products at very attractive prices.

While **Apple** creates customer loyalty by making her customers happy with their only iPhone product, **Samsung** does it by introducing innovative features and guiding them how to better use the product.

By knowing the perceived value of your own product, and pricing based on that value, you'll ensure your customers realize your product's value and how it differs from your competitors. If you succeed in showing your customers a reason to pay more, you can also create customer loyalty with a superior product.

Now, consider your own new product, and reflect on how you can use value-based pricing to win your customers.

13.6.3 Key Strategies for Using Price, Perception, and Value

Price is not just a number – it is closely tied to customer perception and the perceived value of your product. To compete effectively, your pricing must reflect how customers perceive the value of your offering in relation to competitors. The key is to align price with perceived value and use it as a tool to position your product strategically in the market.

- **Price-Value Alignment:** The price must be aligned with the value the customer perceives. If the product is priced too high compared to its perceived value, customers will likely choose a competitor. Conversely, if the product is priced too low, customers may question its quality.

  - **Example: Singapore Airlines** consistently aligns its premium pricing with its brand perception of luxury, superior service, and comfort. Customers are willing to pay more for the premium experience because they perceive the value of the service to be significantly higher than lower-priced competitors.

- **Competing on Value, Not Price:** Competing solely on price can lead to price wars and erode profitability. Instead, businesses should focus on delivering superior value. This involves providing features, customer service, or additional benefits that justify a higher price.

  - **Example: Benjamin Barker,** a local menswear brand, competes not just on the price of its clothing but on the superior value it offers in terms of quality, craftsmanship, and personalized service. The higher price is justified by the tailored experience and premium fabric quality, which differentiates it from lower-cost alternatives.

- **Tiered Pricing:** Offering different price tiers for various product versions allows companies to cater to different segments of the market. Customers can choose the version that aligns with their budget and perceived value.

  - **Example: Shopee** uses tiered pricing by offering a variety of products from low-cost items to higher-end goods. By providing options across different price ranges, **Shopee** attracts a broad customer base while ensuring each segment perceives the value they're paying for.

13.7 Product Packaging Strategies

Packaging plays a crucial role in influencing customer perceptions of value and quality. It's not just about aesthetics – effective packaging can differentiate your product from competitors, enhance brand perception, and drive purchasing decisions.

13.7.1 Why Are We Willing to Pay More

Why are customers willing to pay more for some products, than they are for others?

One of the key reasons lies in how your product is packaged or delivered. When we talk about product packaging, we are not just talking about the physical packaging used to protect your product. We are talking about how customers perceive and engage with your product. Packaging refers to everything that affects the experience your customers have with your product – from purchase, to delivery; from usage, to maintenance and support; and even to how the product is replaced or upgraded.

Thus, packaging includes the cardboard box it comes in, but it can also refer to the way customers purchase the product online, how it gets to their house, how they install it, how it gets used, and much more. All of these aspects of your product have a profound effect on how your product is perceived.

In this section, you'll first explore some of the key reasons that customers are willing to pay more for the way in which a product is packaged, delivered, or supported. Then, we'll explore iTunes' packaging strategy to demonstrate **Apple's** successful understanding of how customers value convenience when it comes to packaging.

Today, we see more and more companies are moving their traditional businesses to the online world. Many of these companies seek to meet customers' new expectations, in terms of ease-of-purchase and the convenience associated with having products delivered to their doors.

Some of the key reasons that customers are willing to pay more for a product, based on how it's packaged to meet their expectations, are listed in Figure 13.5.

Firstly, the product is easier to buy. Perhaps because there is a seamless process on the companies' website and customers are able to make their purchases in a convenient manner.

Secondly, customers value time. This is reflected in the fact that they'll pay more for products that arrive more quickly. As much as 61% of shoppers are in fact willing to pay extra for the convenience that same-day delivery brings, which highlights that customers don't like to be kept waiting and value convenience. From a business perspective, the value of same-day delivery can be a helpful way of increasing your sales volume. There's nothing more convenient for consumers than receiving their orders directly on-site. This level of

FIGURE 13.5 Packaging: Why are we willing to pay more

service, which goes hand-in-hand with same-day delivery, can give you a lot of repeat business from customers.

Products that bring customers prestige are also something that they'll pay more for.

Another reason is a low cost of ownership. This typically refers to the costs associated with installing, or establishing the product. For example, in the **MobileLinQ's** assistive listening product case, universities look at what it will cost them to integrate **MobileListen** into their existing infrastructure. We already know that one of **MobileListen's** selling points is its low cost of ownership, because it integrates very easily with existing infrastructure which means universities don't have to pay for additional hardware or software. For that ease-of-integration, or low cost of ownership, they'll actually be willing to pay more for the product itself.

Friendly customer service is another aspect of how the product is packaged, or perceived. Customers will also pay more for a product that is supported by friendly and efficient customer service.

Customers will also pay more for a better user experience. If, for example, your product offers an easier overall user experience than a competitor's does, then the value of yours will be perceived as greater.

Lastly, a sustainable product that provides environmental, social, and economic benefits while protecting public health and environment over their whole lifecycle is a key factor that affects customers' perception, and therefore what they're willing to spend on your product. More and more people are expressing their concerns about sustainability, through changes in lifestyle and product choices. As such, companies are also taking corporate responsibility more seriously and many are building their products to contribute to sustainability and to society.

13.7.2   How Apple Leverages Its iTunes Packaging

A good example of a company that leverages packaging to add value for customers and users, is **Apple**. Let's look at how they create value through new experiences related to how they package their iTunes product, as shown in Figure 13.6.

The rise of digital music has impacted the way we buy and listen to music. With the launch of the **iPod** and **iTunes**, **Apple** unlocked a new market – or 'blue ocean' – in digital music.

iTunes offered legal, easy-to-use, and highly flexible à-la-carte song downloads. By allowing people to pick and choose individual songs and pricing them reasonably, iTunes broke a key customer annoyance factor: the need to purchase an entire CD when they wanted only one or two songs on it.

FIGURE 13.6 Packaging: The new sound of value

Coupled with the **iPod** and **iPhone,** which enabled customers to keep thousands of songs in their pockets, and the ease of online mobile purchases, **Apple** was able to dominate the digital music market for more than a decade.

13.7.3 Types of Packaging Strategies

- **Luxury Packaging:** Premium products often use luxury packaging to reinforce their high value. High-quality materials, elegant designs, and careful attention to detail in packaging can signal that the product is worth the higher price.

  - **Example:** TWG Tea in Singapore uses luxurious packaging that emphasizes elegance and sophistication. The gold and black designs of its tea canisters reflect the brand's premium positioning, and customers often associate the product's high price with its upscale packaging.

- **Sustainable Packaging:** With growing environmental awareness, many consumers prefer products with eco-friendly packaging. Sustainable packaging can differentiate your brand and align with the values of environmentally conscious customers.

  - **Example:** **Lush** uses minimal and eco-friendly packaging for its beauty products, which reinforces the brand's commitment to sustainability. The use of recycled materials and packaging-free options helps **Lush** stand out to customers who prioritize sustainability in their purchasing decisions.

- **Minimalist Packaging:** In some industries, simplicity can be a sign of high quality. Minimalist packaging focuses on clean designs and limited text, which can appeal to consumers who prefer modern, sleek aesthetics.

- **Example: Muji**, a Japanese home goods and apparel brand, uses minimalist packaging to emphasize simplicity and functionality. This resonates with customers who value understated design and practical products, reinforcing the brand's unique identity.

- **Functional Packaging:** Packaging can also enhance the product experience by being practical and functional. In industries like food and electronics, ease of use and innovative design in packaging can be a significant selling point.

- **Example: Bento Box** packaging in Singapore's food delivery scene is often designed with convenience in mind. The compartments in bento boxes keep food items separate, making it easy for customers to enjoy their meals without needing extra utensils or dishes.

You've seen that product packaging helps companies influence customer perception in their buying decisions. You've also seen some of the key reasons that customers are willing to pay more for the way in which a product is packaged, delivered, or supported.

Apple is one example of a company that has successfully leveraged product packaging to create new experiences for customers in the digital space. Its customers were paying for the actual songs, but they were also paying for the way in which those songs could be downloaded: legally; with an easy-to-use experience; and most importantly – flexibly, as individual songs, free from the other songs on a CD.

Now, consider some of your favourite products. What is it about their packaging, or the way in which you receive or use them, that adds value or enhances your experience? Do you pay more for those products because of those aspects?

13.8 Conclusion

Selecting the right pricing and packaging strategies is essential for ensuring that your product meets customer expectations while driving revenue and market success. Pricing is not just about numbers – it is a powerful tool for shaping customer perceptions and creating value. From value-based and **ROI** pricing, which align price with the perceived benefits, to the freemium model that attracts users with a free tier and converts them to paying customers, every pricing strategy has a role to play depending on the product and market context.

Psychological pricing tactics such as charm pricing, decoy pricing, and anchoring demonstrate how subtle adjustments can influence customer decisions, while tiered pricing allows you to cater to different customer segments by offering various levels of service or features. Additionally, your packaging strategy, whether luxurious, sustainable, minimalist, or functional, is a crucial aspect of delivering value and differentiating your product in the market.

Ultimately, the right combination of pricing and packaging helps your product stand out, appeal to the right customers, and reinforce the value you offer. By understanding customer needs, competitive dynamics, and market expectations, you can use these strategies to position your product for long-term success and growth.

14

CRAFTING A GO-TO-MARKET STRATEGY

14.1 Introduction

A well-executed **Go-to-Market** (GTM) strategy is critical to the success of any product launch. It ensures that your product reaches the right audience, at the right time, through the right channels, with a compelling message. By carefully considering the **5Ws and 1H** (Who, What, Where, When, Why, and How), product managers can develop a structured approach to deploying their next product in a way that resonates with customers and drives market success.

This chapter will explore how to craft a **GTM** strategy using these guiding questions and then outline seven actionable steps to build an effective **GTM** plan.

14.2 Using the 5Ws and 1H

To build a strong **GTM** strategy, you may use a simple technique such as the 5Ws and 1H as illustrated in Figure 14.1, where you need to answer the following key questions:

1 **WHO: Whom Do You Launch To?**
The first step in a **GTM** strategy is identifying the target audience. It's critical to understand **who your users are**, their pain points, and the opportunities your product offers them. Use insights from **Problem Statements**, **Personas**, and **5D Canvas** to ensure you're launching to the right segment.

- **Facebook** famously began its service by targeting college students, focusing on specific schools before expanding its reach. By the time they opened up the platform to the public, they had already achieved significant penetration in US colleges, making broader adoption easier.

DOI: 10.1201/9781003484295-14

FIGURE 14.1 Go-to-Market: 5Ws and 1H

- **YouTrip**, a Singapore-based multi-currency travel wallet, clearly identified its initial target market: **frequent travellers and digital-savvy consumers** who want a hassle-free way to manage and spend foreign currencies without incurring high conversion fees. By focusing on these consumers, **YouTrip** launched its service to users who were already facing challenges with traditional foreign exchange methods. With a focus on international travellers and those who appreciate digital payment solutions, **YouTrip** crafted its marketing and product features around the needs of its target audience, ensuring early adoption among frequent flyers and tech-savvy individuals in Singapore.

2 **WHAT: What Are You Going to Deploy?**
   The next step is to define **what** exactly you are launching. This includes identifying whether it's a new product, a major release, or an incremental update. Consider what additional components you need for a smooth launch, such as support, training, or installation assistance.

- **Thumbtack**, an online marketplace for local services, launched its platform in 2009 to provide home improvement, home inspection, home repair, and home cleaning. However, before targeting users, the founders focused on scraping and building a database of local service providers, understanding that the platform's value lay in having a supply-side ready before reaching out to customers.

- **Ohmyhome**, a Singapore-based real estate platform, provides a great example of considering the 'what' in their **GTM** strategy. Initially, **Ohmyhome** launched as a platform that facilitated **DIY** property transactions, allowing homeowners to buy, sell, or rent properties without needing an agent. However, they soon realized that some users preferred more hands-on assistance. To address this, **Ohmyhome** added a full suite of property services, including agent-assisted services, mortgage advisory, and renovation solutions. By expanding their offering to include both **DIY** and assisted services, **Ohmyhome** ensured that they were providing a comprehensive solution tailored to the varied needs of their customers, improving user experience and market penetration.

3 WHERE: Where Are You Going to Launch?

Deciding **where** to launch is a strategic decision. You might start with a small local market before expanding, testing your product in real-world conditions before scaling.

- **Uber** initially launched in San Francisco, perfecting its ride-hailing service in a single market before expanding to other cities and then globally. Their city-by-city approach allowed them to adapt their services to different market conditions and regulatory environments.
- **Glife Technologies**, a Singapore-based agri-tech company, initially launched its operations in Singapore, focusing on providing digitized supply chain solutions to help restaurants and food businesses source fresh produce directly from farms. As they perfected their product and service in Singapore, **Glife** began expanding across Southeast Asia, including markets like Malaysia, Indonesia, and Vietnam. This phased expansion allowed **Glife** to adapt its business model and technology to fit the unique demands of each regional market, ensuring sustainable growth. The company's strategy involved building strong relationships with local farmers and food businesses in each new market, creating localized supply chains that supported its mission of making farm-fresh food more accessible throughout Southeast Asia.

4 WHEN: When Are You Going to Launch?

Timing can be everything in a product launch. You need to determine **when** is the best time to go live. Consider seasonality, market readiness, competitor movements, and customer behaviour.

- **Apple** traditionally announces its new devices in late summer, aligning with back-to-school and holiday shopping periods, ensuring their products are top of mind when customers are ready to spend.

- **Carousell**, a Singapore-based online marketplace, timed its major expansion and feature rollouts around key shopping seasons. For example, the company often aligns product launches and major campaigns with festive periods such as Chinese New Year and the year-end holiday season. This allows **Carousell** to take advantage of increased consumer spending during these times, maximizing exposure and driving user engagement when people are more likely to buy or sell items. By strategically timing their feature releases and marketing pushes, **Carousell** ensured greater market impact and user acquisition.

5 **WHY: Why Should Your Customers Care?**
The 'why' is at the heart of your GTM strategy. It forces you to be **customer-centric** and to craft a compelling value proposition that communicates why customers should invest in your product.

- **Tesla's** launches are often built around clear value propositions that communicate both product benefits and company mission. For **Tesla's** electric vehicles, the 'why' has been rooted in environmental sustainability, cutting-edge technology, and a luxurious driving experience, giving customers clear reasons to care.
- **Razer**, a Singapore-founded gaming hardware company, built its brand around answering the 'why' for gamers. Their product line, which includes high-performance laptops, mice, and keyboards, is crafted to meet the specific needs of gaming enthusiasts who demand top-tier precision, speed, and aesthetics. **Razer's** value proposition centres on delivering an unparalleled gaming experience with cutting-edge technology and sleek designs. The 'why' for **Razer's** customers is clear: their products offer an edge in competitive gaming environments, where performance is crucial. By effectively communicating how their products enhance gameplay, **Razer** has built a loyal customer base that values the performance benefits their devices provide.

6 **HOW: How Are You Going to Deploy Your Product?**
This question addresses the logistics of the launch. How will the product be introduced to the market? Consider the steps you need to take, from marketing and sales to onboarding and customer support, to ensure a successful launch.

14.3   Developing a Successful Go-to-Market Strategy Plan

Now that we have framed the **Go-to-Market (GTM)** strategy with the 5Ws and 1H, let's dive into the seven steps to develop a successful **GTM** plan. Figure 14.2 shows the seven steps in developing a **GTM** plan.

① Identify Target Market	② Set Objectives and Goals	③ Develop Product Positioning	④ Choose Pricing Strategy	⑤ Create Marketing Plan	⑥ Craft Channel Strategy	⑦ Orchestrate Product Launch
• Market Opportunity • Market Factors • Market Size • Market Segments	• Strategic Alignment • Objectives and Key Results (OKRs) • SMART Goals	• Value Proposition • Elevator Pitch • Perception Mapping	• Superior Perceived Value Pricing • Value-Based Pricing • Personalized Pricing • Psychological Pricing • Packaging	• Marketing Campaign • Marketing Mix • Omni-Channel Strategy • Content Strategy • Campaign Stakeholders	• Growth Channels • Product Distribution • Distribution Channels Considerations	• Product Launch Roadmap • Pre-launch • Launch • Post-launch

FIGURE 14.2 Go-to-Market strategy plan

The **GTM Plan** is a critical roadmap for successfully launching a product into the market, and it consists of **seven key steps**. These steps provide a comprehensive framework for product managers to navigate the entire launch process, from identifying the market to introducing the product.

1 **Identify Target Market**
   A strong GTM strategy starts with understanding the **market opportunity**, defining your **market size**, and segmenting your audience.

   • **Market Opportunity**: Assess the potential for your product in the market. Is there an unmet need or a gap your product can fill?
   • **Market Size**: Define the **TAM, SAM, and SOM** (**Total Addressable Market, Serviceable Available Market, and Serviceable Obtainable Market**) to estimate the market's potential.
   • **Market Segmentation**: Segment your audience into categories based on demographic, geographic, behavioural, or psychographic data.
   • **Example**: When **Netflix** expanded internationally, it carefully assessed market opportunity and adapted its offerings to local tastes and viewing habits, demonstrating the importance of market segmentation.

2 **Set Objectives and Goals**
   Defining clear **objectives** and **goals** ensures your **GTM** strategy is aligned with your company's overall vision. Use the **OKR framework** (Objectives and Key Results) for strategic alignment, and apply **SMART goals** (Specific, Measurable, Achievable, Relevant, Time-bound) to guide the execution.

   • **Example**: **Spotify's OKR** might be to increase its subscriber base by 20% in a specific region within 12 months. **SMART** goals would break down specific actions to achieve this, such as running targeted campaigns and enhancing user retention features.

3 **Develop Product Positioning**
Product positioning defines how your product will be perceived by your target audience. Use tools like the **Elevator Pitch, Value Proposition Canvas,** and **Perception Mapping** to develop a clear and compelling position.

- **Example: Slack** positioned itself as the easy-to-use, fun alternative to traditional corporate communication tools, simplifying team collaboration while offering a playful brand identity that distinguished it from competitors like **Microsoft Teams**.

4 **Choose Pricing Strategy**
Choosing the right pricing strategy is critical to market success. Use a mix of **value-based pricing, personalized pricing, psychological pricing,** and **packaging** to maximize customer appeal and revenue.

- **Example: Straits Times** uses decoy pricing in its subscription plans, where the print-only option is priced the same as the print + digital bundle, driving customers towards the higher-value bundled offer.

5 **Create Marketing Plan**
A marketing plan drives awareness and demand for your product. Use a mix of **omni-channel marketing, content marketing,** and **campaign strategies** to engage with your audience across multiple touchpoints.

- **Example: Nike** runs integrated marketing campaigns that combine traditional media with digital platforms, user-generated content, and influencer partnerships, creating a seamless brand experience that drives engagement and loyalty.

6 **Crafting Channel Strategy**
Your **channel strategy** determines how your product reaches customers. Choose **growth channels** and a **distribution strategy** that best align with your target market.

- **Example: Apple** uses both direct-to-consumer channels (**Apple** stores and its website) and third-party retail partners to distribute its products, ensuring that it can reach a broad audience while maintaining control over the customer experience.

7 **Orchestrating Product Launch**
The product launch is the culmination of your **GTM** strategy. Develop a **product launch roadmap** with clear phases for **pre-launch, launch, and post-launch** activities to ensure everything goes smoothly.

- **Pre-launch:** Generate buzz with teasers, pre-orders, or beta programs.

- **Launch**: Announce the product with a big event, media coverage, and promotional campaigns.
- **Post-launch**: Focus on user feedback, continuous engagement, and feature enhancements to sustain momentum.
- **Example: Tesla** orchestrates its product launches with pre-launch hype (teasers and reservation lists), grand launch events (live product demos), and strong post-launch marketing (continuous updates and new features), ensuring maximum visibility and consumer engagement.

14.4 GTM Components and Key Activities

A comprehensive **GTM strategy** involves various components that ensure your product reaches the right audience, through the right channels, and with a compelling message. For any product to be successful, these components need to be carefully planned and executed with specific activities that align with your overall business objectives. This section breaks down the critical components of a **GTM** strategy and outlines the key activities required to successfully bring a product to market. By understanding and implementing these components effectively, product managers can ensure that their product not only launches successfully but also gains traction, maintains customer engagement, and grows in the market.

Table 14.1 lists the GTM strategy components and key activities.

TABLE 14.1 GTM strategy components and key activities

Component	Key Activities
Market Definition	Identify target audience through market research and surveys
	Create detailed buyer personas
	Analyse competitive landscape to identify gaps and opportunities
	Perform segmentation to target specific customer demographics
Value Proposition	Articulate unique value and differentiation relative to competitors
	Conduct customer interviews to identify core pain points
	Use the Value Proposition Canvas to align product offerings with customer needs
	Ensure alignment with overall business objectives and brand strategy

(Continued)

TABLE 14.1 (Continued)

Component	Key Activities
Product Messaging and Positioning	Develop key messaging that highlights your product's unique value
	Use perception mapping to assess where your product fits in the competitive landscape
	Craft product positioning statements that resonate with your target audience
	Align messaging with sales and marketing teams for consistent communication across all channels
Pricing Strategy	Conduct competitive pricing analysis to set optimal price points
	Consider tiered pricing models to target different customer segments
	Use value-based pricing for products with high perceived value
	Test personalized pricing models where applicable
	Develop discount strategies for early adopters and promotional campaigns
Distribution Channels	Select the most effective distribution channels based on your target audience (e.g., online, retail, direct sales)
	Manage and optimize channels based on performance metrics
	Develop partnerships or alliances to expand reach
	Implement channel-specific marketing strategies to maximize impact
Sales Strategy	Define the sales funnel and customer journey
	Create sales scripts and objection-handling techniques for sales teams
	Provide product training and onboarding resources for sales staff
	Develop incentive programs and bonuses to motivate sales teams
	Implement CRM tools to track sales performance and customer relationships
Marketing and Promotional Plans	Develop a multi-channel marketing campaign to drive product awareness (e.g., digital, social media, traditional media)
	Use content marketing to educate potential customers and generate leads
	Leverage influencer and partnership marketing for broader reach
	Plan promotional events, webinars, or launches to build excitement around the product
	Optimize marketing efforts using data analytics and customer feedback

(Continued)

TABLE 14.1 (Continued)

Component	Key Activities
Market Launch Tactics	Outline a detailed product launch timeline with milestones Create a pre-launch strategy to build anticipation (e.g., sneak peeks, beta versions, waitlists) Coordinate cross-functional teams (marketing, sales, support) to ensure a smooth launch Manage public relations and media outreach for broader visibility Implement a post-launch strategy for continued engagement and retention
Customer Support and Service	Establish customer support plans (e.g., helpdesk, live chat, onboarding materials) Develop a knowledge base and FAQs to handle common issues Implement feedback loops for continuous product improvement Create a system for tracking and responding to customer inquiries in real time Conduct regular customer satisfaction surveys and NPS to gauge service quality
Measurement and KPIs	Define key performance indicators (KPIs) to measure the success of the GTM strategy Regularly monitor metrics such as customer acquisition cost (CAC), lifetime value (LTV), and conversion rates Use A/B testing to refine messaging, pricing, and promotional strategies Create dashboards to track real-time performance of sales and marketing efforts Continuously review and adjust the strategy based on metrics and customer feedback

14.5 Conclusion

Crafting an effective **Go-to-Market** strategy involves careful planning and coordination across multiple areas, from defining your target audience to positioning your product, choosing pricing models, and executing a robust marketing and distribution strategy. By following the **5Ws** and **1H** framework and executing the seven key steps outlined in this chapter, you can ensure your product launch is successful and your product resonates with your target market.

15

THE ART OF PRODUCT PLANNING

15.1 Introduction

Product planning is the cornerstone of successful product management, enabling teams to bridge the gap between market demands, customer needs, and business goals. It involves a series of strategic and tactical processes that ensure products are developed and released effectively, aligned with both internal priorities and external expectations. Effective product planning helps businesses avoid wasted resources, delayed launches, and products that don't meet customer needs.

In this chapter, we'll explore two critical aspects of product planning: product roadmapping and release management, which are essential for laying the foundation for any product's journey from concept to market.

Product roadmapping is the visual representation of a product's evolution over time. It serves as both a planning and communication tool that enables product managers to align internal teams and external stakeholders on key deliverables and product goals. A roadmap articulates the product's vision and provides a high-level overview of how features, iterations, and releases will unfold over months or years. By dividing the roadmap into internal (detailed and tactical) and external (strategic and high-level) versions, product managers ensure that the right information reaches the right audience.

Release management is about the efficient execution of the product roadmap. It involves the meticulous planning and tracking of each release cycle, ensuring that each stage of product development is well-coordinated and on schedule. With modern Agile methodologies, release management has evolved to include flexible and iterative processes such as sprint planning, Agile estimation, and tracking tools like burndown charts. It also involves

DOI: 10.1201/9781003484295-15

defining different release phases (e.g., pre-alpha, beta, general availability) and engaging with beta users to gather real-world feedback before a full release.

Through effective product roadmapping and release management, product managers ensure alignment across all departments, reducing the risk of miscommunication and delays while enabling the product to evolve to meet market demands.

15.2   Problem Space and Solution Space

Product planning begins with a deep understanding of the **problem space** and the **solution space,** terms introduced by Dan Olsen in *The Playbook for Achieving Product-Market Fit.* Figure 15.1 illustrates how these terms relate to market and product concepts.

- **Problem Space ('The What'):** The market in which your product exists, made up of your **target customers** and their **underserved needs.** This space helps define what your product should address. According to Olsen, achieving **Product-Market Fit** occurs when there is a clear alignment between these underserved needs and the **value proposition** your product offers.
- **Solution Space ('The How'):** This covers your **product** and includes its **feature set, user experience (UX),** and the process of **testing with customers.** It outlines how your product will solve the market's problems and meet the customers' needs.

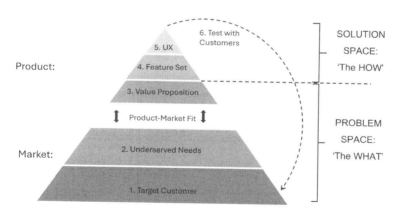

Source: The Playbook for Achieving Product-Market Fit
BY DAN OLSEN ON 13 JULY 2017

FIGURE 15.1   Problem space and solution space

As Einstein famously said, 'If I were given one hour to save the planet, I would spend 59 minutes defining the problem and one minute resolving it'. This quote highlights the importance of thoroughly understanding the **problem space** before diving into the solution space. The ability to clearly define the problem is essential to delivering a product that resonates with users and meets the business's goals.

15.3   Functionality and Value

When thinking about product planning, product managers need to understand both the functionality of the product and the value it brings to users and buyers (Figure 15.2).

Functionality: Refers to the specific features or aspects of the product that make it useful for the end user. For example, when designing a tricycle for a 5-year-old girl, the functionality might include attributes like a lightweight frame, bright and colourful design, and easy-to-turn handlebars. This ties into a product manager's role as an advocate for the customer, ensuring that the user's needs are at the forefront.

Value: Refers to the broader benefits or outcomes that the buyer seeks from the product. In the tricycle example, the buyer is the child's mother, and she may care most about factors like affordability, non-toxic materials, and safety features. Value represents the product manager's responsibility to ensure the business goals are aligned with customer expectations.

The intersection of functionality and value is where successful product planning and product opportunity occurs, and this balance forms the foundation for the product management.

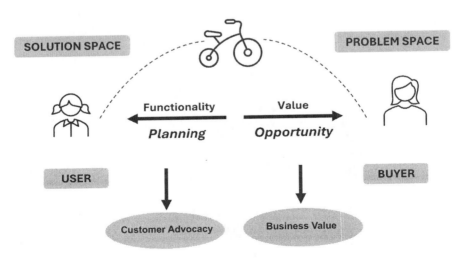

FIGURE 15.2   Functionality and value

15.4   Product Roadmapping

15.4.1   *Internal and External Roadmaps*

A company typically uses two types of roadmaps: an **internal roadmap** and an **external roadmap**.

- **Internal Roadmap:** This roadmap is detailed and often includes confidential information such as specific features, technical challenges, and precise timelines. It is shared with product development teams, sales, and internal stakeholders to coordinate efforts.
- **External Roadmap:** This version is shared with customers, investors, or the broader market. It typically omits trade secrets and confidential development details, focusing instead on high-level goals and future releases. The external roadmap is meant to excite stakeholders and demonstrate the company's commitment to long-term product development without revealing too much information to competitors.

For example, **Apple** provides high-level external roadmaps during its annual product announcement events, revealing major features and product evolution without sharing specific internal development timelines.

15.4.2   *Roadmapping Challenges*

Creating an effective product roadmap can be challenging. Below are some common roadmapping challenges and strategies to overcome them:

15.4.2.1   *Challenge 1: Fixing Dates and Scope*

Problem: One of the biggest challenges in product roadmapping is the expectation to commit to fixed release dates and a defined scope, despite the inherent uncertainties in product development. Market conditions, customer feedback, technological advancements, or internal development challenges may require changes to the roadmap. Fixing dates and scope too rigidly can lead to unrealistic expectations or result in rushed, underdeveloped features.

Solution: To solve this, product managers often create **flexible roadmaps** that accommodate changes in both **time** and **scope**. Instead of hard deadlines, a product roadmap can use **broad time horizons** such as:

- **Now:** Represents the features and initiatives that are currently being worked on or are about to be released in the near term. These are the immediate priorities that are already in development or undergoing final preparations.

- **Next:** Refers to upcoming priorities that are planned for the near future. This includes features and projects that are in the planning or design phase, expected to be worked on in the next development cycle or quarter.
- **Later:** Covers long-term goals and ideas that are further down the pipeline. These features or initiatives are more aspirational and may require more research, development, or resources before they can be started. They provide direction but aren't yet ready for active development.

This level of flexibility allows product managers to adjust as new information becomes available or as unforeseen issues arise.

An alternative approach to structuring a flexible product roadmap is to use **quarters of the year** as time frames. This method divides the roadmap into **Q1, Q2, Q3, and Q4,** corresponding to each quarter of the calendar or fiscal year. This format allows for a more specific yet flexible timeline that helps teams prioritize work over shorter time periods, such as t3-month intervals. Using quarterly designations enables stakeholders to see what will be delivered within a defined time frame while still allowing for adjustments based on evolving market conditions, technical challenges, or changing priorities. For example, features targeted for Q1 might be firm and ready for release, while those in Q3 or Q4 could remain flexible and adaptable to change as development progresses. This quarterly approach can help synchronize efforts across teams, ensuring alignment with other business functions such as marketing, sales, and finance.

- **Example: Spotify** often uses broad timelines for product updates. The company outlines features that are 'in progress' or 'coming soon' without specifying exact dates. This allows Spotify to continuously evolve based on user feedback and technological shifts, while also keeping its roadmap adaptable.
- **Example:** A great example of using **quarterly planning** for a product roadmap comes from **Atlassian,** the company behind tools like Jira, Trello, and Confluence. Atlassian uses a quarterly based roadmap to structure its product releases and internal development milestones.

  For instance, Atlassian outlines its feature development across multiple quarters (Q1, Q2, Q3, Q4), helping the team focus on what's immediately next while leaving room for flexibility in later quarters. Atlassian's quarterly approach also aligns with their Agile development methodology, where features are prioritized for upcoming sprints but categorized into broader quarterly goals.

  In this model, features for Q1 might be almost finalized and ready for release, while Q2 and Q3 represent work that is still being scoped and developed. Q4 could include longer-term initiatives or strategic projects that require more research and may shift in priority as the year progresses.

This structure allows Atlassian to keep both internal teams and external stakeholders informed of the product's development while maintaining flexibility for future changes.

- **Example: Microsoft** has a transparent external roadmap for Office 365, which showcases upcoming features, in-progress developments, and updates. The roadmap is segmented by customer types (enterprise, small business) and product categories (Word, Excel, Teams). By doing so, **Microsoft** keeps its customers informed without revealing specific release dates for proprietary features.
- **Example: Tesla's** internal roadmap is highly flexible, accommodating significant changes based on technological advancements and market conditions. For example, the company frequently updates its timelines and scope for features like autonomous driving and battery advancements while communicating high-level goals in external roadmaps.

15.4.2.2 Challenge 2: Focusing on Solutions, Not Problems

Problem: A common roadmapping mistake is focusing too much on specific **solutions** and features, rather than on the **problems** the product needs to solve. This leads to roadmaps packed with features that may not address the core customer pain points.

Solution: This challenge can be addressed by creating a **problem roadmap,** where the focus is on the problems that need to be solved rather than the solutions. A problem roadmap helps product teams align on user pain points and ensures that the product development process starts from a deep understanding of customer needs.

A problem-centric approach to roadmapping helps ensure that features are built to address genuine problems. As you move forward, each release can focus on solving one or more of these prioritized problems, rather than just adding more features for the sake of it.

- **Example: Slack** has often focused on solving specific communication issues for teams. Early on, instead of just releasing a laundry list of features, **Slack's** product team focused on solving key problems such as **team collaboration, real-time messaging,** and **integration with other tools**. Each release was focused on addressing a specific pain point, which contributed to its rapid adoption among teams and organizations.

15.4.2.3 Challenge 3: Trying to Please Everyone with a Feature Soup

Problem: Stakeholders often want a say in the roadmap, resulting in pressure to include too many features, leading to a bloated roadmap. This 'feature soup' can dilute the focus of the product, overwhelm the development team, and create confusion about the product's core value.

Solution: To avoid a roadmap that tries to 'please everyone', product managers should resist the temptation to pack it with features. Instead, they can organize a **roadmap visioning workshop** where stakeholders come together to align on the product's vision, focusing on the core value propositions.

Product managers can also use **prioritization frameworks** during these workshops to assess which features or problems to address first. These frameworks include:

- **MoSCoW Method:** This method prioritizes features by categorizing them as **Must-Have, Should-Have, Could-Have,** and **Won't-Have.** It helps teams focus on the most critical features without overloading the roadmap.
- **RICE Scoring:** This framework evaluates features based on **Reach, Impact, Confidence,** and **Effort,** helping to prioritize features that will provide the greatest value with the least effort.

By involving stakeholders early and guiding them through these prioritization exercises, product managers can ensure that only the most impactful features are included in the roadmap.

- **Example: Airbnb** faced a similar challenge when it scaled rapidly and was being inundated with feature requests from both hosts and guests. To manage this, **Airbnb** employed a **RICE** scoring system to prioritize features that would have the biggest positive impact on the user experience with the least effort. This helped them avoid over-complicating the platform while focusing on high-impact features like 'Superhost' and 'Instant Book'.

15.4.3 The Role of Product Managers in Roadmapping

For product managers, roadmapping is not just about plotting features on a timeline – it's a tool for **planning, alignment,** and **coordination.** Product managers are responsible for ensuring that the roadmap reflects both the **strategic vision** of the product and the **real-world constraints** faced by the development team.

- **Planning:** The roadmap provides a plan for how the product will evolve over time, helping teams anticipate future needs and allocate resources accordingly.

- **Alignment**: A roadmap serves as a communication tool that aligns the entire company around the product's vision, helping stakeholders stay on the same page regarding what the product will deliver and when.
- **Coordination**: Roadmaps also help coordinate the efforts of cross-functional teams, ensuring that product, marketing, sales, engineering, and support are working towards the same milestones.

15.4.4   Product Roadmapping Conclusion

Product roadmapping is a vital tool in product management. It provides clarity and direction for the product's development and communicates that direction to key stakeholders. By addressing common roadmapping challenges – fixing dates and scope, focusing on solutions rather than problems, and avoiding feature overload – product managers can create more effective and flexible roadmaps. These roadmaps serve not only as tactical guides but also as strategic visions, helping teams stay focused on delivering the highest value to customers.

15.5   Release Management

Release management in Agile product development is essential for planning, tracking, and delivering software or product updates in a fast-paced, iterative environment. This section explores the key concepts of **product planning horizons, Agile estimation,** and release phases, along with real-world examples of successful and failed product releases. It emphasizes the importance of proper release planning and tracking to ensure smooth product launches and customer satisfaction.

15.5.1   Agile Release Planning and Tracking

1 **Product Planning Horizons**

   In Agile methodologies, **Product Planning Horizons** represent different levels of planning, ranging from broad long-term goals to highly specific tasks. Planning horizons break down the scope of work, ensuring that teams are aligned and deliver value incrementally. The **Planning Onion** is often used to visualize how different planning layers work together, with larger strategic goals on the outer layers and detailed tactical plans in the centre. The **Planning Onion** visualizes different levels of planning, starting from broad, strategic goals and narrowing down to tactical, daily tasks. The outer layers (such as **Release Planning**) cover broader product goals, while the inner layers (such as **Task Planning**) focus on immediate, actionable tasks. As teams move closer to the centre of the onion, the scope becomes more detailed and focused.

Here's a breakdown of the planning horizons:

- **Release Planning (3 to 6 months):**
  This is the long-term horizon, where major releases are planned over a period of 3 to 6 months. Each release is defined by clear deliverables and multiple iterations of product development. The output of release planning is delivered to the **end users**, and it often represents major milestones in the product's roadmap.

    - **Example:** A software company may plan for a major feature release by the end of Q2. The release would include multiple iterations leading up to this milestone, with each iteration focused on refining parts of the feature until it's fully ready for user deployment.

- **Iteration Planning (1 to 4 weeks):**
  Within each release cycle, iteration planning focuses on delivering multiple **user stories** that incrementally build towards the release. Iterations are typically 1 to 4 weeks long and deliver functioning features to the **product owner or customer** for feedback.

    - **Example:** In a 4-week sprint, the product team focuses on completing specific user stories that contribute to the larger feature set planned for the release.

- **Task Planning (1 to 2 hours):**
  At the most granular level, **task planning** involves breaking down user stories into manageable tasks. These tasks are specific, small pieces of work that can typically be completed within 1 to 2 hours. Task planning helps teams complete user stories efficiently within an iteration.

    - **Example:** A user story about improving login security might be broken down into tasks like adding two-factor authentication (1 hour), updating the user interface for the login screen (2 hours), and testing for bugs (1 hour).

2 **Agile Estimation**
   Agile estimation is critical for release planning and tracking. Unlike traditional estimation methods that rely on specific time units or deadlines, Agile uses **relative sizing**, where tasks are compared based on their complexity, risk, and effort. This estimation process helps Agile teams prioritize work and provide more accurate projections for when features will be ready.
   The key factors considered during relative sizing include:

- **Complexity:** How difficult or intricate the task is.
- **Risk:** The potential for uncertainty, blockers, or challenges.
- **Implementation:** The effort required to develop the feature.

- **Deployment:** The steps needed to release the feature to production.
- **Interdependencies:** How the task relates to other tasks or systems.

Planning Poker and Fibonacci Scale

Two popular tools used for relative sizing in Agile estimation are **Planning Poker** and the **Fibonacci Scale.**

- **Planning Poker:** This is a collaborative estimation technique where team members assign relative values to tasks based on how complex or time-consuming they believe the task will be. Team members use numbered cards (usually based on the Fibonacci sequence) to vote on an estimate, and the estimates are discussed until a consensus is reached. This technique encourages team collaboration and fosters discussion around task complexities and interdependencies.
- **Fibonacci Scale:** In Agile estimation, the Fibonacci sequence (1, 2, 3, 5, 8, 13, etc.) is often used to assign points to tasks. The further a number is in the sequence, the higher the complexity and effort required to complete the task. This scale prevents false precision by making it harder to differentiate between tasks with small differences in complexity, especially at higher levels of complexity.

  - **Example:** A simple UI bug might be assigned 2 points, while integrating a new payment gateway with multiple interdependencies could be assigned 13 points. The Fibonacci scale helps teams compare tasks based on complexity rather than exact time estimates.

15.5.2 *Release Planning and Tracking Example*

Agile teams plan **release dates** based on backlog items and the team's **project velocity.** Project velocity measures how many **story points** (based on relative sizing) a team can complete within an iteration. By calculating how many story points remain in the backlog and dividing it by the team's velocity, product managers can estimate release dates.

Teams track progress using **burndown charts,** which visually represent the amount of work remaining in a sprint or release. As story points are completed, the team's progress is plotted on the chart, helping to monitor whether they are on track for the release.

In this segment, we will use the product backlog to calculate the total project duration and then generate a release burndown chart, which can be updated as the team works on the product's development. Understanding how to use backlogs and burndown charts will enable you to plan your product releases more effectively.

In Agile approaches, to determine the total duration of the project to build a product, or set of features, product managers need to determine the velocity points as well as the number of sprints.

Sprints refer to short periods of time in which a team works to complete a specific amount of work, or a task.

Velocity is a key metric for release planning – it quantifies the capacity of the product team to complete a sprint. This measure of capacity is measured in story points, much like each item in the backlog.

By using the team's velocity – in other words its capacity – the total number of sprints required for the work to be completed before the release date, can be computed.

Let's walk through a scenario of a product team building an MVP version of a new product to illustrate its release planning and tracking. This product is a mobile application for a carsharing platform for car owners and renters. Let's assume that the team's velocity is 10 user story points.

We know from team's product backlog shown in Table 15.1 that the ten items listed in the backlog are worth a total of 100 user story points.

The number of sprints is determined by the velocity points, divided by the number of backlog items. And so, we can see that ten sprints will be required to complete the development of all ten backlog items.

It is common to factor in an additional pre-release sprint to perform release preparation work, which gives a total of 11 sprints.

If each sprint is 2 weeks long, the total duration for developing the MVP product comes to 22 weeks.

Once the product team has determined the total project duration for developing the MVP of the product, with its ten items, a release burndown chart is created.

TABLE 15.1 Product backlog

Item #	Product Backlog Item	Estimates (Points)
1	Registration and Sign-in: Facebook, Google, Email	6
2	User Profiles	12
3	Rewards: Earn loyalty points / Upgrading	18
4	Rewards: Coupon/discount codes	14
5	Bookings: Manage all bookings – current and upcoming	18
6	Price Comparison	18
7	Car Condition Marking	8
8	Integrated Payment Systems	2
9	Location / GPS Tracking / Maps	2
10	Help Centre	2
	Total:	100

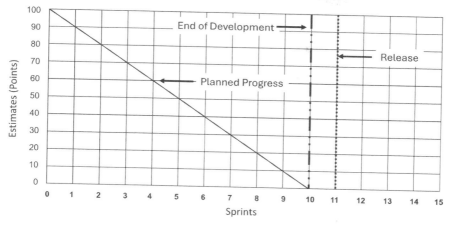

FIGURE 15.3   Release burndown chart

The progress of the product development work can be tracked using a release burndown chart. At the end of each sprint, the team updates the release burndown chart based on the progress.

The burndown chart in Figure 15.3 shows the team's progress towards the release date, by plotting the remaining effort against the planned effort.

The horizontal axis of the burndown chart shows the sprints, while the vertical axis shows the amount of work remaining at the start of each sprint. The work remaining is measured in story points on the vertical axis.

Here you can see a burndown chart for the MVP release. Using the total project duration that we calculated earlier, the team planned to take ten sprints of development work as well as one extra sprint for release preparation work. So, the end of development is plotted at the 10-sprint mark and the release line is plotted at the 11-sprint mark.

The team began with 100 story points of effort for the development work. To finish development within ten sprints, they planned to average ten points per sprint, based on their velocity. And so, we plot the diagonal line, starting at 100 points and ending when the 100 points are used up: at the 10-sprint mark.

As the team works towards the release of the product, it updates its progress in both the release backlog, and the burndown chart.

Let's start by looking at how the product team updated their progress in the release backlog for their first three sprints. The team updates the backlog by updating the estimates for remaining work after each sprint, within each respective column for that sprint, as shown in Figure 15.4.

In Sprint 1, backlog item 1 was completed and so the estimate of remaining work for that item was set to 0. Backlog item 2 was partially completed

S/No	Product Backlog Item	Estimates	Sprint 1	Sprint 2	Sprint 3	Sprint 4	Sprint 5	Sprint 6	Sprint 7	Sprint 8	Sprint 9	Sprint 10	Sprint 11	Sprint 12
1	Registration and Sign-in	6	0	0	0									
2	User Profiles	12	3	0	0									
3	Rewards: Earn loyalty...	18	18	16	10									
4	Rewards: Coupon/...	14	14	14	14									
5	Bookings: Manage ...	18	18	18	18									
6	Price Comparison	18	18	18	18									
7	Car Condition Marking	8	8	8	8									
8	Integrated Payment...	2	2	2	2									
9	Location / GPS ...	2	2	2	2									
10	Help Centre	2	2	2	2									
	Total:	100	85	80	74									

To plot on Burn down Chart

FIGURE 15.4 Release backlog

in Sprint 1. So, the team adjusted the effort points from 12 down to 3, to show their estimate of the remaining effort to complete item number 2.

After Sprint 1, work has not started on the remaining backlog items. The total remaining effort, in the 'total' row, at the bottom of the backlog, shows that there are 85 remaining effort points to complete the remaining backlog items.

One hundred minus 85 equals 15. So, this shows that 15 points-worth of work were completed during Sprint 1. Remember, the team estimated an average of 10 points per sprint, so Sprint 1 went well, since the team burned 5 more points than their velocity of 10 points.

Let's update Sprints 2 and 3. In Sprint 2, backlog item number 2 was completed, so that gets set to 0. In addition, item 3 was started, and its remaining effort after Sprint 2 is now 16 points. In Sprint 3, more progress was made towards the completion of item number 3, reducing its remaining effort to 10 points.

So, by the end of Sprint 3, items 1 and 2 are completed, item 3 is less than half completed, and items 4 to 10 remain uncompleted.

When we update the total remaining work estimates for Sprints 2 and 3, we see totals of 80 and 74, respectively.

We know that if there are, on average, 10 points per sprint, then we should see a total of 70 points remaining at the end of Sprint 3. But, in this scenario, we only see 74. That means there are four more points remaining at this point, than was previously estimated. This could be because the team encountered unexpected problems, added new requirements, or revised estimates of the remaining work.

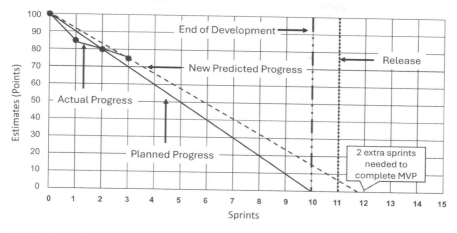

FIGURE 15.5   Updated burndown chart

Next, the team updates the burndown chart to reflect the updates made in the release backlog.

So the remaining estimates of 85, 80, and 74, which you'll recall from the release backlog – updated after each of the first three sprints – are now plotted on the burndown chart in Figure 15.5.

Here, we plot 85 points, 80 points, and 74 points. A line is then drawn to link these points. This line represents the actual progress. So, here we have the planned progress, and an additional actual progress line over the three sprints.

Now, the product manager plots a new dotted line that represents the new (adjusted) predicted progress. This reflects the team's work progress to-date. To draw this line, the product manager starts at the 100-point mark in the top left corner of the chart, and links that line to the remaining estimated 74-point mark, at the end of Sprint 3. This line is then extended to the horizontal x-axis. Where this new predicted progress line hits the x-axis, is the updated forecast of when the development work will be complete. So, in this example, we can see that the team would be late in the delivery, by two extra sprints – which we know to be worth two weeks each. Hence, there is a potential delay of four weeks.

A quick way to use such a chart to determine the actual progress versus the planned progress, is to look at where the actual progress line lies in relation to the planned progress line. If the actual progress line ends above the planned effort line, then the team is behind the schedule. If it is below, the team would be ahead of schedule.

Release planning is an important aspect of working with Agile product teams. Doing so properly ensures that the product is always moving in the right direction, by taking corrective actions as needed.

In this segment you have seen how product managers make use of product backlogs and burndown charts to plan and track a product's development work. Good product managers will review the release backlog and burndown chart regularly, checking to see how the team is performing against the plan and looking for any potential impact to the product delivery date.

If there is a significant gap between the actual velocity and the desired velocity, it should prompt a conversation with the team to understand what's going on. If the delivery date is expected to be delayed, the product manager may need to either reduce the scope or postpone the date of the release.

15.5.3 Phases of Software Product Releases

When managing software product releases, it's essential to understand the different phases a product goes through before reaching the general public. These phases allow for feedback and testing, ensuring that the final product is stable and functional.

1 **Pre-alpha:** This phase focuses on the initial development of the product, where core features are still being built, and testing is conducted on individual components.
2 **Alpha:** In the alpha phase, the product is feature-complete, but significant bugs and issues are expected. This version is tested internally or by a small group of users.
3 **Beta:** The beta phase opens the product up to a larger audience, often external users, who test the product in real-world conditions. Beta testers provide critical feedback on usability and bugs.
4 **Release Candidate (RC):** A release candidate is a nearly final version of the product. If no major issues are identified, it may become the official release.
5 **General Availability (GA):** This phase represents the official launch of the product, where it is available for all users.

15.5.4 The Importance of Beta Testing

Would you drive in a brand-new car that hadn't been tested? Or fly on a plane that had never been tested? For many of us, the answer would be a definite no. If we asked the same question about using a software product, like a mobile app that hasn't been tested, maybe the answer wouldn't be as emphatic. Nevertheless, the software product development process can never be complete without beta tests. Beta testing helps to ensure that your software product is stable and bug-free before you bring it to the market.

Beta testing is crucial for product development, as it allows teams to identify real-world issues and gather valuable user feedback before the official release. By testing the product in various environments, beta users can help the team uncover bugs or usability problems that may not have been discovered during internal testing.

Beta testing also signals to the audience that the product is not final yet, and is still in testing mode. This helps manage the user's expectations of the product.

15.5.4.1 Feature Toggles

Today, we see some product teams beginning to run betas with feature toggles. Feature toggles are mechanisms for controlling the timing and visibility of different software releases. In other words, you can target different users, in targeted rollouts, by selecting which users can see which features. So, a version can be released once, but with certain features disabled. Those can then be enabled, or switched on so that only specific users can see and use those features.

For example, **Pokémon GO** was released on a country-by-country basis: first to the United States and then to other countries. The product team made use of feature toggles to determine which users received specific features first. The best thing about this approach is that you can maintain different regional feature sets, without having to deploy different versions of the application. And of course, it also allowed the team to improve their product, based on customer feedback, before they rolled out the new feature to a wider audience – which they could do, by simply enabling that feature for the wider audience.

Successful Beta Testing Examples

- **Gmail**: **Google** famously kept **Gmail** in **beta** for over 5 years. During this time, millions of users tested the email service, providing **Google** with valuable feedback that allowed them to refine features and fix bugs. **Gmail's** extended beta phase helped it grow into the widely used, reliable email platform it is today.
- **Slack**: Before its public launch, **Slack** went through a successful beta testing phase, where early adopters provided feedback on user interface issues, communication features, and integrations. This beta phase helped **Slack** fine-tune its platform, leading to widespread adoption in the workplace.

15.5.4.2 Failures Due to Lack of Beta Testing

In some cases, beta testing also helps prevent company's losses, caused by product issues that result in damages to reputation.

- **Samsung Galaxy Note 7:** The Samsung **Galaxy Note 7** was rushed to market without adequate testing, leading to catastrophic battery explosions. **Samsung** had to recall 2.5 million **Note 7** phones due to battery explosions. They hadn't done beta testing and sustained heavy financial losses as a result. Not to mention the damage to their reputation. A thorough beta testing phase could have identified the battery issues before release.
- **Google Glass: Google Glass** skipped essential stages of beta testing with consumers, releasing an early version that faced significant privacy and usability concerns. The product failed to gain traction and was eventually pulled from the market.

15.5.5 Release Management Conclusion

Release management is a critical function within product development, ensuring that products are delivered to users in a timely and efficient manner. By using tools like **relative estimation, planning poker,** and **burndown charts,** Agile teams can forecast release dates and manage scope effectively. The various phases of product releases – pre-alpha, alpha, beta, release candidate, and general availability – allow for incremental improvements and ensure product stability. Finally, **beta testing** is essential for validating products in real-world conditions, avoiding potential failures, and ensuring a successful launch.

15.6 Conclusion

The Art of Product Planning is a crucial discipline that brings structure and clarity to the product development process. By mastering the concepts of **product roadmapping** and **release management,** product managers can ensure that their teams work in alignment with business goals and customer needs. A well-constructed roadmap serves as a strategic tool for communicating the product's vision and planning its evolution over time. It provides a clear path from short-term tasks to long-term goals, helping stakeholders understand what is being developed and why.

Release management, on the other hand, ensures that the roadmap is executed efficiently. It introduces flexible, iterative planning through Agile methodologies, enabling teams to adapt to changing market conditions while maintaining focus on delivery. By carefully managing each phase of the product release – through pre-alpha, beta, and general availability – product managers can mitigate risks, gather real-world feedback, and launch successful products that resonate with their target market.

In the end, the art of product planning is about balancing vision with execution, making sure that each step from concept to release is intentional, well-coordinated, and aimed at creating maximum value for both the business and its customers. Through effective planning, alignment, and flexibility, product managers can lead their teams to build and release products that meet market demands and drive business success.

16

MANAGING PRODUCT REQUIREMENTS AND LIFECYCLES

16.1 Introduction

In the rapidly evolving landscape of digital products, successful product management hinges on effectively managing both product requirements and the overall product lifecycle.

Requirements management involves gathering, documenting, and prioritizing features and functionalities that address user needs while aligning with business goals. As digital products continue to evolve, managing these requirements in a flexible and agile way becomes crucial for ensuring that development teams stay focused on delivering value.

Product lifecycle management (PLM), on the other hand, focuses on overseeing the entire journey of a product from its inception to its retirement. Understanding how to navigate the various stages of the product lifecycle – Introduction, Growth, Maturity, and Decline – is essential for ensuring a product's long-term success. Product managers must adapt strategies at each stage to meet shifting market demands, maintain relevance, and maximize revenue.

This chapter aims to provide product managers with the tools and insights they need to manage product requirements dynamically and navigate the complexities of the product lifecycle. By leveraging modern agile techniques and applying lifecycle management strategies, product managers can create a sustainable path for product development, evolution, and eventual phase-out.

16.2 Requirements Management

Requirements management is a critical process in product development, focusing on how to gather, document, and prioritize the various needs and expectations

DOI: 10.1201/9781003484295-16

that shape a product's features and functionality. In modern agile methodologies, this process has evolved to emphasize flexibility and responsiveness to change, allowing product teams to adapt quickly as they build products iteratively.

This section explores the core components of requirements management, including how user stories, epics, features, and a well-maintained product backlog help guide the development process. Additionally, it covers various prioritization techniques that product managers can use to ensure the right features are built at the right time, balancing customer value and business goals.

16.2.1   Agile Requirements Management

In agile product development, requirements are broken down into manageable units that can be developed and tested incrementally.

- **User Stories**: These are the smallest units of work, representing a specific feature or function from the perspective of the end user. A typical user story follows the format:

> As a [user], I want to [do something] so that I can [achieve a goal].

This keeps the focus on delivering value to the user with each story.

- **Example**:

> As a customer, I want to receive email notifications for new product arrivals so that I can stay updated on my favourite items.

- **Epics**: An epic is a large body of work that can be broken down into multiple user stories. It represents a broader functionality or a large feature that cannot be completed in a single sprint or iteration.

- **Example**:

> A new payment system for an e-commerce platform could be an epic, with individual user stories focusing on various aspects such as adding a payment method, processing refunds, and viewing transaction history.

- **Features**: Features are collections of related user stories that together deliver a piece of functionality or value to the product. A feature can consist of multiple stories that address different parts of the same functionality, ensuring that all aspects of a feature are built and tested cohesively.

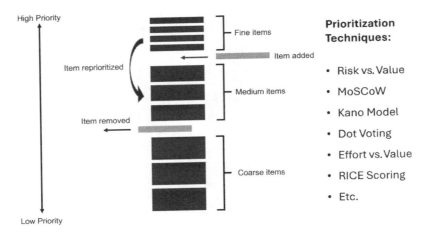

FIGURE 16.1   Prioritization with a product backlog

16.2.2   The Role of the Product Backlog

The **product backlog** is a dynamic, prioritized list of all work items (user stories, epics, and features) that need to be completed. The backlog is constantly evolving as new user stories are added, priorities shift, and some stories are removed based on feedback or changes in scope, as shown in Figure 16.1.

A well-managed backlog allows product teams to:

- Prioritize user stories based on business and customer needs.
- Break down epics into smaller user stories to ensure they are achievable within a sprint.
- Dynamically adjust the backlog over time, adding or removing stories as the product evolves.

The backlog helps teams stay focused on delivering value incrementally, ensuring that they always work on the highest priority items that drive the most value for the product.

16.2.3   Prioritization Techniques for Managing Requirements

Effective prioritization is essential for managing the product backlog, especially as the list of features and user stories grows over time. The following techniques provide structured approaches to ensure the most valuable, least risky items are worked on first:

1 **Risk vs. Value**
   This method helps teams evaluate user stories or features based on their potential value to the customer or business versus the risks involved in

delivering them. High-value, low-risk items are prioritized over low-value, high-risk items.

- **Example**: A high-value, low-risk story might involve adding an FAQ section to a website, which could improve user experience with minimal risk. A low-value, high-risk story could involve integrating an experimental technology with uncertain benefits.

The **Value-Risk Matrix** is structured as a four-quadrant grid with RISK on the X-axis and VALUE on the Y-axis, as shown in Figure 16.2.

Each product or feature is then plotted on the grid, based on the value that it will deliver – either high or low. And the risk of developing or including that product or feature – again, either high, or low.

If a feature will deliver high value and the risks associated with it are low, then it should be prioritized. If, on the other hand, it is of high value, but also comes with high risk, it should be investigated.

If a feature will add some value, perhaps only quite low, and has low risk, it should be considered. And if something is low value and high risk, then it should simply be avoided.

So, we can see that high-value, low-risk features get the highest priority. High-value, high-risk items might be worth the effort, but need to be investigated, and may require risk-mitigation strategies. These are the second priorities.

Then, third-priority items are low-value and low-risk. These can be considered by the team but are secondary to any high-value items.

Lastly, the items features to be avoided are clearly those that should not be prioritized. With the exception that if the item is an essential feature, which is linked to a mobile app's vulnerability, or a weakness in the mobile phone's operating system, it may have to be included, despite the low value and high risk of implementation.

FIGURE 16.2 Prioritization with a Value-Risk Matrix

2 **MoSCoW Method**

Another common prioritization technique is the **MoSCoW** method. Developed by software development expert, Dai Clegg, the **MoSCoW** method categorizes products, items, or product features into four levels of importance. The term **MoSCoW** stems from the four levels of importance that it refers to. The **MoSCoW** method helps product managers prioritize product features in terms of whether they must be included, should be included, could be included, or won't be included. The four levels of importance area as follow:

- **Must Have:** Essential for the product to function. Must-have features are ones that are non-negotiable.
- **Should Have:** Important but not critical. Should-have features are high-priority, but not critical for the first launch. However, these product features are needed in the long run.
- **Could Have:** Nice to have, but not essential. Could-have features are ones that are desirable, but are not important enough to be necessary. These are usually the low-cost tweaking or workaround solutions.
- **Won't Have:** Features that won't be implemented in the current iteration but may be considered later. In other words, the team decides they won't have them now, but agrees they may have them later.
- **Example:** For a new mobile app, user authentication could be a 'Must Have', push notifications a 'Should Have', and social media sharing a 'Could Have'.

3 **Value-Effort Matrix**

This technique helps teams plot features based on their estimated effort and expected value. The result is a visual grid where low-effort, high-value items are prioritized. Like the **Value-Risk Matrix**, the **Value-Effort Matrix** is also structured as a four-quadrant grid, as shown in Figure 16.3.

The X-axis represents EFFORT and the Y-axis represents VALUE. This method is sometimes referred to as the **Lean Prioritization** method. Much like in the **Value-Risk Matrix**, value refers to the value that the feature will add to the product, and therefore to the customer. Instead of rating the risk of implementing each item or feature, this matrix then rates the effort associated with implementing that feature.

If a feature will add high value and will take a low effort to implement, then it should be prioritized above all else. We consider these items to be 'quick wins,' because they add a lot of value, but do not take a lot of effort to develop or implement.

The next features to prioritize are those that add high value, but do require high, or higher, effort. These are referred to as the 'big bets', as

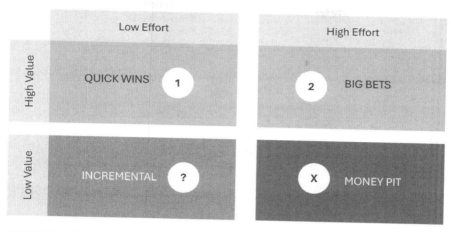

FIGURE 16.3   Prioritization with a Value-Effort Matrix

you are investing a lot of effort into their implementation and hoping for a large payout in terms of value.

The next features in the order of priority are those that are low in value and low in effort. These are termed, 'incremental' These features are typically ones that can be implemented to provide small, incremental improvements to the product.

Lastly, the items that are lowest on the list of priorities, are those that are low in value, and high in effort. These are sometimes referred to as the 'money pit' items, because people end up pouring money or resources into their implementation, but end up deriving little value for those efforts. These features are not worth spending your limited resources on, because they deliver very little value.

- **Example**: A small feature that significantly improves user on-boarding might be high-value but low-effort, and should therefore be prioritized. A highly complex, low-value feature could be deprioritized.

4 **Dot Voting**

Dot voting is a collaborative prioritization technique used to quickly gather input from stakeholders, allowing them to vote on their preferred features or user stories. Each participant is given a limited number of sticky dots to place next to the stories or features they think should be prioritized, as shown in Figure 16.4.

Key Benefit: By limiting the number of dots, this technique forces stakeholders to think deeper about their choices and make hard trade-offs. They can't give every requirement high priority because there aren't enough dots to go around. This encourages stakeholders to carefully consider which

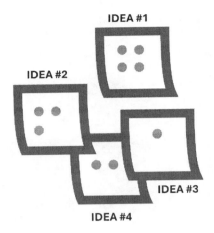

FIGURE 16.4 Prioritization with dot voting

features will provide the most value and impact, helping teams avoid feature bloat and focus on what truly matters.

- **Example:** In a planning session, each stakeholder might receive five dots to distribute among 15 potential features. This limitation requires them to decide which features are most critical to the product's success, leading to a more focused and refined prioritization.

5 **Kano Model**

Your product backlog may contain a seemingly endless list of product features, but you can't build everything in one go, nor should you. You've learned some prioritization techniques to help determine which features to include first. But how do you know which ones will make your customers happy?

The Kano Model is the answer. While other prioritization techniques have their role to play, the Kano Model is the one which puts customer satisfaction first, and is therefore a fantastic tool to ensure your priorities align with customers' needs.

This model was created by a Japanese professor, Noriaki Kano, in 1984, and is still a very useful tool today. It helps determine your customers' needs and measures their satisfaction. That information can then be used to prioritize your products' features.

The **Kano Model** categorizes features based on how they impact customer satisfaction:

- **Basic Needs:** Essential features customers expect.
- **Performance Needs:** Features that increase satisfaction as they improve.
- **Excitement Needs:** Unexpected features that delight users.

- **Example**: In a photo-editing app, basic cropping and filtering functions are 'Basic Needs', while advanced editing tools (like layering) are 'Performance Needs'. An AI-based feature that auto-enhances photos could be an 'Excitement Need'.

Let us take deep dive into the Kano Model to determine how customers feel about specific product features, and what that means for how you prioritize them. To do so, we will use the Kano questionnaire and categorize the results, using the Kano Model.

The Kano graph uses two axes: one for **satisfaction** and one for **functionality**.

Product managers can make use of this approach to prioritize product features based on how likely those features are to satisfy customers, on the one hand. And on the other, the extent to which the feature has been implemented. In other words, its level of functionality: is it functional, or live yet, or is it already fully implemented and therefore fully functional?

Let us take a closer look at the two axes in the model: satisfaction and functionality, as shown in Figure 16.5.

The Y-axis represents the satisfaction scale. It ranges from 'frustrated', at the one end, to 'delighted', at the other. If a customer responds that they like a feature when it is present, and they dislike it when it is absent, then the feature receives a rating of 'delighted'.

In between frustrated and delighted, we have dissatisfied, neutral, and satisfied.

Now let us discuss the X-axis. It measures the degree of functionality. On one end, we have 'none', which means the feature does not yet exist, or has not been implemented yet. On the other end, we have 'best', which means that feature is as functional as possible. In between none and best,

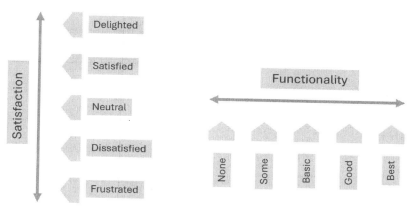

FIGURE 16.5 Satisfaction vs. functionality

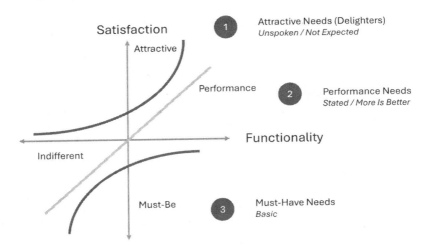

FIGURE 16.6 Three types of customer needs

we have some functionality, basic functionality, and good functionality. When you put the two axes together, you get the Kano Model graph as shown in Figure 16.6. We're going to break this up into three types of customer needs.

The first category is called the MUST-HAVE needs. If these needs are met, the customer is neutral. But if they are not met, the customer will be unhappy.

The second category is called the PERFORMANCE needs. The more of these needs are met, the happier the customer will be. These are needs that customers can tell you about.

The third category is called the ATTRACTIVE needs. These are the needs that are usually not expected by customers, but the customers are delighted by them.

Using the Kano Model to prioritize product requirements entails first using a specific questionnaire. The Kano questionnaire is designed to help customers provide feedback about product features in a quantifiable way, as shown in Table 16.1.

In the questionnaire, each feature is listed separately. For each feature, two questions are asked. First, 'How do you feel, if you have this feature?' And second, 'How do you feel, if you do not have this feature?'

Customers are given a set of five possible responses to choose from.

1 I like it
2 I expect it
3 I am neutral
4 I can tolerate it
5 I dislike it

TABLE 16.1 Kano questionnaire

Functional Question	
How do you feel if you have this feature?	1 I like it
	2 I expect it
	3 I am neutral
	4 I can tolerate it
	5 I dislike it
Dysfunctional Question	
How do you feel if you do not have this feature?	1 I like it
	2 I expect it
	3 I am neutral
	4 I can tolerate it
	5 I dislike it

Let's use the example of a car-sharing platform for car owners and renters. One of key features is the digital key: a means of unlocking a car, using the app on their phone. To determine how customers feel about this feature, the questionnaire would ask how they feel when the feature is present on the app, and how they would feel without it.

For each version of the question, customers must rate whether they like it or dislike it. In other words, whether they like the presence or absence of the feature, or dislike its presence or absence.

So, some customers may like having the feature, some may be neutral, and some may even dislike it. When asked how they feel about not having the feature, some may dislike not having it, some may tolerate its absence, and who knows - maybe some would like not having it.

Once you've elicited customer feedback using the Kano questionnaire, you need to categorize the responses. Based on the responses for a product feature, the feature is placed into one of the six Kano feature categories, as shown in Figure 16.7.

First, there are 'Attractive Features', represented here by the letter 'A'. These features are not expected, but are liked by customers. They make the customers feel happy, or excited and are considered a 'must-invest' feature, because they'll draw customers to the product.

Second, there are 'Must-be Features', represented by the letter M. These are must-have features and customers dislike not having them. They're also known as basic features and must be present and work as customers expect them to. For example, for the car-sharing mobile app, functions such as registration, sign-in, and price-comparison are assumed to be basic, 'Must-be Features'.

Third, we have 'Performance Features'. These are features that customers like having and dislike not having. They are the ones that keep the customers satisfied or happy. And they are responsible for establishing brand

		Dysfunctional (feature is absent)				
		Like It	Expect It	Don't Care	Live With	Dislike
Functional (feature is present)	Like It	Q	A	A	A	P
	Expect It	R	Q	I	I	M
	Don't Care	R	I	I	I	M
	Live With	R	I	I	Q	M
	Dislike	R	R	R	R	Q

A: Attractive Features – These features are not expected but are liked by customers

M: Must-Be Features – These are must have features and customers dislike not having them

P: Performance Features – These are features customers like having and dislike not having

I: Indifferent Features – These are feature that customers are neutral to or can tolerate with

Q: Questionable Features – Conflicting responses from customers

R: Reverse Features – These are features that customers like not having or dislike having

FIGURE 16.7 Six Kano feature categories

loyalty in the market. For example, a feature such as a rewards system, which allows customers to earn loyalty points and upgrade their car model using those points.

The fourth category of features, represented by the letter 'I', are 'Indifferent Features'. These are features that customers are neutral to, or can tolerate. They are the ones the customers do not care about and are typically excluded from the product roadmap.

Fifth, represented by the letter 'Q', are 'Questionable Features'. These features are ones that have received conflicting responses from customers.

Sixth, there are 'Reverse Features', represented by the letter 'R'. They're features that customers like not having or dislike having.

To categorize each feature, you can use an evaluation table. So, for example, if a customer responds with 'I Like It', if the feature is present, and 'I'm Neutral', if it is absent, then you've got an 'Attractive Feature'.

If a customer responds with 'I Expect It', when the feature is present, and 'I Dislike It', when the feature is absent, then the feature is a 'Must-be Feature'.

You can use this type of table to categorize all of your product's features, based on the survey responses.

In the car-sharing mobile app example, a Kano Model can be applied by conducting a survey with a pool of customers to ask for their responses to the mobile app features.

Having evaluated which feature belongs in which category individually for every person surveyed, the product manager then assigns one category to every feature based on the opinions of everybody surveyed.

The evaluation table is used to keep count of how often a feature has been assigned a certain category. In sum, a feature is always assigned the category that most of the people surveyed considered it to belong to, as shown in Table 16.2.

TABLE 16.2 A car-sharing platform's Kano evaluation table

	Must-be	Performance	Attractive	Indifferent	Reverse	Questionable	Category
Login	8% (4)	28% (14)	40% (20)	20% (10)	0% (0)	4% (2)	Attractive
Rewards	4 % (2)	38% (19)	22% (11)	30% (15)	4% (2)	2% (1)	Performance
Manage Bookings	42% (21)	8% (4)	12% (6)	24% (12)	8% (4)	6% (3)	Must-be
Price Comparison	48% (24)	8% (4)	16% (8)	24% (12)	0% (0)	4% (2)	Must-be
Car Condition Marking	50% (25)	14% (7)	20% (10)	14% (7)	0% (0)	2% (1)	Must-be
Notifications of Promotions	14% (7)	8% (4)	10% (5)	58% (29)	2% (1)	8% (4)	Indifferent
Location / Search	4% (2)	22% (11)	44% (22)	26% (13)	2% (1)	2% (1)	Attractive
Mobile Payment	10% (5)	2% (1)	42% (21)	34% (17)	2% (1)	10% (5)	Attractive

As shown in Table 16.2, there are three attractive features (also called 'delighters'), three must-be features, one indifferent feature and one performance feature.

The Kano Model can be used to clearly prioritize the product backlog during product development. A general rule you can use to prioritize features based on their category is must-be > performance > delighter > indifferent.

By implementing not only must-be's and performance features but also making room for delighters can give your products a competitive advantage over the competitors. Obviously, you should exclude the reverse features from your product roadmap.

Measuring and prioritizing product features using customer satisfaction helps to inform the product development and release cycle.

In the Kano Model, we see that the level of customer loyalty is determined by the customer's emotional responses to the product features. However, product functionality alone does not make it 'good' – emotions are as important too.

It is not enough for a product to fulfil the basic need that it is required for. For example, in the car-sharing mobile app example, a customer can use it to complete a task, such as using the mobile app's search function to locate a car.

The search function in this case works and fulfils its purpose, but it can still be boring or 'behind the curve'. For example, a car that has self-driving functionality, or uses virtual reality for navigation, is more impressive. It goes beyond just providing the basic needs, and creates the 'wow' factor.

By using the Kano Model, the product team can increase customer satisfaction by launching a few new and attractive features, rather than just must-be ones. The Kano Model helps the team to prioritize ideas that are most valuable, thereby making effective business decisions on which to drop and which to move forward with.

When it comes to developing product features, the prioritization process helps to identify and separate out important and urgent items, from less important ones, or those for which there is no rush.

Effective prioritization entails striking a balance between delivering value, reducing risk, and managing the limited time and resources you have available.

Key Insight: Features that excite customers today can eventually become basic expectations. This transition happens as competitors adopt the same features and customers begin to take them for granted. The **Kano Model** emphasizes that product managers should continually monitor this progression through periodic Kano analyses to stay ahead of changing expectations.

- **Example: Car Airbags**
  When **Mercedes-Benz** first introduced airbags, they were an **excitement attribute** that signalled a high-end, luxury vehicle. This feature

delighted customers and differentiated the brand. However, over time, other car manufacturers began incorporating airbags into their models, turning airbags into a **performance attribute** – a feature that contributed to customer satisfaction but no longer surprised them. Today, airbags are a **basic need** (threshold attribute) that customers expect to be included as standard, even in budget vehicles. This evolution illustrates how customer expectations shift over time, and what once excited them can become something they take for granted.

• **Example:** In the early days of smartphones, touchscreen technology and app stores were considered **excitement needs,** but over time, these have become basic expectations in any modern phone. Similarly, today's AI-driven personalization features may eventually evolve into basic needs as users come to expect this level of customization in all apps and services.

   This gradual downgrading happens because customers quickly become accustomed to new features, especially as competitors adopt them. The timeline for this shift depends on the type of feature, competitors' designs, and the customer base. To stay ahead, product teams must conduct regular **Kano analyses** to reassess how their features are perceived and ensure they continue delivering value.

6 RICE Scoring

RICE is a more quantitative prioritization technique that considers:

• **Reach**: How many users will benefit?
• **Impact**: How much will it improve the user experience?
• **Confidence**: How confident are we in the impact estimate?
• **Effort**: How much time or effort will it take to implement?

The RICE formula shown in Figure 16.8 helps teams calculate a score for each feature or user story, with higher scores indicating higher priority.

• **Example:** A new onboarding feature for a mobile app might score high on **Reach** (it affects all new users) and **Impact** (it dramatically improves user retention), but low on **Effort** (requiring minimal development time).

1 Reach

Reach measures how many customers will benefit from the feature or initiative within a given time frame, typically the first quarter after launch. The higher the reach, the more potential users or customers will be impacted by the change.

Data Sources:

• Qualitative customer interviews
• Customer requests through Support or Sales
• Surveys

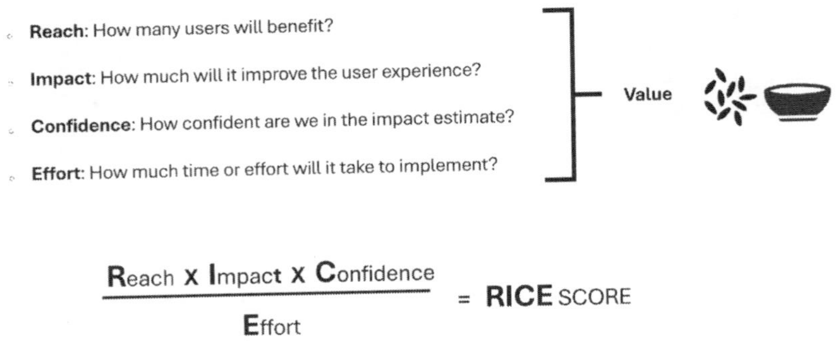

Reach: How many users will benefit?

Impact: How much will it improve the user experience?

Confidence: How confident are we in the impact estimate?

Effort: How much time or effort will it take to implement?

Value

$$\frac{\text{Reach} \times \text{Impact} \times \text{Confidence}}{\text{Effort}} = \text{RICE SCORE}$$

FIGURE 16.8   Prioritization with RICE scoring

Reach Value Scale:

- **10** = Impacts the vast majority (~80% or greater) of users/customers.
- **8** = Impacts a large percentage (~50% to ~80%) of users.
- **5** = Significant reach (~25% to ~50%).
- **3** = Small reach (~5% to ~25%).
- **2** = Minimal reach (less than ~5%).

2 Impact

Impact refers to the degree to which the feature or initiative will affect customers, the company, or both. This factor helps evaluate whether the initiative will drive significant change in key business areas such as revenue, cost savings, or risk reduction.

Factors to Consider:

- Increased revenue potential.
- Decreased risk (to customers or the company).
- Decreased cost (for both customers and the company).
- Revenue-generating vs. non-revenue-generating opportunities.
- Impact on brand perception or loyalty.

Impact Value Scale:

- **5** = Massive impact.
- **4** = High impact.
- **3** = Medium impact.
- **2** = Low impact.
- **1** = Minimal impact.

3 Confidence

Confidence evaluates how well the team understands both the customer problem and the potential solution. Confidence is a way to gauge the risk involved – features with lower confidence values may require more research or discovery before full commitment.

Factors to Consider:

- How well does the team understand the customer's problem?
- How well does the team understand the proposed solution and implementation details?

Confidence Value Scale:

- **100%** = High confidence.
- **80%** = Medium confidence.
- **50%** = Low confidence.

4 **Effort**

Effort is a measure of how much time and resources the feature or initiative will require from the team. It's typically measured in **man-months** or **T-Shirt sizing** (Small, Medium, Large, XL) to give a rough estimate of development complexity. Lower effort scores indicate that the feature is easier and faster to implement, while higher scores suggest greater complexity and time investment.

Effort Value Scale (T-Shirt Sizing):

- **S** = Less than 1 week.
- **M** = 1–2 weeks.
- **L** = 2–4 weeks.
- **XL** = More than 4 weeks.

By combining these factors, product managers can calculate the **RICE score** for each initiative using the formula:

$$\text{RICE score} = \frac{\text{Reach} \times \text{Impact} \times \text{Confidence}}{\text{Effort}}$$

This score helps teams prioritize features with the highest impact and least effort, while also accounting for the reach and confidence in the initiative's success.

Software tools such as **Roadmunk** can streamline the RICE scoring process, enabling product teams to organize, visualize, and prioritize initiatives more efficiently. Roadmunk offers built-in templates for RICE scoring, allowing teams to input the four factors (Reach, Impact, Confidence, and Effort) and automatically calculate a prioritization score. The visual interface helps product managers see the relative importance of different initiatives at a glance, ensuring a data-driven approach to decision-making, as illustrated in Figure 16.9.

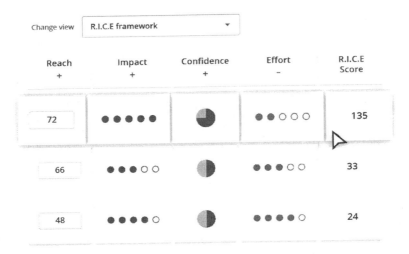

Change view | R.I.C.E framework ▾

Reach +	Impact +	Confidence +	Effort −	R.I.C.E Score
72	●●●●●	◕	●●○○○	135
66	●●●○○	◑	●●●○○	33
48	●●●●○	◑	●●●●○	24

FIGURE 16.9 Roadmunk's version of RICE prioritization

Roadmunk RICE Scoring Interface:

Another popular tool is **Productboard,** which also supports RICE scoring and integrates with product roadmaps. Productboard's interface allows teams to align RICE scores with overall product strategy and track initiatives throughout their lifecycle. These tools make it easy to adjust priorities dynamically as new information or user feedback becomes available.

These tools simplify the RICE scoring process, reduce manual calculation errors, and provide clear visuals that help teams focus on the most impactful initiatives.

16.2.4 Managing Agile Requirements Summary

Effective **requirements management** is essential for successful product development, especially in fast-moving, agile environments. By breaking down features into **epics, user stories,** and managing them dynamically within the **product backlog,** teams can maintain flexibility while ensuring that the most valuable and feasible work is prioritized.

Through structured **prioritization techniques** like MoSCoW, RICE scoring, and the **Effort vs. Value Matrix,** product managers can guide their teams to focus on delivering maximum value in every sprint, ensuring the product evolves to meet both customer and business needs.

16.3 Product Lifecycle Management

Product lifecycle management (PLM) refers to the journey of a product from its ideation to its eventual exit from the market. Understanding this lifecycle is critical for product managers as it helps them align strategies with each phase of the product's development. Two important frameworks – the **Innovation Adoption Curve** and the **Product Lifecycle** –provide foundational insights into product growth, customer adoption, and business strategies throughout a product's lifespan.

16.3.1 Innovation Adoption Curve

The **Innovation Adoption Curve** in Figure 16.10 is a graphical model that represents the rate at which new products or innovations are adopted by different segments of the population. Developed by professor and scientist Everett Rogers in his 1962 book, *Diffusion of Innovations,* this model explains how innovations spread across a population, and why some people adopt new technologies faster than others. Rogers' model classifies adopters into five groups:

1 **Innovators:** The first to adopt new technology. They are risk-takers and willing to try new products even in their early, untested stages.
2 **Early Adopters:** Opinion leaders who embrace new products after seeing the success experienced by innovators.
3 **Early Majority:** More cautious than early adopters, but they adopt innovations before the average person.
4 **Late Majority:** Sceptical and only adopt innovations once they have been widely tested and proven.
5 **Laggards:** The last group to adopt new technology, usually resistant to change and only doing so when necessary.

This curve highlights how different segments of the population adopt innovations at varying speeds, with early adopters driving initial product growth and the majority of the population following suit as products become more widespread. The key takeaway for product managers is to align

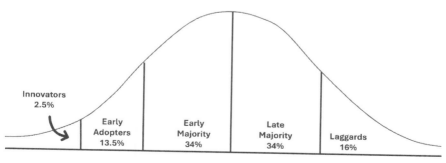

R. Everett's Diffusion of Innovation model (1962)

FIGURE 16.10 Innovation Adoption Curve

marketing and product development strategies with these adoption phases to maximize impact.

Product Growth Insights: Product growth often stems from understanding how innovations are adopted and spreading them through the population. As new technology progresses from early adopters to the mainstream market, product managers need to track where their product falls on the curve. Aligning this with an **ideal market share curve** – one that gradually increases as adoption accelerates – helps guide product scaling strategies.

16.3.2 The Chasm

In his 1991 book *Crossing the Chasm*, **Geoffrey Moore** introduced the concept of the **chasm**, a gap that exists between the early adopters (technology enthusiasts and visionaries) and the early majority (pragmatists). According to Moore, crossing this chasm is one of the most critical challenges in bringing a product from early adoption to mainstream success. The early majority, consisting of pragmatists, have very different expectations from early adopters, which creates a disconnect that can cause many innovations to fail to reach mass-market success. Figure 16.11 is a diagram that depicts the chasm (or gap) between the early market and the mainstream market.

Moore suggests that early adopters are excited by the innovation and willing to deal with a less polished product, whereas the early majority are more pragmatic and demand a proven, reliable solution. This divergence in expectations creates a 'chasm' that companies must bridge to transition from niche success to mainstream market adoption.

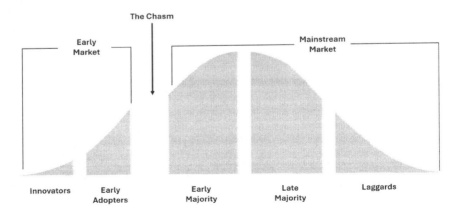

FIGURE 16.11   The chasm

16.3.2.1 *Strategies to Cross the Chasm*

Moore outlines several strategies that companies can adopt to successfully cross the chasm:

1 **Choose a Target Market:** Focus on a specific niche within the broader early majority that shares the same values and needs as early adopters. This helps build momentum within that segment.
2 **Understand the Whole Product Concept:** The whole product includes not just the core product itself, but also additional services, customer support, and other factors that the early majority expects.
3 **Position the Product:** Create a compelling narrative that positions the product as a solution to a pressing problem for the target market. Pragmatists are more likely to adopt a product if it solves a specific problem and is easy to implement.
4 **Build a Marketing Strategy:** Tailor marketing efforts to address the needs and concerns of the early majority. Use case studies, testimonials, and success stories from early adopters to provide proof of the product's value.
5 **Choose the Most Appropriate Distribution Channel:** Ensure that the product is available in places where the early majority expects to find it. This might involve partnering with established vendors or using distribution channels trusted by the pragmatists.
6 **Pricing:** Pragmatists are less likely to take risks on expensive products unless the value proposition is clear. Consider setting pricing that reflects the product's value while providing incentives or trial periods to encourage adoption.

Practical Steps to Cross the Chasm

1 **Gather Feedback from Early Adopters:** Early adopters are a key source of feedback, which can help refine the product before it reaches the early majority. Companies should actively seek feedback from these users to identify any shortcomings or areas for improvement.
2 **Evolve the Product:** Based on feedback, make necessary adjustments to the product to meet the expectations of the early majority. This may involve improving user experience, adding critical features, or enhancing support and documentation.
3 **Assess and Remove Barriers:** Identify and address any barriers that could prevent the early majority from adopting the product. This might involve simplifying the onboarding process, ensuring scalability, or making the product more user-friendly.
4 **Refine Features and Scalability:** Pragmatists expect a product to be reliable and scalable. Product managers should prioritize refining indispensable features and resolving any bottlenecks that could hinder scalability. This ensures the product is not only appealing to the early majority but also able to grow with demand.

16.3.2.2 How the Chasm Relates to Product Growth and Success

Successfully crossing the chasm is essential for turning an innovative product with niche success into a mainstream success story. By aligning the product with the expectations of the early majority and addressing the differences between visionaries and pragmatists, companies can accelerate growth and reach their full market potential.

Moore's concept of the chasm highlights that the early majority's cautious nature can stall growth if the product fails to meet their expectations. Therefore, crossing the chasm is not just about improving the product but also aligning the business strategy, marketing, and distribution with the needs of pragmatic buyers. If a company successfully crosses the chasm, it positions the product to rapidly gain adoption and enter the **growth stage** of the product lifecycle.

16.3.3 Gartner Hype Cycle: Managing Innovation and Adoption

After discussing **Geoffrey Moore's Chasm** in the **Innovation Adoption Curve**, it's essential to also understand how technologies evolve beyond early adoption and how market expectations shift over time. The **Gartner Hype Cycle** is a complementary framework that helps product managers navigate the stages of technological adoption, particularly in understanding the relationship between innovation, market expectations, and the eventual value a product or technology brings.

16.3.3.1 Gartner Hype Cycle

The **Gartner Hype Cycle** as shown in Figure 16.12 provides a graphical representation of the maturity, adoption, and social application of new technologies. This model is particularly useful for product managers, as it highlights the typical lifecycle of innovations and helps to identify risks, opportunities, and the appropriate timing for adopting or investing in emerging technologies.

The Hype Cycle consists of five key phases:

1 **Technology Trigger (Innovation Trigger):**
   This phase starts when an innovation or technological breakthrough, such as a new product launch or research discovery, generates significant interest. At this point, there is high visibility, and the innovation is often seen as revolutionary, leading to early excitement and media buzz. However, real-world applications are limited, and there may not be a working prototype yet.

   • **Example:** The initial excitement around **blockchain technology** when it was first introduced as a revolutionary way to enable decentralized

VISIBILITY

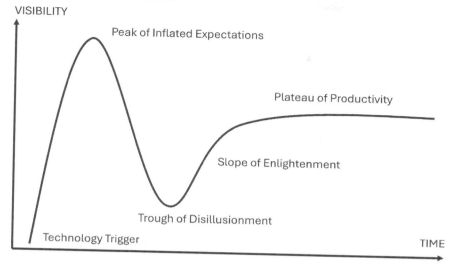

FIGURE 16.12 Gartner's Hype Cycle

systems. Many saw it as the future of finance and data security, even though practical applications were still in the early stages of development.

2 **Peak of Inflated Expectations**:

At this stage, early adopters begin experimenting with the technology, and media coverage drives inflated expectations. While there are some success stories, the hype often outweighs the actual performance of the technology. Organizations rush to adopt, expecting immediate results, but most projects either fail or fall short of the overblown expectations.

- **Example: Virtual Reality (VR)** experienced a surge in interest during this phase, with many believing it would rapidly transform gaming, education, and healthcare. However, the technology's practical applications lagged behind the initial excitement.

3 **Trough of Disillusionment**:

As the hype fades, early adopters begin reporting performance issues, challenges, and a lack of return on investment (ROI). At this point, the initial excitement wears off, and many organizations give up on the technology. However, some persistent organizations continue to refine the innovation, leading to incremental improvements and lessons learned.

- **Example**: After the initial excitement around **3D printing**, many users realized the limitations in terms of speed, cost, and material compatibility, causing interest to wane. However, some industries continued to develop the technology to address these shortcomings.

4 **Slope of Enlightenment:**
In this phase, early adopters who stuck with the technology begin to see real benefits. The understanding of how the innovation can be applied to real-world problems improves. Gradually, more organizations realize how to adapt the technology for practical use cases. Documentation, best practices, and case studies start to emerge, making it easier for others to adopt the technology with fewer risks.

- **Example: Artificial Intelligence (AI)** applications in healthcare and business have gradually matured as organizations found specific use cases (e.g., predictive analytics, personalized medicine) where AI delivers real value.

5 **Plateau of Productivity:**
The technology has now matured and reached mainstream adoption. The initial hype is gone, but the innovation's practical benefits are evident. More organizations adopt the technology as they see proven results. The product or technology becomes a standard solution in its industry.

- **Example: Cloud computing** has now reached the Plateau of Productivity, as organizations across various industries recognize its benefits for cost savings, scalability, and data storage.

16.3.3.2 How Product Managers Can Use the Gartner Hype Cycle

The **Gartner Hype Cycle** helps product managers assess where a new technology or product sits in its lifecycle, allowing them to make informed decisions about adoption, investment, and timing. Here's how product managers can apply the Hype Cycle to avoid common pitfalls and capitalize on emerging opportunities:

1 **Avoid Adopting Too Early:**
Jumping on a new technology at the **Technology Trigger** or **Peak of Inflated Expectations** phase without a clear understanding of its practical applications can lead to wasted resources and failed projects. Product managers should monitor these innovations carefully and wait for initial proof-of-concept implementations before committing fully.

2 **Don't Give Up Too Soon:**
During the **Trough of Disillusionment,** many organizations may abandon the technology due to early setbacks or unmet expectations. However, product managers who recognize the potential of the innovation should continue refining it or wait for better implementations as the technology matures.

3 **Adopt at the Right Time:**
The ideal time to adopt a new technology is when it moves into the **Slope of Enlightenment.** By this point, early adopters have paved the way by refining the technology and developing best practices. Product managers can

learn from these examples and apply the technology in ways that minimize risk and maximize impact.

4 **Understand Long-Term Viability**:

Product managers should also evaluate whether a technology will reach the **Plateau of Productivity** or if it is likely to fade away. By tracking industry trends and observing how well the technology performs in real-world environments, product managers can better assess whether it is worth long-term investment.

16.3.3.3 *Gartner Hype Cycle and Product Managers Today*

For modern product managers, the **Gartner Hype Cycle** provides a valuable framework for assessing the risks and opportunities associated with new technologies. It highlights the importance of timing and encourages a thoughtful approach to adopting innovations.

- **Use in Technology Adoption**: The Hype Cycle helps product managers identify when to engage with new technologies based on their maturity and real-world use cases. For example, if a product manager is considering adopting **AI for product personalization**, they can use the Hype Cycle to see if AI applications have reached the **Slope of Enlightenment** or **Plateau of Productivity** – indicating that it's a good time to invest.
- **Practical Risk Management**: The Hype Cycle emphasizes the importance of managing risk when adopting new technologies. By understanding where a technology sits on the curve, product managers can avoid adopting something too early or holding onto a failing innovation for too long.
- **Informed Decision-Making**: The visual nature of the Hype Cycle provides product managers with a straightforward map to assess technologies, allowing them to make informed decisions about investments, roadmaps, and strategic direction.
- **Adapting to Market Shifts**: In an age where technological advancements move quickly, the Gartner Hype Cycle helps product managers stay ahead of trends, ensuring their products remain competitive and relevant in rapidly evolving markets.

16.3.3.4 *The Intersection of the Chasm and the Gartner Hype Cycle*

By integrating **Moore's Chasm** and the **Gartner Hype Cycle**, product managers gain a comprehensive view of the challenges and opportunities involved in driving technology adoption.

- **Crossing the Chasm** focuses on moving from early adopters to the early majority, while the **Hype Cycle** provides a broader perspective on the trajectory of technological innovation.

- Both frameworks stress the importance of timing, user feedback, and adaptability, helping product managers navigate the complex landscape of innovation adoption and ensuring long-term product success.

By understanding both frameworks, product managers can better predict when and how their product will reach mainstream adoption, avoid common pitfalls, and align their strategies with real-world technology maturity.

16.3.4 Product Lifecycle

The **Product Lifecycle** as shown in Figure 16.13 defines the stages through which a product evolves, from its initial concept to eventual market exit. There are four key stages:

1 **Introduction**: The product is launched in the market, and awareness is low. The focus is on educating customers and driving early adoption.
2 **Growth**: The product gains traction, and sales increase rapidly. Competitors may enter the market as demand grows.
3 **Maturity**: The product reaches peak market penetration. Growth slows as the market saturates, and competition intensifies.
4 **Decline**: Demand starts to decrease as new technologies emerge, and the product may eventually be phased out or replaced.

In today's fast-moving digital world, product lifecycles are often shortened, and digital products must be managed continuously from **cradle to grave**. Regular iterations and updates help keep digital products relevant and competitive. In this environment, product managers must think strategically about each phase of the lifecycle and adapt quickly to market changes.

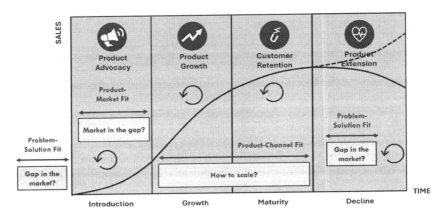

FIGURE 16.13 The Product Lifecycle

16.3.4.1   Strategies for Each Stage of the Product Lifecycle

Each phase of the **Product Lifecycle** requires a unique approach tailored to the specific challenges and opportunities present at that stage. Below is a detailed overview of the strategies product managers should apply at each phase to maximize product value, ensure growth, and strategically extend the product's lifespan.

1 **Introduction Stage – Product Advocacy Strategy**

In the introduction stage, the product is newly launched, and the main focus is on building awareness and educating potential customers. The strategy here is **product advocacy** – championing the product, establishing its value, and differentiating it from competitors.

- **Key Focus Areas:**

  1 Establish a clear brand identity to make the product stand out in the market.
  2 Build customer awareness around the product's unique value proposition.
  3 Differentiate the product from competitors, highlighting what makes it better.
  4 Generate early demand by attracting initial paying customers.

- **Role of the Product Manager:**

  - Collaborate with marketing, sales, and design teams to position the product effectively.
  - Validate product assumptions by gathering early feedback from customers and testing their willingness to pay for the product.
  - Refine user personas based on the behaviour of early adopters.
  - Track product usage metrics and ensure the product is moving towards **Product-Market Fit**.
  - Iterate the product to address customer needs as they evolve.

- **Metrics to Track:**

  a. Product activation rates.
  b. Conversion rates from landing pages.
  c. Feedback from MVP (Minimum Viable Product) users.
  d. NPS (Net Promoter Score).
  e. Feature adoption rates.
  f. Customer acquisition costs.
  g. Initial revenue.

2 **Growth Stage – Product Growth Strategy**

In the growth stage, the product gains traction, and the focus shifts towards scaling adoption and market share. The strategy during this phase is **product growth** – maximizing market reach and improving the product based on user feedback.

- **Key Focus Areas:**

  1 Optimize pricing strategies to balance competitiveness and profitability.
  2 Drive deeper product engagement by encouraging usage and adoption.
  3 Gather customer feedback and incorporate it into the product road-map to enhance features.
  4 Conduct market research to solidify customer preference for the product.

- **Role of the Product Manager:**

  - Work with marketing and sales to maintain competitive pricing that drives growth.
  - Focus on customer satisfaction by adding new features that meet evolving needs.
  - Maximize revenue and market share by aligning the product with customer expectations.

- **Metrics to Track:**

  - Revenue growth rate.
  - Customer lifetime value (LTV).
  - Key acquisition channels.
  - Stickiness (user engagement).
  - Expansion revenue (upselling, cross-selling).
  - Referral rates.
  - Customer satisfaction.

3 **Maturity Stage – Customer Retention Strategy**

As the product reaches maturity, growth stabilizes, and the emphasis turns to retaining existing customers and maintaining market share. The strategy here is **customer retention** – focusing on loyalty and optimizing the product to keep customers engaged.

- **Key Focus Areas:**

  1 Provide exceptional customer support to ensure high satisfaction.
  2 Use data to guide product improvements and keep it competitive.
  3 Reduce customer churn by focusing on retention initiatives.
  4 Leverage data-driven marketing to target loyal customers with personalized offers.

- **Role of the Product Manager:**

  - Focus on retaining market share by continuing to differentiate the product.

- Explore new markets or segments to extend product reach.
- Keep innovation alive by launching incremental product improvements.

- **Metrics to Track:**

  - Feature usage metrics.
  - User feedback loops.
  - Innovation rates.
  - Churn rate (percentage of customers leaving).
  - Retention rate (percentage of customers staying).

4 Decline Stage – Product Extension Strategy

In the decline stage, the product faces diminishing demand, and the focus is on either revitalizing the product or gracefully phasing it out. The strategy here is **product extension** – finding ways to extend the product's life or transitioning customers as the product nears its end.

- **Key Focus Areas:**

  1 Pivot the product strategy to address changing market conditions and customer needs.
  2 Explore new solutions to meet evolving demand.
  3 Plan for a smooth product sunset (retirement) when necessary.
  4 Retain customer loyalty through ongoing support during product phase-out.

- **Role of the Product Manager:**

  - Analyse the reasons behind the product's decline and explore opportunities to pivot or extend its lifecycle.
  - Re-engage inactive users through targeted marketing and product updates.
  - Manage the offboarding process, ensuring minimal customer disruption.
  - Facilitate the product's market exit if necessary.

- **Metrics to Track:**

  - Customer churn rates.
  - Re-engagement metrics for inactive users.
  - Offboarding success rates.
  - Market exit data (if applicable).

16.3.5 *Product Growth Engine: Strategic Planning Questions*

The **Product Growth Engine** in Figure 16.14 provides a systematic approach to driving product growth by addressing three fundamental strategic questions.

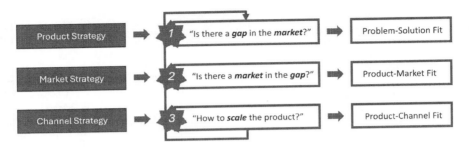

FIGURE 16.14 Product Growth Engine

Each question is linked to a specific strategy and goal that helps product managers navigate the complexities of product development and scaling.

Question 1. Is there a gap in the market?

- **Product Strategy**: Establish **Problem-Solution Fit.**
- **Goal**: Identify a gap in the market and develop a product that addresses it.

The first step to building a successful product is identifying an unmet need in the market. This involves conducting in-depth customer research to find pain points and creating a solution that addresses those issues. Achieving **Problem-Solution Fit** means the product provides a compelling solution that resonates with the target audience.

- **Example: Uber** and **Grab** identified an unfulfilled need for reliable, on-demand transportation. Their ride-hailing platforms provided a convenient solution to a widespread problem, making it easy for users to book rides anytime, anywhere.

Using tools like the **Value Proposition Canvas** helps product teams align the product's features with the customer's needs and jobs-to-be-done. Once a **Problem-Solution Fit** is established, the product is ready for the next step – market validation.

Question 2. Is there a market in the gap?

- **Market Strategy**: Achieve **Product-Market Fit.**
- **Goal**: Validate that there is demand for the product and a sizable, sustainable market to support growth.

After ensuring the product solves a real problem, the next step is to validate whether there is a large enough market willing to pay for it. A

Product-Market Fit is achieved when the product meets market demand and resonates with a broad audience.

- **Market Size Analysis (TAM, SAM, SOM)**: Product managers use the TAM, SAM, SOM model to evaluate market size:

  - **TAM** (Total Addressable Market): The total market demand for the product.
  - **SAM** (Serviceable Available Market): The portion of TAM the product can target.
  - **SOM** (Serviceable Obtainable Market): The realistic portion of SAM the product can capture.

- **Example: Spotify** faced challenges when it expanded into a number of new markets that comprise developing countries in Asia, Africa, the Pacific and the Caribbean in 2021 without fully accounting for the region's **purchasing power parity (PPP)**. Spotify projected a TAM of over a billion users but didn't factor in that the relative affordability of its service in a country like India was five times more expensive than in the US Spotify's actual market reach should realistically be much lower than anticipated, highlighting the importance of considering economic and market factors in the TAM, SAM, SOM model.

Question 3. How to scale the product?

- **Channel Strategy**: Ensure **Product-Channel Fit**.
- **Goal**: Scale the product by optimizing distribution channels to reach a broader audience.

To scale effectively, product managers must ensure the product is distributed through the right channels – both physical and digital. **Product-Channel Fit** refers to the alignment between the product and its distribution methods, ensuring that it reaches customers efficiently.

- **Criteria for Product-Channel Fit**:

  1 The distribution method should be convenient and accessible to the customer.
  2 The product must be delivered at the right place, time, and quality while controlling costs.
  3 The channel strategy should be designed to maximize market reach while maintaining efficiency.

- **Scaling Tactics**:

  - Increase customer retention.
  - Create customer advocacy.
  - Drive customer lifetime value (CLTV).

16.3.6 Three Ways to Scale a Product

Scaling a product requires strategic focus on building long-term customer relationships, creating advocates for the brand, and maximizing the value each customer brings over their lifecycle. To achieve sustainable growth, product managers need to focus on three critical areas shown in Figure 16.15: **customer retention, customer advocacy**, and **customer lifetime value (CLTV)**. Each of these areas contributes to a scalable, profitable product strategy.

1 **Increase Customer Retention**

Customer retention is a key pillar in scaling a product. Acquiring new customers is significantly more expensive than retaining existing ones. In fact, **customer acquisition costs** are often **four to ten times higher** than retention costs, which makes it much more profitable to invest in keeping current customers happy. Repeat customers tend to spend more, are more loyal, and can become long-term users, thereby increasing profitability.

To retain customers, product managers should focus on:

- Offering personalized experiences and features based on customer preferences.
- Providing excellent customer service and support, addressing issues promptly.
- Continuously improving the product based on feedback, ensuring it evolves with user needs.

By prioritizing retention, product managers can build a loyal customer base, reduce churn, and maximize revenue without having to continuously invest heavily in acquiring new customers.

2 **Create Customer Advocacy**

In today's market, **most consumers trust other consumers** more than they trust brands. This is particularly true for **Millennials**, who are more likely

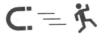

1. Increase Customer Retention

2. Create Customer Advocacy

3. Drive Customer Lifetime Value

FIGURE 16.15 How to Scale the Product?

to make purchase decisions based on their emotional connection with a brand rather than through traditional sales pitches. As a result, brands must create a sense of trust and relationship-building, rather than focusing solely on a hard sell.

Customer advocacy involves turning your satisfied customers into brand advocates who will promote your product through word-of-mouth, social media, and reviews. Here's why customer advocacy is essential for scaling:

- Advocates can provide authentic, trustworthy recommendations to potential customers.
- Organic promotion by advocates is often more effective than traditional advertising in building credibility.
- Advocacy helps generate free, high-quality leads from trusted sources, reducing marketing costs.

Brands build advocacy by:

- Engaging with their customers meaningfully through storytelling, social media, and personalized content.
- Offering loyalty programs, incentives, or referral bonuses that encourage customers to share their positive experiences.
- Fostering a community around the product where customers feel connected and empowered to share their views.

By creating customer advocates, brands can leverage the power of word-of-mouth marketing to scale their product and increase customer acquisition without the heavy reliance on traditional advertising.

3 **Drive Customer Lifetime Value (CLTV)**

Maximizing **customer lifetime value (CLTV)** is critical for generating sustained revenue. A large portion of revenue for many businesses comes **after the initial sale**, through renewals, upselling, and cross-selling. This means that the longer a customer stays engaged with your product, the more valuable they become.

Here's how product managers can drive up CLTV:

- **Renewals:** Keep customers on board by offering subscription-based services or contracts, ensuring they continue to benefit from the product over time.
- **Upselling:** Offer premium versions, additional features, or higher-tier packages that add value to the customer's experience.
- **Cross-selling:** Introduce complementary products or services that enhance the user's experience with the core product, thereby increasing their overall spend.

For example, companies like **Amazon** and **Apple** have perfected the art of maximizing CLTV by continually offering additional products and services that cater to their customers' evolving needs. Amazon, through **Prime memberships**, cross-sells streaming services, groceries, and exclusive deals, all of which increase the customer's value to the company beyond their initial purchase.

To optimize CLTV:

- Use customer data to understand purchasing patterns and behaviour.
- Personalize offers to fit the customer's preferences and needs.
- Ensure continuous engagement through marketing campaigns, loyalty programs, and tailored recommendations.

Increasing CLTV is essential because it allows businesses to extract more value from each customer over time, making the growth model more sustainable and reducing the reliance on acquiring new customers.

16.3.7 The Flywheel Effect and Business Growth

The **flywheel effect** is a concept that illustrates how small, consistent actions can build momentum over time, leading to sustained business growth. Unlike a funnel, where customers move through a linear process and exit at the bottom, the flywheel is a continuous cycle where customer engagement drives ongoing growth. This approach focuses on creating value at every stage of the customer journey, which in turn accelerates growth as the flywheel gains momentum.

16.3.7.1 The Flywheel Diagram

The flywheel can be visualized as **three concentric circles**, as shown in Figure 16.16:

1 **Centre Circle: Growth**

- The ultimate goal of the flywheel is **growth**, which is achieved through the actions taken at the outer layers of the flywheel.

2 **First Outer Layer: Key Actions (Attract, Engage, Delight)**

- **Attract**: The process of drawing in potential customers (strangers) by offering valuable content, insights, or solutions to their problems.
- **Engage**: Once attracted, these prospects are engaged through meaningful interactions, such as personalized offers, helpful content, or direct customer service.
- **Delight**: After a purchase, customers are delighted with exceptional experiences, support, and continuous value, turning them into promoters who advocate for your brand.

FIGURE 16.16 The flywheel effect

3 **Second Outer Layer: Customer Journey (Strangers, Prospects, Customers, Promoters)**

- **Strangers**: Individuals who are unfamiliar with your brand or product.
- **Prospects**: Potential customers who have shown interest or engaged with your brand but have not yet made a purchase.
- **Customers**: Those who have purchased your product or service.
- **Promoters**: Satisfied customers who advocate for your brand, recommending it to others through word-of-mouth, reviews, or referrals.

16.3.7.2 How the Flywheel Works: Turning Strangers into Promoters

The flywheel is designed to turn **strangers** into **prospects**, then into **customers**, and ultimately into **promoters** who help fuel further growth. Here's how the process works:

1 **Attract Strangers to Become Prospects**:
At this stage, the goal is to **attract** strangers to your brand by offering them something of value – whether that's educational content, insights, or solutions that speak to their needs. This is often achieved through content marketing, SEO, social media, and other inbound marketing techniques.

- **Example**: A SaaS company might publish helpful blog posts, guides, or case studies that address common pain points for their target audience, drawing in potential prospects.

2 **Engage Prospects to Convert Them into Customers**:
Once prospects have engaged with your brand, the next step is to **nurture** them through personalized communications, offers, and direct engagement. This could involve emails, product demos, or free trials designed to convert prospects into paying customers.

- **Example**: E-commerce businesses use personalized email campaigns and abandoned cart reminders to encourage prospects to complete their purchases.

3 **Delight Customers to Turn Them into Promoters**:
After converting prospects into customers, the focus shifts to **delighting** them with an exceptional post-purchase experience. This includes top-notch customer service, personalized product recommendations, loyalty programs, and continuous value. By delighting customers, businesses increase the likelihood of retaining them and turning them into promoters who will advocate for the brand.

- **Example**: A subscription-based service might offer free gifts, exclusive content, or priority support to loyal customers, making them more likely to refer friends and family.

16.3.7.3 How the Flywheel Drives Business Growth

As the flywheel spins, it generates momentum, turning satisfied customers into promoters who advocate for your brand and attract more prospects. This self-sustaining cycle helps reduce customer acquisition costs and increase customer lifetime value, driving long-term growth.

Here's how each stage contributes to growth:

- **Attracting Strangers** brings in new prospects to fuel the growth pipeline.
- **Engaging Prospects** converts them into customers, increasing sales and revenue.
- **Delighting Customers** ensures retention and turns customers into promoters, further fuelling growth by bringing in new prospects through word-of-mouth.

16.3.7.4 Starbucks' Digital Flywheel: A Real-World Example

A prime example of the flywheel effect in action is **Starbucks' Digital Flywheel** strategy, which has helped the company achieve phenomenal growth. Starbucks' flywheel focuses on:

1 **Attract**: Starbucks attracts customers with a wide variety of offerings and a compelling brand presence across physical stores, social media, and digital platforms like its mobile app.

2 **Engage:** The company uses its loyalty program and **Mobile Order & Pay** feature to engage customers by offering personalized recommendations, discounts, and a frictionless shopping experience. Customers can order ahead via the app, reducing wait times and making it easier to interact with the brand.

3 **Delight:** Starbucks delights its customers by using data from its loyalty program to offer personalized incentives, rewards, and experiences, ensuring that customers feel valued and remain loyal. For instance, customers receive free birthday drinks and tailored promotions based on their purchase history.

Through this approach, Starbucks turns **strangers** into **prospects** by attracting them with a strong brand and social presence. It then converts these **prospects** into **customers** through engagement with its mobile app and loyalty program, and ultimately turns **customers** into **promoters** by delivering seamless, personalized experiences. These delighted promoters help fuel the flywheel by bringing in new customers, creating a continuous cycle of growth.

Starbucks leveraged the **Digital Flywheel** to fuel growth by focusing on personalized incentives, seamless customer experiences, and technology-driven convenience. The flywheel effect helped Starbucks drive continued growth through four main strategies:

1 **Personalized incentives:** Starbucks' loyalty program offers personalized rewards based on customer purchase history, encouraging repeat visits and higher spending.

2 **Data-driven personalization:** Starbucks uses customer data to offer tailored experiences and promotions, making each interaction feel personal and relevant.

3 **Mobile Order & Pay:** The integration of mobile ordering has made transactions faster and more convenient, increasing order frequency and reducing wait times.

4 **Seamless digital experience:** The unified digital experience across mobile apps, rewards, and in-store interactions ensures a frictionless journey for customers, boosting engagement and loyalty.

By continually applying force through these initiatives, Starbucks was able to create a self-reinforcing growth cycle, where increased customer engagement led to higher sales, more data-driven insights, and further personalization – all of which propelled the company forward.

The **flywheel effect** is essential for product scaling and business growth, as it builds momentum over time, helping businesses sustain and accelerate their growth.

16.4 Conclusion

Managing Product Requirements and Lifecycles is essential for ensuring that products evolve in alignment with both user needs and business objectives. Effective **requirements management** enables teams to prioritize high-impact features, ensuring that development efforts focus on delivering value incrementally. By utilizing agile techniques such as user stories, epics, and prioritization methods like **MoSCoW** or **RICE** scoring, product managers can dynamically manage product backlogs and respond to changing market conditions.

At the same time, mastering **Product Lifecycle Management (PLM)** allows product managers to strategically guide a product through its various lifecycle stages. Whether a product is in the Introduction, Growth, Maturity, or Decline phase, having a clear understanding of the lifecycle allows managers to employ the right strategies – be it product advocacy, growth, customer retention, or product extension. These lifecycle strategies ensure the product remains competitive, relevant, and profitable for as long as possible.

In summary, by mastering both requirements and lifecycle management, product managers can not only build products that resonate with customers but also ensure their long-term success and adaptability in a rapidly changing digital landscape.

17
BRIDGING STRATEGY WITH EXECUTION

17.1 Introduction

As we conclude Volume 1, we've explored the key elements of strategic planning and market opportunity that form the foundation of digital product management. However, strategy alone is not enough to ensure success. The transition from strategy to execution is where true value is realized, and this is the focus of the upcoming volume. This chapter serves as a bridge between the two volumes, connecting the theories and methodologies of strategic planning with the practicalities of product development, market launch, and ongoing product support. By understanding these dynamics, product managers will be better equipped to move from planning to execution, ensuring their products not only meet but exceed market expectations.

In this chapter, we will also introduce emerging trends such as the increasing role of AI and automation, the growing emphasis on customer-centric products, and the transformative power of data-driven innovation. As digital product managers, it is essential to stay ahead of these trends while preparing to face the challenges of tomorrow's competitive market. We will also touch on the importance of continuous learning and how product managers can adapt to the ever-changing demands of the digital age. We will discuss five key areas that bridge the gap between strategy and execution: Emerging Trends in Digital Product Management, Leveraging AI and Automation, Data-Driven Product Innovations, Customer-Centric Products, and Preparing for Future Challenges. These topics provide a roadmap for navigating the complexities of executing your digital product strategy.

DOI: 10.1201/9781003484295-17

17.2 From Strategy to Execution

In Volume 1 of the Digital Product Management series, we have explored the theories, methodologies, and tools that guide product managers in identifying opportunities, conducting market research, and crafting a solid product strategy. These foundational elements serve as the blueprint for everything that follows in product development, launch, and support, which will be covered in Volume 2.

Product managers will also face the challenge of turning those plans into reality – building products that meet market needs, launching them successfully, and managing them through their lifecycles. This section will serve as a bridge between the two volumes, connecting the strategic planning aspects covered in Volume 1 with the hands-on execution processes that will be explored in Volume 2.

17.2.1 Digital Product Management Framework

The **Digital Product Management Framework** provided in Volume 1 introduced the **five core process groups**: Product Opportunity, Product Planning, Product Development, Product Launch, and Product Support, as shown in Figure 17.1.

Volume 1 concentrated on the first two groups, which are directly under the responsibility of product managers. In Volume 2, the focus will be on the remaining three: **Product Development, Product Launch**, and **Product Support**, where product managers orchestrate cross-functional teams and stakeholders to execute the strategy effectively. In this volume, we will delve into the practicalities of product execution: how to lead product development, craft marketing strategies, manage sales channels, and support

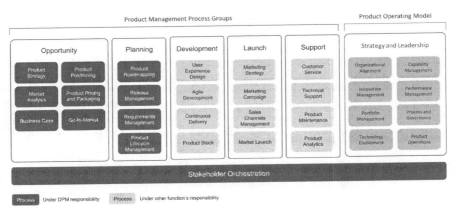

FIGURE 17.1 Digital Product Management Framework

products post-launch. Readers will have a complete understanding of how to move from concept to market success, ensuring their product's growth and longevity. This section serves as a critical pivot point for the content, tying together the high-level strategies of the Volume 1 with the actionable steps required to lead digital product management teams to success in the real world.

17.2.2   Product Vision to Planning to Execution

In digital product management, the journey from **product vision** to **execution** is a carefully orchestrated process that ensures every step aligns with the overarching goals of both the organization and its customers. This section explores the key stages that product managers need to navigate to transform a product from an idea into a reality – while ensuring its ongoing success and relevance in the market. Figure 17.2 illustrates the journey from vision to plan, roadmap, development, launch, and support.

1 **Product Vision**

The product vision is the foundation upon which the entire product development process rests. It serves as a guiding light that defines why the product is being built, what problems it seeks to solve, and the value it aims to deliver to customers or users. A clear product vision helps the team stay focused on the core objectives and differentiates the product from competitors.

Example: Apple's vision for the **iPhone** was to reinvent the mobile phone by creating a device that could seamlessly integrate communication,

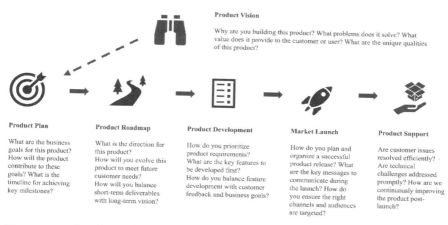

FIGURE 17.2   Product vision to planning to execution

entertainment, and internet browsing. The goal was to solve the problem of cumbersome user interfaces and bring a product that combined ease of use with powerful capabilities.

Key Questions:

- Why are you building this product? (To revolutionize the mobile phone industry by making devices easier to use)
- What problems does it solve? (Complex interfaces, lack of integrated experiences)
- What value does it provide to the customer? (Simplified, seamless communication and entertainment)
- What are the unique qualities of this product? (Seamless integration with the **Apple** ecosystem)

2 **Product Plan**
Once the vision is clear, the next step is translating it into actionable business goals. The product plan outlines how the business will achieve its objectives, focusing on product milestones, target markets, and resource allocation. It acts as a high-level blueprint for executing the product vision while considering business constraints.

Example: Tesla's business goal for the **Model 3 (Tesla Model 3)** was to bring electric vehicles (EVs) to the mass market. The product plan focused on producing a high-volume, affordable EV that maintained the quality and performance **Tesla** was known for. The plan involved setting clear production goals and expanding **Tesla's** manufacturing capabilities.

Key Questions:

- What are the business goals for this product? (To become a leading manufacturer of mass-market EVs)
- How will the product contribute to these goals? (By being an affordable, high-quality EV with **Tesla's** brand cachet)
- What is the timeline for achieving key milestones? (To achieve full-scale Cybertruck production by 2025, regulatory-approved autonomous vehicles by 2026, and mass-market energy product integration by 2030)

3 **Product Roadmap**
A product roadmap outlines the long-term direction for the product, helping to evolve it over time. It includes a strategic view of the product's development path, detailing planned features, timelines, and how those features align with both customer needs and business objectives. The roadmap ensures that teams have a clear direction while remaining flexible enough to adapt to market or technology changes.

Example: Zoom's product roadmap evolved rapidly due to the unexpected demand during the COVID-19 pandemic. The company focused on adding features like enhanced security (end-to-end encryption) and virtual backgrounds to meet the needs of both businesses and individual users. Zoom's roadmap balanced immediate needs with a long-term focus on collaboration tools.

Key Questions:

- What is the direction for this product? (Enhanced features for remote work and education)
- How will you evolve this product to meet future customer needs? (By adding more features for both personal and professional users)
- How will you balance short-term deliverables with long-term vision? (By continuously enhancing its platform while investing in future innovations like AI-driven collaboration and immersive experiences)

4 Product Development

This phase focuses on prioritizing and executing the necessary requirements to bring the product to life. The product development process involves breaking down the roadmap into prioritized tasks and features, often stored in a product backlog. Prioritization is typically based on factors such as customer impact, business value, and feasibility.

Example: Slack prioritized key communication features in its product development process, including instant messaging, file sharing, and integration with third-party tools like **Google** Drive. This allowed teams to collaborate more efficiently. **Slack's** development process was highly iterative, continuously evolving based on user feedback.

Key Questions:

- How do you prioritize product requirements? (By focusing on features that improve collaboration and productivity)
- What are the key features to be developed first? (Instant messaging, file sharing, integrations)
- How do you balance feature development with customer feedback and business goals? (By prioritizing user-driven improvements that align with strategic objectives, ensuring both customer satisfaction and long-term business growth)

5 Market Launch

The product launch is a critical step that requires detailed planning and coordination across marketing, sales, and support teams. A successful product release hinges on timing, positioning, and ensuring that both internal teams and customers are ready for the new product or update.

Example: When **Netflix** expanded into new markets, it tailored its marketing strategy to local cultures and preferences, ensuring that its content resonated with the target audience. For example, in India, **Netflix** launched with Bollywood films and localized pricing options to attract new users.

Key Questions:

- How do you plan and organize a smooth and successful product release? (Localized content, pricing, and marketing strategy)
- What are the key messages to communicate during the launch? (Using local content partnerships and promotions)
- How do you ensure the right channels and audiences are targeted? (Through personalized algorithms, data analytics, and localized content strategies)

6 **Product Support**
Once the product is launched, ongoing support is crucial to ensure a positive user experience and sustained customer satisfaction. This element includes customer service, technical support, and continuous improvement based on user feedback. Efficient product support allows teams to address customer pain points, solve technical issues, and continually refine the product to meet evolving customer needs.

Example: Amazon Prime offers exceptional customer support with its fast shipping, easy return policies, and around-the-clock technical support for streaming services. Continuous improvement is driven by customer feedback, with **Amazon** consistently introducing new features such as same-day delivery and enhanced video streaming.

Key Questions:

- Are customer issues resolved efficiently? (24/7 customer support)
- Are technical challenges addressed promptly? (New features like faster delivery and exclusive content)
- How are we continuously improving the product post-launch? (Through customer feedback, data-driven insights, and rapid feature iterations)

The above examples demonstrate how successful companies like **Apple, Tesla, Zoom, Slack, Netflix,** and **Amazon** navigate the product journey from vision to execution, ensuring that each stage builds on the previous one to deliver high-value products that meet customer needs.

By structuring your product journey through these elements, you create a seamless process from vision to execution. Each step informs the next, helping to build a product that not only meets market needs but also sustains long-term growth and customer satisfaction.

17.3 Emerging Trends in Digital Product Management

To execute a strategy successfully, product managers must stay ahead of industry trends. Technology and consumer behaviour change quickly, and products that are relevant today might become outdated tomorrow. Emerging trends such as artificial intelligence (AI), automation, big data, and omnichannel customer engagement are reshaping the digital product landscape.

One example is the rise of **subscription-based business models,** as seen in products like **Netflix** and **Adobe Creative Cloud**. These models have shifted away from one-time purchases to ongoing relationships with customers. Product managers must now focus on creating recurring value, maintaining high engagement, and ensuring continuous innovation. This trend requires a shift in how success is measured – not just by how many users are acquired, but how long they stay and how deeply they engage.

Another significant trend is the **growing influence of AI and machine learning in product development and customer interaction**. Companies like Spotify and TikTok have capitalized on AI to create personalized user experiences, leveraging algorithms to recommend content that keeps users engaged. The challenge for product managers is to stay informed about these technologies and ensure their teams integrate them effectively into the product.

17.4 Leveraging AI and Automation in Product Management

Artificial intelligence and automation are no longer optional add-ons; they are fundamental to scaling and efficiency in digital product management. AI can drive innovation in user experience, automate tedious processes, and enhance decision-making with data-driven insights. For example, **Tesla** uses AI not only in its cars but also to optimize production and predict maintenance needs. This AI-driven approach allows **Tesla** to deliver continuous improvements to its vehicles, pushing the boundaries of traditional product lifecycles.

Chatbots and **virtual assistants** are another area where AI is transforming customer service and engagement. Many businesses, including **Amazon**, use AI-powered customer service bots to handle routine customer inquiries, allowing human representatives to focus on more complex issues. By incorporating these technologies, product managers can improve the efficiency of product support, reduce operational costs, and improve the overall user experience.

Automation also plays a critical role in product delivery through **Continuous Integration/Continuous Delivery (CI/CD)** pipelines. For instance, companies like **Netflix** have embraced automation for delivering frequent, small updates to their platform, ensuring they stay ahead of bugs and maintain optimal performance without disrupting the user experience.

17.5 Data-Driven Product Innovations

In today's digital economy, decisions based on gut feeling are a thing of the past. Data-driven innovation is at the core of successful digital products. Product managers must embrace a culture of experimentation and iterative development by using real-world data to guide product improvements.

For example, **Google** uses A/B testing extensively to compare different product features, website designs, and user flows. By testing these features with real users, they gather concrete data to determine which version provides the best results. Product managers at **Google** use these insights to continuously refine and enhance their offerings.

The role of data analytics extends beyond product development into customer engagement. **Airbnb** is a prime example of how a company uses data to personalize the customer experience and optimize its platform. By analysing user behaviour, **Airbnb** can suggest the most relevant listings to potential travellers, maximizing engagement and satisfaction.

Product managers need to set up systems for gathering and analysing data to drive product decisions, enabling them to improve user engagement and optimize business outcomes continually.

17.6 The Increasing Importance of Customer-Centric Products

In the digital age, products that do not revolve around the needs of the customer are unlikely to succeed. The customer-centric approach focuses on creating products that align with the evolving demands and preferences of users. As we move into execution, product managers must ensure their strategies are flexible and responsive to user feedback.

Apple is a powerful example of customer-centricity. Every product they design, from the iPhone to the MacBook, is built around the user experience. Product managers can learn from **Apple's** attention to design, usability, and ecosystem integration. By focusing on what users need, **Apple** has been able to create products that are not only functional but also desirable, driving long-term brand loyalty.

Similarly, **Starbucks** has leveraged customer feedback to design its mobile app, which offers features like pre-ordering and loyalty rewards. By integrating technology into its customer service, Starbucks provides a seamless and personalized experience, which has helped the brand maintain its competitive edge.

17.7 Preparing for Future Market Challenges and Opportunities

The rapid pace of technological change and evolving consumer preferences means that product managers must always be prepared for future challenges and opportunities. Disruptions such as new market entrants, regulatory changes, or shifts in consumer expectations can drastically affect a product's success.

Rolls-Royce, for example, has embraced digital transformation by creating a new revenue model around '**power-by-the-hour**' in its aviation division. Instead of selling engines outright, **Rolls-Royce** provides customers with access to engines and guarantees a certain number of operational hours. This model relies heavily on predictive analytics and AI to monitor engine performance in real time, reducing downtime and improving service delivery. Such innovations demonstrate the importance of preparing for the future by leveraging data and technology.

Product managers must anticipate potential disruptions and remain adaptable. This involves continuous learning, staying updated on industry trends, and cultivating a mindset that embraces change as an opportunity for growth.

17.8   Conclusion of Bridging Strategy and Execution

Effective digital product management is about transforming vision into reality. By linking strategy with execution, product managers ensure that their products not only meet immediate business goals but also evolve to meet customer needs and market shifts. This chapter has highlighted the critical steps, from defining a clear product vision to executing a market launch and providing continuous product support. By focusing on both strategic and operational elements, product managers can guide their teams towards success while maintaining flexibility and foresight in an ever-changing digital landscape.

By staying ahead of trends, embracing AI and data analytics, and focusing on customer-centric solutions, digital product managers can ensure their strategies translate into successful product outcomes. These methods will not only help product managers execute their plans effectively but also empower them to adapt to a fast-changing digital landscape. The next Volume 2 in the Digital Product Management series will provide practical guidance on how to manage the execution side of product management, where these strategies meet real-world challenges and opportunities. In that volume, we will explore the hands-on processes that product managers must lead during Product Development, Product Launch, and Product Support in greater details.

INDEX

Printed in the United States
by Baker & Taylor Publisher Services